HISTORIC GAINESVILLE & HALL COUNTY

An Illustrated History

Compiled and edited by William L. Norton, Jr.

William L. Norton, Jr.

Published for the Hall County Historical Society, Inc.

Historical Publishing Network
A division of Lammert Publications, Inc.
San Antonio, Texas

ISBN: 1-893619-13-3

Library of Congress Card Catalog Number: 00-112324

Historic Gainesville & Hall County: An Illustrated History

compiler and editor:	William L. Norton, Jr.
historical consultant and contributor:	Charles S. Gurr
historical consultant and contributor:	M. Garland Reynolds, Jr.
contributing writer for "sharing the heritage":	Stephen Gurr
cover artist:	George Evans
photography consultant:	Richard Stone

Hall County Historical Society, Inc.

president:	Ken Cochran
chairman:	William L. Norton, Jr.
secretary/treasurer	Adelaide Gregory Norton
administrative assistant:	Susan M. Corby

Hall County Historical Society, Inc. Directors

Steven T. Arminio	Jeff D. Gay, Sr.	Dale Jaeger	Lydia Sartain
Vicki L. Bentley	Curtis George	Happy Garner Kirkpatrick	Curtis Segars
Eugene Bobo	Dr. Eugene Green	Abit Massey	Dr. Martin Smith
Allen Carter	Robert Hamrick	William H. Maxey	Warren Stribling III
Roger Brown	Linda Henry	Richard Banks McCrary	Charles Strong III
Ben H. Carter	Nathaniel Hewell	Charles Musselwhite	Jim Syfan
Lucille Carter	Martha Norton Hodge	Mark Musselwhite	Colonel Harold Terrell
Ned Carter	Ron Hollis	Professor Tom Nichols	Charles J. Thurmond
Anne Davenport	Heyward Hosch, Jr.	David Peters	Robert Vass
Rosemary Johnson Dodd	Charles House	Karen Peters	Frank T. Waggoner
Barbara Ward Edmondson	William M. House	Richard Pilcher	Jim Walters
Myrtle Figueras	Patricia Hudson	Wilbur Ramsey	Tharpe Ward
Charles Frierson, Jr.	Kelly Hulsey	M. Garland Reynolds, Jr.	Fleming Weaver

Hall County Historical Society, Inc. Chapter Officers

Flowery Branch Chapter

president:	Ken Cochran
vice president:	Vicki L. Bentley

Gillsville Chapter

president:	Charles House
vice president:	Nathaniel Hewell

Historical Publishing Network

president:	Ron Lammert
vice president:	Barry Black
project managers:	Lou Ann Murphy, Lisa Kennard
director of operations:	Charles A. Newton, III
administration:	Angela Lake, Donna M. Mata, Dee Steidle
graphic production:	Colin Hart, John Barr

PRINTED IN SINGAPORE

CONTENTS

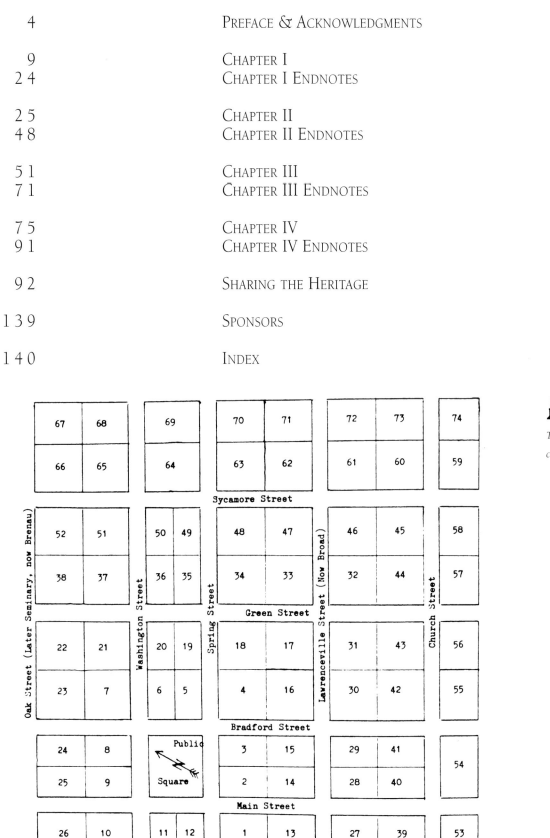

The original design of Gainesville, Georgia., c. 1821.

PREFACE & ACKNOWLEDGMENTS

HISTORIC GAINESVILLE & HALL COUNTY: An Illustrated History had its genesis several years ago. The Hall County Historical Society adopted a desire in the 1970s to publish a local narrative history. Board Chairman William LaFayette Norton, Jr., Lewis W. Richardson, and President William H. House, began to assemble and inventory materials and information on various aspects of the history of Hall County. L. W. Richardson, an accomplished serious historical researcher and writer, was named official Hall County historian in the 1970s, later followed by Ruth Waters in the 1980s and Judge Norton in the 1990s.

Photographs, pamphlets, newspaper articles, personal histories, monographs on particular interests of Hall County were gathered. Having insufficient storage facilities, the Society routinely gave the Hall County Library copies of photographs, monographs, walking tours, riding tours. Lew Richardson prepared several walking and driving tours of Gainesville and Hall County which the Society published and shared with others. In the 1970s the Society invited the Georgia Archives to visit Gainesville to photograph pictures brought by citizens of Hall County and surrounding counties. In two publicized visits these photographs were recorded, itemized, catalogued and preserved on microfilm and negatives at the Georgia Archives.

In the 1970s a video-audio thirty-five-millimeter photo slide history was prepared by Richardson/Norton and a professional video-audio consultant under a grant to the Society by Heyward Hosch, Jr., and The Citizens Bank, now Bank of America. For several years the twenty-minute presentation was offered to groups by the bank and Society.

Gainesville is indebted to a Society committee: Committee Chairwoman Adelaide Gregory Norton; Marion Ledford Chrisner; Marie (Claud) Carter; Annadell (Robert) Moore; and Lura (Carl) Whitehead worked diligently to produce the applications, approved in 1975, for North Green Street and Brenau College neighborhoods to be historic districts on the National Register of Historic Places. The Society has been concerned continuously about the preservation of Green Street and Brenau Historic Districts. Since 1967 the Post Office on Green Street has been an unfortunate magnet for excess traffic and commercialism on Green Street.

In 1998 Historical Publishing Network contacted Judge Norton to propose the publication of a narrative and pictorial history of Hall County. They specialize in publication of local histories sponsored by historical groups. Norton furnished them a list of possible chapters of subjects and sequence. Norton explained that the Society could sponsor a publication with its full approval but could not furnish financial assistance to the publication. The publisher offered to finance the publication by using its experienced sales force to solicit support from local institutions to include historical "profiles" in the book and that future sales of the book could provide income to the Society. The publisher offered to employ a qualified writer to author the history at no cost to the Society. After negotiation of a contract the Society, recognizing the legal writing and publication experience of Judge Norton, requested him to organize, author, manage and complete the process. However, he felt he was too busy to author it alone and preferred to recruit a local team to help produce

The Pruitt-Wheeler House. *This house, now owned by attorney Jim Whitmer, is located at 539 Green Street in Gainesville's Historic District.*

COURTESY OF GEORGE EVANS. WATERCOLOR, 2000. LIMITED EDITION PRINT. SIZE 9 ½ X 14 INCHES. AVAILABLE FROM THE HALL COUNTY HISTORICAL SOCIETY.

the history instead of relying on the publisher to supply an author. He solicited Charles S. "Steve" Gurr, a known editor and biographer and retired professor of history and dean of the History Department of Gainesville College, who the publisher employed for research and consultation to assist Norton and the Society. M. Garland Reynolds, Jr., agreed to write a manuscript primarily devoted to the history of the railroads, hotels, General Longstreet, Woodrow Wilson, and the Gainesville Square. Norton and Gurr contacted numerous historical and photographic sources. The Society appreciates the input of Professor Gurr for research, some initial text, and identification of photography during the latter part of 1999 and the early part of 2000. In spring 2000 Gurr concluded that he did not have the time to devote to the continuation and completion of the endeavor and he withdrew from the project. Norton and other members of the team persisted and finished the project in June 2001.

The Society is fortunate to have recruited the talents of local artist George Evans to create the original artwork for the book jacket cover. In 1999 M. Garland Reynolds, Jr., persuaded Evans to paint a montage of the Longstreet Piedmont Hotel and the surviving rooms to be restored. Reynolds, an architect and amateur historian, is the discoverer of the remains of the hotel and founded The Longstreet Society as the protector of the post Civil War reputation of General Longstreet for his policies of "peace and reconciliation" which he advocated in Gainesville, Georgia, where he owned and operated the Piedmont Hotel. The hotel is being restored by the Gainesville-Hall Trust for Historic Preservation with the assistance of the Hall County Historical Society and The Longstreet Society. In addition to the design of the book jacket cover, HISTORIC GAINESVILLE & HALL COUNTY is distinguished by several reproductions of the original art of George Evans. The original watercolor paintings included on the cover and other original art within HISTORIC GAINESVILLE & HALL COUNTY will become signed and numbered prints available through the Hall County Historical Society.

Norton recruited a professional photographer, Richard Stone of Talmo, to restore and improve old photographs, search for historical photographs, and to take new requested photographs. Recommended by Norton, Historical Publishing employed Stephen Gurr, journalist at the Athens Banner Herald, to prepare some of the historical "profiles" of the distinguished institutions which support the publication. Lou Ann Murphy and Lisa Kennard of Historical Publishing Network were also valuable in soliciting institutional support. The Society appreciates the business and other institutions that provided necessary support to the project through "profiles" written by our profile writer. Without the civic support of these history-inclined institutions, the Society could not have produced this book.

Photographs and information were solicited from numerous individuals. Norton and Stone took numerous photographs for possible illustrations, excessive to this project, which were made into negatives, prints, and slides for retention in Society files for future use. Thousands of photographs were reviewed. One objective has been to minimize reproduction of photos previously published. Except for period postcards, generally only original unpublished photos are included. United Kolor Camera Video, performed skilled, professional reproduction of old photographs and slides, and developed new photographs.

Special thanks to Wilbur and Dixie Ramsey for their courtesies, cooperation and generosity in offering the files of several hundred photos from Ramsey Studio, taken by her father and grandfather, prominent professional photographers from 1900 to the 1960s. The Ramsey collection is quite distinguished.

Robert and Caroldene McEver of Talmo, Georgia, provided access to several thousand photos taken by Cicero Simmons of Talmo in the period of 1895-1925. This is a most important collection purchased by the McEvers from the estate of Simmons which is being carefully processed from the original glass plate negatives and preserved by our consulting professional photographer, Richard Stone. Miraculously, these historical glass plate negatives had been stored and well preserved in secure wooden boxes in an attic in Talmo for some seventy-five years.

The available collections of professional photographers Milton Hardy, Leonard Cinciola, and Ed Beasley were reviewed. Walter Byrd graciously provided his notebook of railroad photographs and information reference the career of fifty or so years of Byrd's father, Van Leland Byrd, with the Gainesville Midland Railroad.

Norton's business firm, without expense to the Society, employed Susan Corby, a professional word processor and editor, as associate manuscript editor to process and research terms and verify dates, names and places for numerous revised drafts of the manuscript. Office Manager Joyce Seabolt, Adelaide Norton, and Martha Norton Hodge performed management, word processing, and other services, and Lee Wood provided bookkeeping. A team effort resulted in the Norton offices at 380 Green Street Historic District and information from many individuals and other sources was compiled.

James DeLong furnished information on the development of the airport, automobile dealers, the Square and the 1936 tornado. Richard Pilcher, a historian on General Longstreet and the Civil War, Harold and Joe Terrell, Dr. Larry Tomlin, senior pastor of the Central Baptist Church, William H. Maxey, Eugene Bobo, Charters Smith Embry, Loyd Strickland, the late Henry O. Ward, Sr., former mayor and chairman of the Hall County Historical Commission, Edith Quinlan Rankin, Judge Sidney O. Smith, Jr., and Carl Lawson supplied valuable information. Tharpe Ward, owner of Johnny's Barbecue of Parkhill Drive, gave the researchers access to the photographic collection which hangs on the wall of his restaurant, some of which were supplied by Tim Reed. Although Norton had been general counsel for the Georgia

Poultry Federation and most of the organized poultry industry from 1957 to 1971, Ben Carter, Richard Harris, Abit Massey, Jack McKibbon, Jack Prince and Homer Wilson filled in facts about the poultry industry.

Anne Amerson, a historian and author from Dahlonega, Georgia and publisher of several history books and articles, was a valuable resource especially on the proposed Gainesville-Dahlonega Railroad and hydroelectric dams. Clara Head, a ninety-one-year-old native of Clermont, now residing in Athens, Georgia, was a source of lively conversation and valuable historic background, especially on the Gainesville Northwestern Railroad branch line to the pyrites mine.

The Society appreciates the contributions of M. Garland Reynolds, Jr., for consultation, advice, and considerable researched information and written memoranda. The Norton, Reynolds, and Gurr manuscript drafts, along with several other writings on segments from enlisted local knowledgeable persons, were edited, integrated, and expanded by Norton.

During the writing of this book, numerous persons of good knowledge were solicited. But frequently, information and memories were incomplete. Some periods of history and some known events are devoid of recorded or reliable information. Many photographs fail to reveal names or dates. Although most facts are cited to sources, in the interest of brevity references have been omitted in several general information quotes. It was recognized all along that there are others in the community that may have information or know more about a particular subject than the editors, consultants, and members of the Society who responded to this effort. Perhaps the publication of this book will encourage others to offer facts to the Society.

In the final stages, Norton asked several members of the Society and other persons to critique various drafts of chapters and particular subject matter in the quest for accuracy, additional information and clarity. Special thanks go to Ben H. Carter, Professor Tom Nichols, Adelaide Norton, and Susan Corby who served as literary reviewers on the final drafts of the manuscript. It is recognized that the subject is broader than the allowed publication space and there are omissions and possibly inaccuracies and errors. The Society appreciates input given to Norton by numerous individuals having varied and long Hall County tenures (see Acknowledgements), but the Society ascribes no responsibility for error or inaccuracy as Judge Norton and the Society are totally responsible for the text.

Despite mandated publisher limitation as to number of pages, hopefully the publication is an informative, accurate, easily read and understood illustrated narrative history. The objective has been to present a definitive, comprehensive, concise narrative history that can be read at one sitting or in segments and also serve as a reference source.

As you read this book, we hope you will write suggestions to the Society as to how the publication can be improved if expanded in future years. You will be doing us a favor to point out additions which would clarify sections that are incomplete, unclear, inaccurate, and inconsistent.

The Society will continue to solicit, collect, and organize materials on Gainesville and Hall County history. Some day, expanding on the substantial materials that the Society has accumulated and will continue to acquire, a different type history may be written. Individuals, estates, librarians, businesses and institutions are urged to advise the Society of available photographs, letters, objects and historical information. After reproduction the Society will return the original. Present plans are to solicit monograph histories of communities such as Bark Camp, Belmont, Belton, Braselton, Brookton, Candler, Chestnut Mountain, Chicopee Village, Clermont, Flowery Branch, Gainesville Mill Village, Gillsville, Glade Falls, Klondike, Lula, Maysville, Mossy Creek Campground, Murrayville, New Holland Village, Oakwood, Sardis, Skitts Mountain, Tadmore, Talmo, and Wauka Mountain.

Also the Society seeks monographs and information on particular subjects such as banks, cemeteries, churches, commerce, corn grist mills, cotton gins, cotton warehouses, courts, dairies, electricity, families, hospitals, Lake Lanier, law, manufacturing, medicine, mica, gold, and diamond mines, poultry industry, railroads, retail, rock quarries, schools, sports and athletics, textiles, wholesale, and others. The Society is encouraging students in local high schools, middle schools, and area colleges to become research historians of modest subjects which we are listing on our agenda. These brief monograph histories would be interesting education to citizens and students. Please contact the Society if interested in a project for students.

Together we can preserve historical materials and sources and perhaps some day a more comprehensive volume of local history can be produced. The rich historical heritage of Gainesville and Hall County must be preserved for future generations.

HALL COUNTY HISTORICAL SOCIETY, INC.
380 Green Street Historic District • Gainesville, Georgia 30501
Tel. 770-503-1319 • Fax 770-536-7072
www.hallcountyhistoricalsociety.org

All paintings by George Evans featured in this publication and on its dustjacket are now available as limited edition prints, numbered and signed on acid-free karma stock paper. All receipts to benefit the Hall County Historical Society.

The authors appreciate input from numerous individuals having varied and long Hall County tenures, including:

Bob Adams	Judge Andy Fuller	Abit Massey	Lamar Scroggs
James J. Adams	Curtis George	Kay Ann Massey	Robert Sealey
JoAnn Adams	Leila B. Grigg	James Mathis	Curtis Segars
Anne Amerson	Mayor Bob Hamrick	William H. Maxey	Richard Shockley
Dr. Steven Arminio	Richard Harris	Frances Wheeler McBrayer	Jim Shuler
George Austin	Mike Harrison	Caroldene McEver	David Shumake
Jimmy Bagwell	Clara Head	Robert McEver	LeTrell Simpson
Colonel John (Judge) Beaver	Connie Healan	Gabriel R. McClure	William Slack
Herbert Bell	Linda Henry	Richard Banks McCrary	John H. Smith
Benjamin Blatt	Gene Hollis	Olive Price McKeever	Dr. Martin Smith
Frank Eugene Bobo	Frank Hooper	Jack McKibbon, Jr.	Patsy Horkan Smith
Rev. Fulton Boswell	Homer Hope	Sylvan Meyer	Judge Sidney O. Smith, Jr.
Bimbo Brewer	Skip Hope	Hugh Mills	Charles Smithgall
Roger Brown	Heyward Hosch, Jr.	Charles Morrow	Lessie Smithgall
Dr. John Burns III	Marian Hosch	Frances Nalley	John Souther
Walter Byrd	Mrs. Ed Hughes, Jr.	Dr. Martha Nesbitt	Virginia Parks Souther
Ethel Carras	John Burl Hulsey	Barbara Jean Newton	Robert Spriggs
Alan Carter	Walton Jackson III	Professor Tom Nichols	Newt Stepp
Ben H. Carter	Jay Jacobs	Violet Lee Nicholson	Dr. W. D. (Dick) Stribling, Jr.
H. Chambers	John Jacobs, Jr.	Judge William C. O'Kelley	Loyd Strickland
Joe Chipman	Bob Jaeger	Marvin Orenstein	Daniel Summers
Dallas Chrisner	Dale Jaeger	Bob Painter	Chandelle Summers
Marion Ledford Chrisner	Ed Jared	J. Ernest Palmour III	Jim Syfan
Ken Cochran	Dora Kimbrough Jenkins	Mrs. Tom (Mary Foote) Paris, Sr.	Col. Harold Terrell, Jr.
Lewis Coker	Tom Jenkins	Curtis Parks, Jr.	Joe Terrell
Judge Pattie Cornett	Dr. Henry Jennings	Willie Partolow	Charles Thurmond, Jr.
Rev. Jorge Cristancho	Katherine Hosch Jessup	Eula Mae Grigg Pearce	Lib Thurmond
Richard Crow	Charlie Johnson	Susan B. Pierce	Dr. Larry Tomlin
James DeLong	Nellie Joiner	Richard Pilcher	Sheriff Bob Vass
Harold DeLong	Lynn Jones	Bobby Poole	Dr. Frank Waggoner
Dr. Pierce K. Dixon	Richard Harris	Larry Poole	James Walters
Rosemary Johnson Dodd	Jane Reynolds Hemmer	Mr. and Mrs. Jack Prince	Henry O. Ward, Sr.
Candler Dozier	Lydia Banks McCrary Henley	Harry Purvis	Tharpe Ward
Edgar B. Dunlap, Jr.	Judge A. Richard Kenyon	Wilbur and Dixie C. Ramsey	J. Foster Watkins
James A. Dunlap	Lois Kenyon	David and Edith Quinlan Rankin	Mr. and Mrs. Alan Wayne
Jimmy Echols	Happy Garner Kirkpatrick	Janet Reed	Bob C. Wayne
Austin Edmondson	John Kollock	Dr. John Reed	Gene Wayne
Charters Smith Embry	Robert Latham	Tim Reed	Gus Whalen
Frances Bogdon Fennell	Carl Lawson	M. Garland Reynolds, Jr.	Perry Whatley, Jr.
Myrtle Figueras	Johnny Lawson	Dr. William Roberts	Mrs. Carl Whitehead, Sr.
Lou Fockele	Robert Lawson, Sr.	Dr. R. L. Rogers, Jr.	A. Frederick Young
Robert Fowler	Margaret Luther	Carl Romberg II	Willie B. Young
Walter L. Fowler	Elizabeth Hulsey Marshall	George Romberg	W. Rogers Young
Charles Frierson	Clifford B. Martin	Mrs. Danny Scroggs	Martha Zoller

Pearce Auditorium. *The auditorium is*
located on the campus of Brenau University,
Gainesville, Georgia.

Built - 1818

1977

Burned - 1882

1938

1885 - 1936

HALL COUNTY COURT HOUSES

CHAPTER I

HALL & GAINESVILLE – EARLY BEGINNINGS

In the 1780s Northeast Georgia was an inviting destination for the restless and ambitious expansioneers of the older settled parts of the state and beyond. For generations the region had been the domain of the first native Americans. There had been Creek Indians in what was later Hall County but by the mid-eighteenth century the Cherokees had driven them out. In 1785 the Cherokees signed the Hopewell Treaty with the federal government allowing white settlement on the frontier near what was to become the Jackson-Hall line. There were white interlopers on the Indian side of the line by 1798, and in 1802 the land east of the Chestatee and Chattahoochee Rivers was assured for whites as the natives were granted tracts to the west.

"Booger Bottom," an earlier Indian site now covered by Lake Lanier, included a large oval mound reported to be seven feet high, 250 feet long and 200 feet wide. A sample trench dug at the start of the dam project in 1950-51 revealed evidence of the influence of pre-Cherokee populations: coiled clay pottery fragments, signs of ties to tobacco and other agriculture, and elaborate burial rites.

Most of Hall County, as well as Gwinnett and Habersham Counties, were created from the 1818 Cherokee Treaty of Session through federal negotiations with the native population. Some of the land was carved out of Franklin County and, in 1819, additional lands ceded in the Treaty of Washington were added to the western portions of both Hall and Habersham Counties. Hall County[1] was carved out of a large Jackson County to the east and named for Dr. Lyman Hall from Augusta, signer of the Declaration of Independence and the Constitution. War Hill, a fort said to have been near present-day

A drawing of the Hall County Courthouses over the years by William Rensburg, 1977.

COURTESY OF JUDGE RICHARD AND LOIS KENYON.

CHURCHES OF GAINESVILLE GA

The 1906 First Methodist Church (must be preserved), 1906 First Baptist Church (destroyed 1959), First Presbyterian Church (destroyed 1960s), postcard, c. 1910.

COURTESY OF ED DUNLAP AND THE HALL COUNTY HISTORICAL SOCIETY.

Gillsville, was established for defenses against the Indians during the early period of pioneer-native disputes in Northeast Georgia. Several Indian trails in the region became the footprints of roads.

The pioneering white settlers found the land almost completely forested. Trees grew to the banks of the Chattahoochee, the Chestatee, the Oconee, and the Little River. The old trails followed lines of least natural resistance and led to springs named Mule Camp, Gower, Limestone, and White Sulphur. Game was plentiful, streams were pure and the soil was virgin sandy clay loam and clay subsoil. In time the earth would yield lead, mica, rubies, iron cyanite, garnets, agate, asbestos, and GOLD! Also, diamonds were predicted near Glade Falls and some other gold mines in White and Lumpkin Counties.

In the early 1800s, people had come to farm the rivers' rich bottomland producing grain, cattle and hogs, cotton, and vegetables for home consumption. Corn was conveniently converted to whiskey, a marketable, portable trade item as well as a product for home use. The writings of famous naturalist John Muir[2] suggest that life on these farms and for these farmers and their families changed very little between the white settlement of Hall and the coming of the railroads in the 1870s.

These foothills were populated by white farmers working small farms producing little which brought cash. Most did a little trading among themselves and valued their independence from any serious market system which might subject them to forces beyond their control.

A town which later became known as Gainesville grew from a natural geographical occurrence that created two crossing ridge top trails. This crossing had the additional feature of a large spring, known as "Mule Camp Spring," where travelers could stop to camp, trade goods and conduct business.

Native Americans had long used the place for the same purposes as the early settlers and continued to do so until their removal west by the U.S. government in 1838. Activity around the spring continued to grow as the primary site for trade with settlers and Indians so that by the time Hall County was established in 1818 and needed a seat of government, the area was chosen and incorporated in 1821 as Gainesville[3]. The name Gainesville, as with several other towns in the United States, was in honor of General Pendleton Gaines who had gained national prominence as a soldier in campaigns in the Mexican War and in displacing the Seminole Indians from northern to southern Florida.

Joseph McCutchen, a schoolteacher and Revolutionary War veteran and surveyor, was the census taker for Hall County in 1820. McCutchen had trouble taking the census:

"The inhabitants were very dispersed, there are but few roads, a great part of the country is very mountainous" and it was "difficult to get nourishment for either myself or my horse."

Due to the quagmire that had developed around the mosquitoes-plagued spring, the center of the new town was located two hundred yards north to higher better-drained land. Timothy Terrell IV, a young surveyor from Alabama and member of a family which later became prominent in Gainesville[4], was employed to lay out the town in a classical grid pattern[5]

Because of the major ridge running northeast/southwest, Terrell positioned the Main Street axis of the town perpendicular to this geological phenomenon. This ridge, now known as the Brevard Cataclysmic Ridge, divides Hall County into two almost equal parts and helps form the eastern U.S. Continental Divide. One ridge from the Square runs out Oak Street, another out North Green Street via Riverside Drive to the Chattahoochee River. A large open area measuring three hundred feet square was carved out for the center of the new town. On Terrell's map the Square is referred to as "Public Square." A 150-foot diameter circle of land in the center of the Square was deeded to the County for the Courthouse and a simple log courthouse was quickly erected on the spot.

CHURCHES

As the streets were named, one was designated "Church Street." It was located two blocks off the Square with four lots specified for Methodist, Baptist, Presbyterian, and Episcopal. However, only one church ever located there. Circa 1840, the log courthouse was moved from the Square to Church Street and became the First Methodist Church. A new larger clapboard wooden courthouse was located in the Square. It burned in 1885.

Subsequently, in the late 1800s, the First Methodist Church relocated, then again in

Above: Churches continued to provide a great influence over life in the community. Baptists and Methodists at Gainesville Mill Church shown here.

COURTESY OF DIXIE RAMSEY & THE RAMSEY COLLECTION.

Below: The church at Spring and Grove Streets, originally built as an Episcopal Church, became First Presbyterian and then Saint Paul Methodist. The church was destroyed by the tornado of 1936.

COURTESY OF CATHERINE COLLINS.

DEWBERRY CHURCHES

The original Dewberry Church was established in 1821. Members George Chapman and Philip Byrd in early the 1830s had begun a local debate over the doctrine of "Election" or what some might more simply call "predestination."

A meal of fried chicken and biscuit set the stage for the famous clash. Byrd held up a piece of chicken claiming that he was predestined to eat the piece of chicken before the world began. Chapman apparently realizing he could disprove that theory, pulled the piece of chicken from Byrd's hand and as it flew across the room, a dog caught it in midair and devoured it. Chapman won a great laugh on friend Byrd, but Byrd's angry reaction led to Chapman and his followers, a majority of the membership of the church, leaving to meet at an abandoned Methodist Church not far from Dewberry until a new building could be constructed. This explains why there are now two Dewberry Baptist Churches—Church #1 the newer and Church #2 the older. Hall County's earliest experience with secession may have had a more lasting impact than the later one.

Above: The 1906 First Methodist Church, North Green, Academy, and Brenau Streets, 2000. The church complex was purchased in October 2000 by Charles and Lessie Smithgall. The Smithgalls donated the church to the Arts Council, Inc. which Lessie Smithgall helped form in 1970. The facility is now being renovated as a performing arts and cultural center.

COURTESY OF WILLIAM L. NORTON, JR.

Below: The Central Baptist Church (1890), South Main and High Streets, 2000.

COURTESY OF WILLIAM L. NORTON, JR.

1906 to North Green Street at Academy Street and Brenau Avenue. No other church ever located on Church Street. The First Baptist Church, the First Presbyterian Church, the Grace Episcopal Church, and the St. Paul Methodist Church were each located on more than one site before their present locations. The Central Baptist Church had two sites near Myrtle Street before locating on South Main Street at Myrtle Street (now Martin Luther King Boulevard).

The Presbyterians constituted the larger group in Hall County at the beginning of its settlement history. There were four Presbyterian Churches by 1829; Gainesville Church, Concord, Nazareth, and Hickory Grove. Among the earliest Baptist churches were Hopewell, Sardis, Flat Creek, Timber Ridge, and Harmony Hall.

It took almost a decade (1821-1831) for the Methodists to get a foothold and organize a town church. The Baptists established Shiloh (Shilo), the precursor to the present day First Baptist Church, as the town church in 1831, meeting in a variety of temporary quarters including the Academy building, the Presbyterian meeting house and at Limestone and later Mule Camp Spring. By 1845 a wooden structure was built between Main and Bradford near the site of the present Georgia Mountains Center. The church has had three other locations, i.e. on the lot on the opposite side of Main in 1882; in 1911 on the corner of Green and East Washington Streets; then, after a fire in 1960, moving to the present location, 751 North Green Street in 1962. The 1826 establishment of the Chattahoochee Baptist Association at Hopewell Church was the beginning of one of the area's most vital organizations in the religious life of its people and their communities. Nevertheless, the propagation of churches was not always pleasant or based on need.

SCHOOLS IN THE MID-1800s

In addition to a courthouse, all counties were required by Georgia law to have a "learning academy." The Gainesville Academy was founded soon after Gainesville was established and located just off the Square on a block site between Main and Maple facing the beginning of College Avenue[6]. The success of early education in this area was like that in many others, uneven with numerous fits and starts. In 1821 the "Academy of Hall" was formed by a group of interested citizens and occupied a place near the present Hall County Library System headquarters at West Academy and South Main Streets. Another school, this one for girls, was established by the 1830s and eventually came to be known as the "Female Academy." So-called "district schools" sprang up around the County in the antebellum period. At the end of that decade the Academy of Hall had begun accepting females as well as males. Milton P. Caldwell advertised his own "Chattahoochee Academy" six miles north of

Gainesville, "suited in a pleasant, healthy section, where society is good."

In the 1870s Main Street School, a magnificent two-story brick building with colonial front columns and full usable basement was constructed on the site at Main Street facing College Avenue. It served as a Gainesville Elementary School until it closed in 1969. In 1977, some groups of alumni, historical preservationists, including the Save Main Street School Committee and the Hall County Historical Society, made plans to preserve and convert it to other beneficial civic uses including theater (it had a stage and auditorium). Unfortunately, after the groups appeared and presented a preservation resolution signed by numerous citizens for adoption by the City Council, which the Council took under advisement, the Council instead demolished the building and sold the lot to the County for the erection of a jail[7].

During the late 1800s some private schools, for example Mrs. G. R. Bickers School, established by the mother of Bessie Bickers, founder of the Humane Society and a longtime teacher of second grade classes at Candler Street School; and Beulah Rucker, provided valuable educational services. Thus, government, churches, and education[8] were planned simultaneously.

LAND EXPANSION

The land lottery of 1820 provided for a second wave of settlement to the area prior to the period of final Indian removal. For an $18 fee with payments made over the period of a year (or sometimes up to as much as fifteen years) and a successful draw, 250-acre lots were made available in the northern and western portions of Hall. Six hundred lots were opened in this fashion. Apparently recognizing patriotism and need, those who qualified to draw included veterans of the Revolutionary War, the War of 1812, and Indians wars, disabled veterans, widows, and orphans.

GOLD

From their earliest entry into the area of Hall County white settlers had acknowledged a potential conflict with the Indians. As early

BLACK HALL COUNTIANS

A 1908 *Voter's Oath Book* for Hall County includes names, ages, occupations, and "color" of eligible voters. This record not only tells of the early participation of blacks in Hall County politics, but it helps define the occupational roles of the black community at this time: house and yard work, well digger, public work, physician, clerk, minister, cook, wholesale grocer, shoemaker, teacher, farmer, tailor, carpenter, insurance man, driver, white washer, laborer, teamster, city employee, and railroad employee.

The history of Gainesville reveals that race relations were generally tranquil and seldom did confrontations erupt. Beulah Rucker's School made a strong contribution to the community before public schools existed. In April 1912 "colored people" organized a "Law and Order League." Its leadership included Professor C. E. Williams, Dr. N. A. Doyle, R. A. Chamblee, John Reed, Sam Ashe, Fred Mathews, Len Reed, G. S. McCrary, Jennie E. McCrary, Aaron Wyatt, and A. P. Butler. The *Gainesville News* said, "This movement should be given the hearty encouragement of everybody, white and colored." Such an organization reflected concerns for the moral betterment of the community in the same way that white versions of such organizations did in Hall County where "blind tigers and dives[9]" continued to cause problems and endanger the peace and welfare of citizens, black and white.

Before integration of public schools and public facilities in Georgia in the 1950s, the City Commission appointed two black individuals on the thirteen-member Gainesville School Board[10] and black policemen were employed by the police department.

as 1826 a militia unit, the "Hall County Rifles" was formed with forty-five members to protect the security of the white settlers on the borders of the Cherokee lands. In the 1830s the Cherokees located just beyond the Chattahoochee and Chestatee Rivers were still around and came to town to see the sights and to trade. They brought gold, moccasins, beadwork, and chestnuts to exchange for blankets and other items. Those days, however, were numbered.

In 1826, while deer hunting in North Hall near Murrayville and the Chestatee River, Benjamin Parks, Jr., picked up something that

During his brief stay in Gainesville (1830-32) Templeton Reid coined what would become some of the rarest and most valuable American coins. Shown here are three of the four types of gold coins minted in Gainesville by Reid (obverse and reverse). The dated $10 coin is not shown. Reid's were the first gold coins minted with a dollar value on the coin. These three are estimated to be worth half a million dollars on the 2001 coin market.

COURTESY OF WILLIAM HOUSE.

caught his eye, examined it and decided it was gold. This triggered the North Georgia gold rush and the site became the Calhoun Mine. Gold was discovered in 1828-29 in the Loudsville region of what is now White County, on Duke's Creek in White County and Bear Creek at Dahlonega. It has been said that by 1830 there were thirty thousand gold hunters in Hall County.

The 1818 Cherokee Treaty of Session was a significant stimulus to the spread of local farming in the bottomlands of the Chattahoochee River and eventually to the growth of Gainesville's commercial/service role in Northeast Georgia. Because of its trade route location through the Indian Territory and because it was the closest point of civilization, Gainesville quickly became the center for prospectors to purchase provisions for their expedition to the northern gold fields. The town had tradesmen equipped to assay and sell gold for the miners.

Gainesville quickly grew with all the commercial and entertainment establishments of a boomtown. Such a promising gold rush situation brought many to the area. Among them Templeton Reid who arrived in Gainesville from Milledgeville in the summer of 1830. Reid established a private mint about one block west of the Square on West Washington and Maple Streets. Reid minted gold two and one half, five, and ten-dollars marked with the value and "Templeton Reid, Assayer." He stayed in Gainesville, only a year or so until a federal mint was located in Dahlonega, but in that time created what today

Above: Wagon and buggy building were important local industries well into the twentieth century.

Below: A 1952 photo of the "last" Bagwell Wagon getting final attention from old hands of this locally important industry.

COURTESY OF TONY PECK.

4

G. W. WALKER,

MANUFACTURER OF

PHAETONS and BUGGIES.

REPAIRING DONE

In all its Branches.

Main Street.   Near Square,

GAINESVILLE, GA.

are some of the most desirable and valuable coins in American coin collecting.

Between 1820 and 1830, Hall's population more than doubled from something just over 5,000 to almost 12,000. Most were white newcomers attracted by the lure of gold. When the gold miners abandoned Lumpkin and Hall Counties in 1849 and moved on to California and Colorado, the Gainesville population declined by the late 1850s to about twenty-five hundred. But, by 1900, the population had swelled again to four thousand.

EARLY DEVELOPMENT

From 1828 to the beginning of the Civil War in 1861 the Gainesville Square steadily grew with an assortment of wooden buildings along board sidewalks with hitching posts. During this period fires were frequent but structures were replaced as quickly as they were lost. In 1885 the small outdated wooden courthouse located in the center of the Square burned. A new large Victorian-styled brick courthouse was built in 1885 one block away between East Broad, South Bradford, South Green and East Spring. This had the advantage of visually opening up the Square and relieving some of its congestion.

In 1867 when John Muir came to Hall County on his "thousand mile walk to the Gulf," his route took him through Gainesville which he described as a "comfortable, finely shaded town." He spent the night with the Praters, "a plain backwoods family," whose son was a friend of Muir. Muir spent a day with Prater on the Chattahoochee "feasting on grapes that dropped from overhanging vines[11]." Muir reported that he "was intoxicated with the beauty of those glorious riverbanks[12]."

Beginning in the late 1800s and continuing to the 1940-50s, Gainesville hosted several wagon and carriage manufacturing businesses. George W. Walker Carriage Factory and Evans Carriage Company, both located on Main Street one block off the Square, built complete lines of carriages and wagons. Their covered wagons were commonly seen on the Oregon, Santa Fe and other trails. Bagwell Carriage Manufacturing Company, located until the 1930s at the east side of Athens and Summit Streets, was widely known for sturdy wagons. With the increase in the number of motor vehicles after the 1920s, the use of wagons and carriages declined correspondingly.

Next door to the Bagwell Carriage Manufacturing firm was a livery stable also owned by the Bagwell Brothers that continued until the 1950s. The urban renewal program of the 1960s removed those deteriorated facilities and redeveloped that block and other

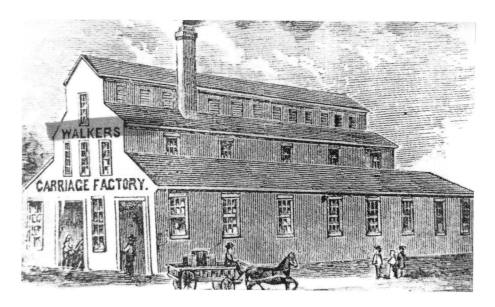

blocks along Athens Street, College Avenue, and South Green Street.

Cultural opportunity in Gainesville accelerated toward century's end. A Library Association was organized in 1877. Fraternal orders and lodges were established among the black as well as the white citizens. There was a local Agricultural Society (1878) and a Ladies Literary Club (1894). In 1888 Hall County's first local fair honored General James Longstreet, proprietor of the Piedmont Hotel, as grand marshall.

Along with "town team baseball" and the bicycling "craze," the Chautauqua was an important part of recreation in 1890s Gainesville. The Chautauqua (organized in Gainesville in 1898) was a spreading cultural-

Above: George W. Walker's Carriage Factory, 53 South Main Street, 1876.

Below: The Square before "Ole Joe," postcard, c. 1900.

Above: The Harrison Taylor Martin and Son Livery Stable, Spring Street, 1879.

Below: This building served as the Hall County Courthouse from 1885 to 1936. This image was taken from a postcard, c. 1900.

Descriptions of farm life in the area tell much the same story anytime from the 1830s well into the last years of the nineteenth century. Spring, the plowing season, saw the man of the house and the older children in the fields from first light till sundown, taking breaks for water and food at midday, usually biscuits or cornbread, a little pork, maybe an onion. In July crops were "laid by," and fodder pulled. September brought harvest, first peas, then cotton and now even the smallest of the family went to the fields. Sweet potatoes, peanuts, and cane needed attention, too, along with mother's garden and house orchard. As the cool weather came, the women dried beans, made kraut, and canned vegetables. In the winter months quilting provided a break in the routine of soap making, washing, scrubbing, and tending to the children and babies. With seasonal relief from field chores, the men and boys turned to building and making repairs. Cutting trees, sawing logs, gathering rocks for chimneys and pillars, riving shingles, piling up firewood, weaving oak split baskets, readying tools for the next season, and hunting filled the shorter days of the year.

It is difficult to find detailed accounts of farm life among specific families in Hall County during this period, but town settlements have a way of leaving more historic evidence of their times. From this point on it is often the case that the documented and written history of Gainesville has to serve as much of the history of the entire County.

Reverend Adiel A. Sherwood offered a description of Hall's County seat: "31 dwelling houses, 8 stores, 4 law offices, 3 doctors and 5 mechanic shops. C.H. [Courthouse] and Jail, 3 houses of public worship, for Baptists, Methodists, and Presbyterians[14]."

Politics was not considered very important. Political campaigns were largely based on personalities; the driving issue of antebellum politics and states-rights was of minor interest in this part of Georgia right up to the verge of secession and war. Georgia mountain folks were usually more stirred up over individual rights than states rights. In discussions of who was in charge, Hall Countians certainly did not think it was the federal government, but neither did they think it was the government in the capitol at Milledgeville.

entertainment-educational American phenomenon of the late nineteenth century. Lectures, speeches, and talks, and demonstrations were provided by a wide array of traveling personalities[13]. Politicians, scientists, preachers, and perhaps a few "humbugs" roamed the hinterlands, appeared in open air forums, under canvas tents, or in large halls and presented sessions of inspiration and promise not entirely unlike the motivational seminars of late twentieth century America.

COURT LITIGATION

The Square witnessed litigation and court decisions that sometimes attracted notoriety and brought folks from all over into Gainesville. Relations with the Cherokee changed as gold seekers scoured the countryside. The Cherokee turned to the Federal Government for protection against encroachments on their lands by the gold seekers, yet the State of Georgia, in a show of fierce state's rights independence extended Georgia law into the Indian Territory.

In 1830 a Hall County jury at the wooden courthouse on the Square convicted an Indian named George (Corn) Tassel of killing a white man trespassing on Indian land. The verdict was appealed to the U.S. Supreme Court which reversed its opinion by Chief Justice Marshall ruling that Georgia had no jurisdiction over the Cherokee Indian Territory. However, it was the decision of the Georgia governor and local authorities to carry out the original sentence and Corn Tassel was hung on December 24, 1830 two blocks south of the Square on College Avenue, Main and Grove Streets near the spring (Mule Camp). Hundreds of "people came from miles around to witness the event[15]." This became a landmark case for U.S. Indian Affairs. A new treaty calling for Indian surrender of their lands to the State brought the opening and settlement of these new lands by whites.

Top: A handsome reminder of the thirties, 1938 Federal Courthouse, addition to the 1911 Post Office.

COURTESY OF RICHARD STONE.

Above: The 1938 Hall County Courthouse from inside the courtyard of the Georgia Mountains Center and government complex, c. 2000.

COURTESY OF RICHARD STONE.

Left: A busy day on the Gainesville, Georgia, Square. Bradford Street can be seen in the background and Spring Street on right.

COURTESY OF CURTIS PARKS, JR.

Top, left: William G. B. Hosch (1845-1914) Company E, Confederate States Marines, c. 1864. He came to Gainesville from Hoschton following the Civil War and established a family and business.

COURTESY OF HEYWARD HOSCH, JR.

Top, right: Robert Garner (b. 1842) of Murrayville area of Hall County CSA, c. 1863.

COURTESY OF IRIS FRY.

Bottom, left: Early entrepreneur, John J. Huessey began a short-lived business, a hand rolled cigar factory, in 1894.

Bottom, right: The Whelchels were a pioneer family whose importance continued into the twentieth century. This photo is a studio portrait of Dave Whelchel, c. 1870.

COURTESY OF DIXIE RAMSEY & THE RAMSEY COLLECTION.

Another trial in 1911 took place in the 1885 Courthouse when the notoriously famous stagecoach, bank, and train robber, Bill Miner, robbed the train near Air Line Station and White Sulphur Springs, five miles from Gainesville. Miner was found guilty and sentenced to life. It was said that one of the railroad protectors (private police), Allan Pinkerton of the Pinkerton National Detective Agency, himself, attended the trial. Miner was called the "Gentleman Bandit" and "The Grey Fox." He made famous the quote "Hands up[16]!"

and was the subject of a major motion picture *The Grey Fox*, starring the late actor Richard Farnsworth as Miner.

A FINE PLACE TO LIVE

One of the area's attractions for the years to come was already apparent at the time of Adiel Sherwood's *Gazetteer of Georgia* of 1837. "This

is," he wrote, "a place of considerable resort during the summer season." Sherwood mentioned gold mining in the area and "pretty good, tolerable, or rough" roads. He observed that the land "with a little work can be made smooth but it will ever be hilly." Sherwood noted the "fine view of the Yonah Mt., on the road to Clarksville."

An 1831 Athens newspaper account of the prosperity which was coming to Gainesville mentioned "great advantages to the capitalist: enterprise of its inhabitants, rich gold mines, civilized men, various types of employment, luxuries and refinement of a town destined to rival…many of the old more populous."

Gainesville and Hall County by the end of the 1830s were populated by many who came from the northeast, beyond Georgia, of a Scotch-Irish stock that had its most immediate previous experience and cultural molding in the Carolinas and Virginia rather than from the coastal origin of Savannah or cotton-rich middle Georgia.

In the early 1900s, Hosch Brothers Wholesale, Claud Peck Wholesale Grocery, and Whitaker, Garrett Wholesale Grocery, Palmour Hardware Company, and, after World War II, Paris-Dunlap Harware Company competed in North Georgia until the chain store system of merchandising eliminated many of the independent North Georgia institutions.

EDUCATION AT THE TURN OF THE CENTURY

Murrayville Yellow Creek Baptist Church, founded in 1823, and Hopewell Methodist Church were the spiritual anchors of the community and the people of these congregations were keen on creating educational opportunities for their young folk. There are attendance records for a Murrayville Boarding School as early as the 1840s. A 1915 brochure advertising Murrayville High School describes the building and grounds as "well located on a large elevated plot of ground," with

Above: Following the Civil War, William Hosch, a Civil War veteran, began a dry goods store in Hoschton (later in Flowery Branch) with others as partners. In 1892 Hosch went to Gainesville and opened up Hosch Bros. & Sons (1892-1901) with his brother and then Hosch Bros. Company (1901 onward). Hosch family members involved in these enterprises included William Hosch, John H. Hosch, William H. Hosch, Walter E. Hosch, G. Carlton Hosch, Lester W. Hosch, and Ralph Hosch. The wholesale dry goods and notions wholesaler became a prominent business managed by the Hosch family.

COURTESY OF LESTER HOSCH & HEYWARD HOSCH, JR.

Left: A float created by Hosch Brothers & Co. Note the initials of the family members on the float. In 1907 the Hosch family led the founding of the Citizens Bank (later changed to Bank South in the 1990s and Bank of America in 1998). In the years following the Civil War other wholesale enterprises, including Carter Grocery Company, owned by S. C. Carter and his sons Lint, Roy, and Jimmy, and Gainesville Grocery, the predecessor of H. A. Terrell and Son Grocery Company, became prominent.

COURTESY OF LESTER HOSCH & HEYWARD HOSCH, JR.

a "large, modern and convenient school building, one of the best in Northeast Georgia." Following World War II the community, through all kinds of fundraisers and thousands of volunteer hours, built and equipped a new lunchroom and installed indoor restrooms. The County sold the building within a decade of these great efforts and closed the school in 1957.

Out in the County in 1875 there were nineteen white schools and one black school under some general county supervision but in reality they were governed by individual boards of trustees who took the lead in the distribution of the meager state funds. Because students paid tuition the "system" was less than free public education. A private prep school was opened in 1899 as Piedmont High School and became Georgia Military Institute in 1900.

Brenau University began in 1878 as Georgia Baptist Female Seminary, a college for women. It was renamed Georgia Female Seminary and Conservatory of Music in 1890. Pearce Auditorium, completed in 1897[17], seats 733. When purchased by H. J. Pearce in 1900, the seminary was renamed Brenau College and Conservatory. Brenau Academy, a female,

Brenau College, Gainesville, Ga.

residential college-preparatory high school, was created in 1928. In the 1990s Brenau College attained university status.

The State of Georgia took its first steps toward a state system of education in 1872 and Gainesville and Hall County were among the first communities in the State to organize public education. What was called "Gainesville College" was opened in 1874 in a structure erected by the City located on Main Street at College Avenue. It was not really a college, more of what would today be considered a high school and while it was a public effort, students were still required to pay tuition. In 1892 the City created a Board of Education and opened

the Gainesville High School at the old Gainesville College location. The first graduating class with eleven grades was in 1894. Subsequently, when a Gainesville High School building was constructed in the 1920s at West Washington Street one block off the Square, the "college" structure became Main Street Elementary School until 1957. In 1899 a new school, Northwestern, for black students was completed.

Educational concerns for the youth prompted individual Hall County communities outside Gainesville to establish some impressive schools prior to the full consolidation of an educational system in the County in the late 1920s. Concord

Above: This image of Brenau College was taken from a postcard, c. 1910.

Below: The students at attention, Riverside Military Academy boys on parade ground before World War I.

Academy was established in the northern part of the County around 1890 and in 1901 the Chattahoochee Baptist Association founded Chattahoochee High School at Clermont. For a time the Concord Academy Elementary School met with the Chattahoochee High School. There were 150 students in the first term of the combined schools. Despite a disastrous fire in 1908 enrollment reached 350 by 1910. In the early 1920s the school was a secondary school of Mercer University but soon returned to its former status with expanded support from

Left: The Prior Street football team 1922: 1-Melvin Ramsey, 2-Major Nuckolls, 3-Joe W. Robertson, 4-Bill Johnson, 5-Frank Cash, 6-Edward Bowen, 7-Bob Montgomery, 8-Emmett Lilly, 9-Otto Ramsey, 10-Rufus Brown, 11-Ben Nuckolls.
COURTESY OF DIXIE RAMSEY & THE RAMSEY COLLECTION.

Below: Fourth grade Candler Street School students in Gainesville on the eve of the Great Depression.
COURTESY OF DIXIE RAMSEY & THE RAMSEY COLLECTION.

associated churches in the region. At the close of the 1920s it became part of the newly consolidated Hall School System, continuing as Chattahoochee High School until the end of World War II. Its famous basketball teams of the 1930s produced such notables as John "Whack" Hyder who was inducted into Georgia Institute of Technology's Baseball Hall of Fame (1956) and Basketball Hall of Fame (1960) while employed as Georgia Tech's basketball coach (1952-1973).

CHAPTER 1 ENDNOTES

[1] Hall County was created December 15, 1818.

[2] John Muir. *A Thousand-Mile Walk to the Gulf* (1916).

[3] Gainesville was incorporated November 31, 1821.

[4] H. A. Terrell & Son Wholesale Grocery, Maple Street at West Spring Street, c. 1900-56; Henry Earl Terrell, manager, Coca-Cola Bottling Plant, North Green Street, c. 1915-50.

[5] The Terrell plat of Gainesville. The lots were numbered and the streets were named.

[6] According to M. Garland Reynolds, Jr. (b. 1935), a Gainesville-based, nationally respected architect, and Jane Reynolds Hemmer (b. 1947), the first female local Georgia state senator, their great, great grandfather, Bartimous Reynolds, was one of the first five trustees of the Gainesville Academy.

[7] Candler Street School, where classes first began after construction in 1911, was vacated by the City School System in 1978 with plans to abandon the facilities. The Hall County Historical Society advocated preservation and restoration to civic and/or business uses. The City offered the school for sale under conditions of preservation by the purchaser. Purchased in 1981 by Don Carter Realty and Bates Carter & Co., P.C. (owned by Jim Bates and John Carter), the school was approved on the National Register of Historic Places in 1982. The inconsistent adjoining school addition, erected in 1947, was torn down for construction of quality condominium apartments on the playground and athletic fields which surround the historic school building.

[8] Gainesville has been fortunate in the attraction of schools: Brenau University, formerly Brenau College and originally the Georgia Baptist Female Seminary (1878); Riverside Military Academy (1907); Gainesville College (1963), formerly Gainesville Junior College; Lanier Technical College (1963), formerly Lanier Technical Institute; Lakeview Academy (1970); Enota School; Candler Street School; Fair Street School; E. E. Butler High School; Gainesville High School; now extensive good County schools. A review of the development of the schools would be an interesting history itself.

[9] Unlicensed saloons.

[10] D. S. (Doc) Lowe, along with Austin Brown, Reverend A. D. Hawks, Reverend C. T. Hester, J. Wesley Merritt, John Morrow, and Roy Stephens served successively on the school board in the 1950s.

[11] "This remarkable species of wild grape…fall into the river (and) are often found in large quantities in the eddies along the bank (and) sometimes made into wine. I think another name for this grape is the Scuppernong, though called 'muscadine' here."

[12] Muir.

[13] According to a pamphlet published by the Gainesville Chamber of Commerce around 1910 that was written by Dr. M. S. Stephenson, scientist, "The Auditorium of Brenau College, which is used during the Chautauqua and on other occasions, is one of the most beautiful in the state."

[14] Adiel Sherwood. *A Gazetteer of Georgia*. Washington, P. Force (1837).

[15] *Gainesville Eagle*, May 11, 1888.

[16] Mark Dugan and John Boessenecker. *The Grey Fox*. University of Oklahoma Press (1992). Inside cover page, see photo of Bill Miner at sixty-four-years-old, after capture in Gainesville, Georgia, for the Southern Railroad train robbery in 1911 at night near Air Line Station and White Sulphur Spring; page 156, a composite photo of Miner and two others; and pages 168-70, photos of prisoners, all photographed by W. J. Ramsey of Gainesville.

[17] Today, with its distinctive fresco ceiling, Pearce Auditorium remains a tribute to local educational and cultural concern and support.

CHAPTER II

RAILROADS & NEW TECHNOLOGY

Gainesville escaped the ravages of the Civil War, primarily because there was no railroad and the area had little strategic value. The Square actually prospered during this time because of its location as the principal Northeast Georgia trading center.

Earlier, corporate charters in 1847 and again in the mid-1850s advocating rails to Hall County had failed. The Civil War halted talk of railroad development. But by early 1869 workers of Atlanta Charlotte Air Line, later Richmond and Danville Railroad (later Southern Railroad), began locating the route for the new rail line from Washington, Atlanta, and New Orleans. A debate arose as to whether the main rail line depot should be at Lula or Gainesville. Once Gainesville was selected, Gainesville leaders pressed for the railroad route that would run close by the Square. The Railroad demurred and the Square area ultimately lost to the route one mile south completed in 1872. Subsequently, Main and Bradford Streets from the Depot to the Square became major transportation routes to the Square.

The Northeastern Railroad, circa 1876, which connected Athens with Gainesville via Lula, Gillsville, Maysville, and Commerce was taken over about 1900 by Southern Railroad, now Norfolk Southern.

THE GAINESVILLE MIDLAND RAILROAD

In 1872 the Gainesville, Jefferson, and Southern Railroad line (GJS) was chartered. Operated by the Georgia Railroad and Banking Company, it was a narrow-gauge track running fifty-two miles eastward from Gainesville, Candler, Belmont, Braselton, Winder to Monroe to Social Circle[1].

Gainesville's first radio station, WGGA (Athens Highway), began shortly before WWII. Shown here are staff, management, studio, and the station's mobile unit in the late '40s. Charles Smithgall and Lessie Smithgall are seated on the far left with Jim Hartley standing behind them.
COURTESY OF LESSIE SMITHGALL.

This Gainesville and Northwestern train ran from Helen to Gainesville between 1913 and 1933 hauling lumber which was used for much of the construction of Gainesville prior to the 1936 tornado. Note the swastika-like symbol within the logo of the railroad. This symbol has held individual meanings for thousands of years in different cultures and in this case was a Native American symbol of "good luck."

Around 1900, Georgia Railroad Company bought from GJS the thirteen miles from Social Circle to Monroe. Then GJS built a branch line from Belmont to Athens via Talmo, Pendergrass, Jefferson, Redstone, Attica, and widened the existing narrow gauge track to standard from Gainesville to Belmont and Monroe. When the branch line was extended from Belmont to Athens, the GJS name was changed to Gainesville Midland Railroad Company. By August 1924 when Wylie Cronic (now age ninety-six residing on North Avenue) started working with Gainesville Midland along with Van Leland Byrd, father of Walter Byrd, the Gainesville Midland was operating both its line from Belmont to Pendergrass, Jefferson, and Athens, and continued the newer route from Belmont, Braselton, Hoschton, and Winder to Monroe. In 1959 Seaboard Railroad bought Gainesville Midland and soon abandoned the older line from Belmont to Braselton, Winder, and Monroe and continued the newer route from Belmont, Talmo, Pendergrass, and Jefferson to Athens. The Belmont to Athens line of Seaboard Railroad Company (now CSX) competed with the Southern Railroad Company (now Norfolk Southern) branch line via Lula, Gillsville, Maysville, and Commerce to Athens.

The line from Candler to Belmont, Talmo, Pendergrass, Jefferson, and Athens had its share of idiosyncrasies. One story told about

this line was that of the lady passenger who, frustrated by the slow pace of the journey asked the conductor "can't you run faster than this?" "Yes," he replied, "but regulations require that I stay with the train." First hand accounts recalled the train stopping for blackberry picking along the route.

THE GAINESVILLE-HELEN RAILROAD

The Gainesville Northwestern Railroad, ran from New Holland parallel to Clark's Bridge Road to Brookton, Clermont, Cleveland, Nacoochee Valley, Helen and Robertstown. About 1912 rail magnate Henry C. Bagley, after the White County gold boom, discovered the mountains had quantities of large virgin pine and poplar trees, some of them twenty-five feet in circumference. He built the Gainesville Northwestern Railroad to Cleveland, Helen, and Robertstown, and Byrd and Matthews Lumber Mills built a substantial lumber mill ("one of the world's largest") on the banks of the Chattahoochee River at Helen[2]. The main line was standard gauged track, but from Helen and Robertstown, narrow gauge tracks ran into the mountains to haul large logs to the lumber mill in Helen. Until about 1925, a passenger train was operated daily to Gainesville. It was comprised of "a steam locomotive, a coal car, a combination baggage, mail and a passenger car with an observation platform at rear[3]." The north Georgia timber forests were effectively exhausted in the late 1920s, and the lumber mill at Helen, then owned by Morris Brothers Lumber Company, was reduced in operations in the early 1930s. With little lumber being manufactured, the railroad hauled only feeds, foodstuffs, and other consumer products which was also terminated by 1933.

BRANCH TO PYRITES MINE

Beginning in 1916, for defense purposes following the entry of the U.S. into World War I, the Chestatee Pyrites and Chemical Corporation built and owned a branch line from Clermont, which was completed in July 1918, to the pyrites mine[4] on the Chestatee River in Lumpkin County. At Clermont it connected with the Northwestern Railroad line which owned, operated, and maintained the branch trains. Before the railroad was constructed, pyrites ore was transported via vehicles owned by the mine operator and by farmers along the route hired to haul to the Northwestern stop at Brookton. The hilly dirt road was rough and impassable in rainy weather. The pyrites ore was shipped to Copper Hill, Tennessee, to be smelted for sulfuric acid to make explosives.

Soon after gearing up for the war effort, the end of WWI in 1918 terminated the pyrites contract with the federal government and the mining and shipping of pyrites ended in 1920. Quarrying thereafter at this location in a new tunnel was for crushed stone for road building. When the pyrites mine closed in 1928, the rail line was abandoned[5]. The railroad line ran from the small depot across from the Clermont Hotel at the location of the present Clermont City Hall on a route parallel to the highway to the intersection with Shoal Creek Road, then along Shoal Creek Road by the northern and eastern base of Wauka Mountain to Shoal Creek, and past Mt. Zion Church to the Chestatee River.

The Gainesville-Helen tracks and the branch line from Clermont to the pyrites mine were removed starting around 1936 and the steel reputedly was sold to Japan.

THE PROPOSED GAINESVILLE-DAHLONEGA RAILROAD

Plans for a railroad line from Gainesville or Lula to Dahlonega which never materialized were occasionally mentioned in newspaper accounts, but the planned route and the development facts are mainly mysteries. The most interesting information concerning the proposals from the 1870s to 1906 is contained in a chapter entitled "The Railroad That Almost Came to Dahlonega" in *I Remember Dahlonega*, Volume 2, pages 21 through 28, authored by Anne Amerson (second printing published in 1998 by Chestatee Publications). According to Amerson, following earlier proposals begun through a state charter originally obtained in 1847, the prime mover, planner, and persistent constructor of a line

from Gainesville to Dahlonega was Colonel William P. Price, state legislator, U.S. congressman, and mayor of Dahlonega[6]. During these years, the newspapers *Dahlonega Signal*, *Dahlonega Nugget*, and *Gainesville Eagle*—published letters and statements from various individuals about the line, sometimes alternatively referenced as the "Gainesville and Dahlonega Railroad," the "Athens, Lula, Tate Railroad," and the "Dahlonega-Dawsonville Railroad;" one article mentioning that the routes and some tracks had been laid from a Chattahoochee railroad bridge several miles to Bark Camp and "Price" (a planned "stop" at the intersection of Cool Springs Road and Price Road near Murrayville)[7]. In December 1879 Colonel Price reported that the railroad from Gainesville to Bark Camp was under construction and had crossed the Chattahoochee River[8]. Apparently the Price group built a bridge allegedly costing $40,000 that crossed the Chattahoochee River near Gainesville, then to the Chestatee River near Leather's Ford. No railroad trestle seems to have been built across the Chestatee River[9].

The *Gainesville Eagle* reported on May 7, 1880 that a surveyor had "located" the line "to Aurora[10]." The closer it got to Dahlonega, the more difficult the construction became because of the terrain. References to the location of a planned route are even more confusing.

An article in the *Signal* in July 1884 reported: "Capt. Neisler and Mr. James Dune, contractors

According to news accounts, this would show the end of the last narrow gauge section of the old Gainesville Midland line, c. 1908. Railroads, faced with new competition from the automobile, consolidated and began to update their technology.

COURTESY OF THE HALL COUNTY LIBRARY.

Big Bear Café, erected in 1936, on South Main Street at Southern Railroad Depot, 2000.
COURTESY OF WILLIAM L. NORTON, JR.

RAILROAD & HIGHWAY DISPUTES

Dr. Rafe Banks, Jr. (1919-1985), prominent medical doctor, urology specialist, and businessman, was a son of banker-businessman Rafe Banks, and fourth generation of the Hall County Banks family. He was cautious in his own dealings and once related an interesting thought. His great-grandfather, Dr. Richard Banks, settled in Gainesville in 1820s where he became a prominent medical doctor, large landowner, banker, and legislator. After the exodus of miners from Gainesville and Dahlonega upon the Gold Rushes to California in 1849 and to Colorado in 1858, desperate landowners sold land to Dr. Banks and others at bargain prices of a few cents per acre in Hall and Banks Counties (named for the Banks family). Dr. Rafe Banks, Jr., related that, when the Southern Railroad was surveying the route (c. 1870), they tried to acquire adequate land near Lula for the local major depot and switching tracks. The Banks family held out for more money. The Railroad decided to locate the depot near Gainesville on cheaper land. Gainesville prospered while Lula became a satellite. Dr. Banks in the 1960s speculated "If the railroad had persuaded my family to sell Lula area land, would Lula and Banks County have been what Gainesville developed into?" He offered the philosophical comment that "sometimes it may not be wise to continually refuse to sell something."

A similar dispute as to a highway transportation route involved a State Highway Department offer to widen U.S. Highway 23 from Flowery Branch[17], through Chicopee and Gainesville, and past New Holland Mill. In fall 1945, funds having been released by the end of WWII, Governor Ellis Arnall called State Senator W. L. Norton and offered the four-lane highway from Flowery Branch which Gainesville had sought prior to WWII. The City accepted but insisted the route follow Broad Street between 1938 City Hall and 1938 County Courthouse to New Holland rather than the route proposed by Highway Department which left West Broad Street to follow Myrtle Street to New Holland. The Highway Department adamantly refused, saying it would never build a new major highway across several lanes of railroad track such as near the Gainesville Midland Depot. The City was unyielding and the project was lost. Later Broad Street at the Government Center was closed for construction of the Georgia Mountains Center and the City-County Administration Building on the campus of the historic "Civic Center" composed of President Franklin Roosevelt's historic 1938 Courthouse and City Hall. During the years intervening, the Myrtle Street (now Martin Luther King Boulevard) widened route to New Holland was repeatedly planned to move some traffic off Broad and Church Streets (now Jesse Jewell Parkway), but is not completed to date.

for the trestle work of the Gainesville and Dahlonega Railroad have gone to work getting things in readiness to commence construction of the trestles[11]." According to Amerson, no further newspaper references appeared until the April 9, 1886 issue of the *Signal* reported "the company has already graded the road from Gainesville to the Chestatee River, a distance of twelve miles and laid about four miles of track. It has also built a substantial bridge costing $15,000 across the Chattahoochee River[12]." What was completed and happened to "the Gainesville and Dahlonega Railroad remains a bit confusing[13]."

ELECTRICITY PLANS FOR GAINESVILLE

Around 1900 the story of the plans of the Colonel Price group for a railroad line from Gainesville to Dahlonega becomes merged with the story of the plans of the Warner group for electricity. In 1898 General Adoniram Judson Warner, an engineer, migrated to Gainesville from Ohio. Warner was an officer in the Union forces in the Civil War, a Democratic Ohio congressman, a friend of President Lincoln, who came south possibly on doctor's advice to search for a more acceptable climate and perhaps to investigate mining potentials around Dahlonega. He was skilled in both mining and railroad engineering. He became impressed with the North Georgia rivers and streams and the potential for construction of hydroelectric dams[14] to provide electricity.

A year later he returned to Gainesville from Ohio where he had raised capitol for Georgia electric development enterprises. He founded the North Georgia Electric Company in 1902 (D. M. Stewart, president; W. A. Carlisle, whom Warner had brought from Ohio, vice president; W. H. Slack, Warner's son-in-law, secretary) as well as a subsidiary, the Gainesville and Dahlonega Electric Railway Company, also in 1902 (A. J. Warner, president and general manager; C. M. Merrick, vice president; W. A. Carlisle, secretary and treasurer)[15]. He also attracted some capitol from locals including Colonel Samuel C. Dunlap. Between 1901-1905, they acquired land and easements along the Chattahoochee, Chestatee and Etowah Rivers for potential hydroelectric facilities[16].

THE CREATION OF COMMUNITIES

Cotton gins, trains, textile mills, and increasing commercial farming and exchange fostered a number of small communities around Hall County. The communities sometimes started as "stops" or "stations" along Railroad lines at roads where warehouses were located to hold fertilizer and feed and other farming supplies. Belmont was established in 1881 as a station on the Gainesville, Jefferson, and Southern Railroad (GJS). Belton (also called Bellton) approximately one mile from Lula, was laid out in the 1870s as the Atlanta Charlotte Air Line Railroad (later Richmond and Danville) was being built. Lula was established as "Lula Junction" in 1876. Candler and Braselton each started about 1881 as stations along the Gainesville-Jefferson line. Clermont was originally Concord Church Community; the post office was named Dip until it was changed in 1905 to Clermont. Brookton and Clermont became stops in 1913 on the Northwestern Railroad line to Cleveland, Helen and Robertstown. New Holland evolved from New Holland Station (1877) and as a springs resort previously known as Limestone Springs (and New Holland Springs), a name revived as Limestone Parkway in 1990. Other well-known Hall County communities, for example: Gillsville, first called "Stone Throw," which may deserve to be considered Hall's first settlement, and Murrayville, are properly considered pioneer communities by coming into being with the creation of the County. Chicopee was a late 1920s wholly owned, planned textile community of Johnson & Johnson, Inc.

The North Georgia Electric Company and the Gainesville and Dahlonega Electric Railway Company, planned to build hydroelectric plants on these rivers. First in 1902 they began a dam and hydroelectric plant at "New Bridge," (also called Leather's Ford) on the Chestatee River at a cost of $100,000. By 1903 it generated electric power and for the operation of a proposed railroad to Gainesville over "a 14-mile" transmission line "by copper wires" along the railroad right-of-way to supply electricity to the streets, hotels and businesses and to electrify the existing horse-drawn Gainesville and Hall County Street Railroad streetcar line in Gainesville (chartered in 1884.); the New Bridge Chestatee Plant was treated as a part of the Gainesville and Dahlonega Electric Railway project[18]. The dam was 200 feet long, 27 feet high, and the power plant had a 1,200-horsepower output. The New Bridge dam was built with timbers and continued in operation until 1927 when the dam was abandoned because of poor repair and rotting timbers by its successor, Georgia Power Company[19].

In Gainesville, with electricity by 1903 from the New Bridge plant, an electric motor trolley line soon replaced the mule and horse-drawn streetcar line from the Southern Railroad Depot via South Main Street. It traversed around two sides of the Square and then ran via East Washington and East Spring Streets to New Holland Spring Hotel (Limestone) via North Green to near Gower Spring Hotel and Riverside Drive to the Chattahoochee River at a recreation area known as "Chattahoochee Park." A pavilion was built circa 1898 at Chattahoochee Park and the streetcars circled it to repeat the route. After the pavilion burned a new pavilion was constructed circa 1903-06 which is still at the American Legion Marina site. The former "Chattahoochee Park" (circa 1880s-1928), then "Georgia Power Club" (1928-58), then American Legion Marina (1958-2001) is one of Gainesville's most historic sites. Streetcars also traversed via East Washington and East Spring Streets through Brenau College to New Holland Spring Hotel and textile mill.

A. J. Warner, while promoting electrical facilities on the Chestatee and Chattahoochee Rivers in the early 1900s, also headed the Crown Mountain Mining and Milling Company which had a dam and hydroelectric generating plant known as Gorge Dam Power Plant for its mining operations[20].

In 1906 the Warner group completed a transmission line from Gainesville to Atlanta, allegedly the first steel tower transmission line built in the southeast and the second in the United States[21]. In the same year the North Georgia Electric Company erected a substation and office building at Edgewood Avenue between Piedmont Avenue and Courtland Street preparatory to obtaining a license to provide electric power in Atlanta[22].

In 1908 the Warner group constructed Dunlap Dam and a hydroelectric plant[23] at a bend of the Chattahoochee River at the

GAINESVILLE, GA.   Chattahoochee Park

Chattahoochee Park on Lake Warner,
terminus of the streetcar tracks, Riverside
Drive, postcard, c. 1910.

terminus of Riverside Drive in Gainesville. Built of logs cut in the area, it was 500 feet long, 36 feet high, and 80 feet wide at the foundation. It cost $150,000[24] and created a nine-mile-long Lake Warner and Chattahoochee Park for boating, swimming, and other recreation.

About July 1900 Colonel Price offered to donate his "unfinished track, including the piers at the Chattahoochee River with all of his road" to the Warner group which "proposed" to complete building the railroad[25]. This was about the date of arrival of the Warner group to Gainesville. It is not known what relationship the Price group had with the Warner electric and railroad company enterprise prior to the announcement of Price in July 1900 to sell the Price group railroad enterprise to the Warner group[26]. By 1900, the Price railroad group had acquired land and partially graded the right-of-way from Gainesville to New Bridge at the Hall-Lumpkin County line where the Warner group desired to build an electric plant[27]. Prospects for the Warner group completing the Price group's Gainesville-Dahlonega Railroad seemed high. After the Warner group had built the hydroelectric dam and plant at New Bridge by February 1903 the Gainesville Street Railroad (Warner group), according to the *Dahlonega Nugget*, "had recently begun to run on four miles of finished track on Gainesville streets and work would soon begin on the railroad line to the Chestatee Power Plant at New Bridge and thence Dahlonega[28]." In

August 1903 the *Gainesville Eagle* reported its confidence that the Gainesville and Dahlonega Electric Railway Company (Warner Group) "will soon begin work on the line to Dahlonega[29]." It was also reported that a branch line was to be built from the main line up Long Branch "to the Pyrites Mine." Pyrite was allegedly in great demand at the time for conversion into sulfuric acid used in making fertilizer[30].

In 1903 the *Eagle* reported a transfer of ownership of all the rights to the partially constructed Dahlonega rail route by Colonel Price to the Warner group[31]. The *Eagle* reported that the rail line would run from the Gainesville Railroad Depot along Gainesville Midland line across Broad Street and Washington Street to the Chattahoochee River where a bridge would cross and proceed to "Price" and thence to Lumpkin County across the Chestatee River. But it is difficult to know the route with accuracy because all of the references are quite vague. Sometimes the newspaper references circa 1880-1908 concerning the Gainesville-Dahlonega Railroad are two or three years apart with no mention of anything to indicate that any progress of construction had been made in the interim.

On April 26, 1905, the stockholders of the Gainesville and Dahlonega Electric Railway Company (chartered by Warner in 1902) sold all of the rights of its railroad line to the Gainesville-Dahlonega and Northern Railway Company (chartered by Warner April 15, 1905) for $500,000[32]. The transfer from one Warner corporation to a new Warner corporation included "the railroad right-of-way, roadbed, easements, franchises for railroad purposes and for the railroad from Gainesville along what is known as the Price line or the line of the old Gainesville and Dahlonega Railroad to Dahlonega[33]." It did not transfer to the corporation ("Northern Ry") the rights to electric transmission lines from New Bridge to Gainesville[34]. Thus, apparently the electric facilities along the railroad route stayed with North Georgia Electric Company.

The transfer agreement[35] and other information indicate that the proposed line from the Southern Depot area crossed Broad and Washington Streets, went through the valley which during the 1930-50s was the site of the Gainesville Golf Course, along "Black's Branch[36]," which is now a cove covered by Lake Lanier. Apparently, the route followed that "Black's Branch" valley and crossed the Chattahoochee River to proceed north to "Price Station" (near Bark Camp at Price Road and Cool Springs Road near Murrayville) and thence to New Bridge at Leather's Dam at the Chestatee River. Verification of that railroad route near Gainesville may be the alleged sightings of trough diggings of the route on the peninsula at the marina near the clubhouse of the present Chattahoochee Country Club. All evidence of the bridges over the Chattahoochee and Chestatee Rivers and much of the route were covered by Lake Lanier.

After the transfer of the rights from the Price group to the Warner group and from one Warner corporation ("Electric Ry") to another Warner corporation ("Northern Ry") in April 1905 available records fail to disclose any announcement of the continuation, demise or termination of efforts to build the railroad. But, it was never completed. In the late 1920s the North Georgia Electric Company became a part of Georgia Power Company.

Despite the efforts of some consecrated individuals primarily in Lumpkin County, always led by Price, during the years 1878-1905, the absence of demonstrated interest from Gainesville and others outside of Lumpkin County and other factors defeated the project. When Lake Lanier was constructed in the 1950s, easements to such Dahlonega railroad line were abandoned by heirs of the original owners[37].

SPRINGS, RESORTS & HOTELS

Following the Civil War years and the location of the railroads, an impressive number of hotels rose largely in support of the resort clientele which had been attracted to the region for years earlier than 1845 by the location of various springs thought to have curative powers and health benefits. These included Limestone Spring Resort; the Gower Spring Hotel at Thompson Bridge Road and Green Street Circle; White Sulphur Spring outside of Gainesville property and on the Square; the brick, three-story Arlington at

Spring and Main Streets; the Hudson House, another brick building, at Washington and Main Streets; and the Richmond on the north side of Main Street. On Main Street at Spring Street was the Hunt House, on Bradford Street, the Merchant's House, and the Piedmont Hotel on the block bounded by Main, High, Myrtle, and Maple Streets.

Promotional publications touted Gainesville for "low taxes, no ruts or cliques, accessibility, cheap land, good schools and churches, and two railroads." The chief attraction, however,

Top: The Dixie Hunt Hotel (formerly the Arlington Hotel), c. 1930.
COURTESY OF WILLIAM L. NORTON, JR.

Above: The rear of the Dixie Hunt Hotel, c. 1933.
COURTESY OF WILLIAM L. NORTON, JR.

GENERAL JAMES LONGSTREET

Lieutenant General James Longstreet, c. 1863.

General James Longstreet was transformed from war and hostility to the realization that the only proper course for the South was for the Confederate States to rejoin the Union in peace and reconciliation, and become an effective participant in a stronger United States. He remained a close friend of Ulysses S. Grant from their time spent at the West Point Military Academy in 1842. Grant married Longstreet's cousin, Julia Dent, and Longstreet was a groomsman in the wedding. President Grant appointed Longstreet to several important federal posts, including customs director of the Port of New Orleans.

After the war, Longstreet adopted the philosophy that the South, for its own good, should forget and forgive and join the new Union as a full participant in political affairs, which meant joining the party of Lincoln, as Longstreet did. He relocated to New Orleans and began a prosperous business. Appointed by the governor as head of the Louisiana militia, he defended the state government, which had decided to rejoin the Union, from a mob of several thousand who were advocating the overthrow of the state government unless the state legislature agreed not to rejoin the Union. Longstreet agreed that rejoining the Union and allowing blacks to vote was necessary if the South was to revive its economy. In the confrontation between the state militia, which included blacks, and a mob that included some Confederate veterans, the outnumbered militiamen were overwhelmed. Longstreet was wounded, captured, and held prisoner.

Leading black militiamen against former Confederate soldiers put Longstreet's life and reputation in peril. His business collapsed. Persuaded by his brother, Longstreet came to Gainesville in 1875 and purchased the new Piedmont Hotel on Main Street and a plantation facing Park Hill Drive near the present City Park. He established pastures, an orchard of fruit trees and an extensive grape vineyard.

In January 1879 Longstreet was appointed postmaster of Gainesville and served in that capacity until his appointment as minister to Turkey in 1880, returning to Gainesville in 1889. The seventy-six-year-old Longstreet married thirty-four-year-old Helen Dortch in 1897. The following year he was appointed U.S. railway commissioner. Longstreet was the leading local and state representative of the Republicans.

During the thirty post-war years he spent in Gainesville, Longstreet continued to advocate "Peace and Reconciliation" as a policy and argued that active participation of the former Confederate states in the Union would gain advantages to the Southern people and make the national government stronger. He urged citizenship, voting, and civil rights for former slaves. The "Peace and Reconciliation" argument for partnership with the North was not an attitude embraced by many in the South, including some former Confederate Army officers who became critics of Longstreet.

Neither was this policy appreciated by some citizens in Gainesville. Some ostracized Longstreet socially and in church. The fire which destroyed his residence at his farm on Park Hill Drive[38] (now the Longstreet Hills subdivision) on April 19, 1889, and a fire which damaged the Piedmont Hotel in 1903 were coincidental, suspicious, and tragic. Such socially "liberal" views were still controversial in the 1960s, the era of Martin Luther King, Jr. The soldiers who fought under Longstreet, however, throughout his life were uniformly devoted, loyal and admiring of their former commander. And General Robert E. Lee, never a critic, was always an admirer of General Longstreet.

On January 2, 1904, General Robert E. Lee's "old war horse" and "staff in [his] right hand[39]," died in Gainesville. The Candler Horse Guards escorted Longstreet's body to the Hall County Courthouse where he lay in state in the rotunda under the American flag. Mayor Howard Thompson proclaimed a suspension of business for citizens to attend the funeral service at the Courthouse at 11 a.m. on the 6th of January. Georgia Governor Joseph Terrell came with his following in two special trains from Atlanta. General James Longstreet's body is buried at Alta Vista Cemetery, Gainesville. President Theodore Roosevelt in a letter to Helen Longstreet, his widow, proclaimed General Longstreet "as patriotic to the Union after the war as he had been to the South during the war."

Longstreet's son, Garland, was an architect VMI graduate. He designed several buildings in Gainesville. They include City Hall and Fire Station, destroyed by the Tornado of 1936; Yonah Hall (Pearce Auditorium), Brenau College; and Colonel C. C. Sanders' house on Main Street as well as several Atlanta homes. He is buried next to General Longstreet at Alta Vista Cemetery in Gainesville.

Continued on next page

GENERAL JAMES LONGSTREET (Continued)

Another son, Robert Lee Longstreet, inherited the homeplace farm north of City Park from General Longstreet and sold the acreage in 1938 to W. L. Norton, Sr. for development of the Longstreet Hills subdivision, the first FHA-approved residential subdivision north of Decatur[40]. Robert Lee, who was General Robert E. Lee's godson, and his brother, James, Jr., both Army officers, are buried side by side in Arlington National Cemetery. The Longstreets' only daughter, Louise, who lived in Gainesville, produced two WWII naval officers who are buried near their uncles in Arlington Cemetery.

The dedication of the historic marker by the Historic Preservation Division of the Department of Natural Resources, in front of the Historic Piedmont Hotel, c. 2000. In attendance are (from left to right) Mayor Robert Hamrick, Jim Syfan; County Commissioner Jerry Carpenter; Lieutenant Governor Mark Taylor; Representative Carl Rogers; Burt Weerts, director of the State Parks and Historic Sites Division of the Department of Natural Resources; Ray Luce, director of the Historic Preservation Division of the Department of Natural Resources; M. Garland Reynolds, Jr.; Tevi Taliaferro; and Richard Pilcher.
COURTESY OF WILLIAM L. NORTON, JR.

was "a great health resort—winter and summer." Gainesville, it was said, was located in the ideal spot in regard to climate and elevation. It was a reasonably proximate location to escape the problems of the heat, mosquitoes, bugs, and malaria evident further south. The described resources had an additional attraction, their accessibility by means of "cheap railroad fare." There was described an abundance of excellent hotels and boarding houses which offered "fresh, nutritious food" and interestingly singling out fresh eggs and fat chickens, "Gainesville being the greatest chicken and egg market perhaps in the South."

From the Southern Railroad Depot, Gower Spring Hotel just north and west of Green Street on Thompson Bridge Road at Green Street Circle was easily accessible via the streetcar line and was considered "one of the chief attractions of our city." The water there was considered "valuable" as a tonic for "general debility, all kidney troubles, indigestion, and hemorrhoids." Proprietor P. B. Holtzendorf assured his hotel was "excellently kept."

Oconee White Sulphur, later the thirty-two-room White Sulphur Spring Hotel, was located six miles east of Gainesville and one mile from the Air Line Station on the Richmond and Danville Railroad line (which became Southern on July 15, 1894). Developed around 1920 by Colonel J. W. Oglesby, a railroad magnate, it was advertised as one of the most "attractive" and "fashionable" watering places in the South, with a "well appointed hotel" (until 1933, when it burned) and "modern cottages" near the spring. The hotel had a resident physician in addition to the waters which were "noted for marvelous cures...in cases of rheumatism, blood poisoning, dyspepsia and other complaints." A swimming pool, bathhouses, a bowling alley, a

The local resort period was nearing its end when this photo of the White Sulphur Spring Hotel was made in the late 1920s.
COURTESY OF THE HALL COUNTY LIBRARY.

HOME OF GENERAL JAMES LONGSTREET, GAINESVILLE, GEORGIA

Top: General James A. Longstreet's on home, Park Hill Drive, c. 1876.

Above: A postcard of General Longstreet's Piedmont Hotel (1875-1903), c. 1900.

large ballroom where dances were held in the evening, and a wide porch surrounding some of the hotel were part of the local accommodations.

GROWTH AFTER RAILROADS: THE QUEEN CITY OF THE MOUNTAINS

The rail connections following 1872 made Gainesville the primary market for the crops of northeast Georgia: cotton, pork, chickens, sorghum syrup, and apples. A host of new building materials was made available for Square construction, including wire nails, wood moldings, cast iron, brick and stone. Making the most dramatic change of all was cheap coal for better, easier, and safer heating. The town experienced tremendous growth as a commercial center. With the impetus of the railroads, it assumed its new role as the "Queen City of the Mountains[41]" by the end of the Civil War.

The gold activity in Lumpkin County and North Georgia progressed from the panning of gold and manual labor excavation of mines to the use of machinery and high-pressure water via hydroelectric power, a technique which had been developed in the gold operations of Colorado and California. Gainesville provided wholesale distribution of dry goods, hardware, machinery, and food products to not only the local retail stores, but east, west, and north to the borders of South Carolina, North Carolina, and Tennessee.

The Gainesville Street Railway Company was formed in 1875 and a streetcar line was constructed with horse and mule-drawn trolley cars, which were later replaced with electric cars. In 1884 and 1885 it was chartered as the Gainesville and Hall County Railroad with officers H. H. Dean, president, secretary, and treasurer; A. D. Candler, vice president; and D. E. Evans, manager. The route went from the Railroad Depot up Main Street, around the Square, up Green Street to the Gower Spring Hotel, and Riverside Drive to the springs at the Chattahoochee River, and out East Washington and Spring Streets to the New Holland Spring Hotel. Residential houses, including some large stately residences began to be erected along Main and Bradford Streets to the Square.

In 1872 the Piedmont Hotel was built by Alvah Smith two blocks from the Depot in the block bounded by Main, High, Myrtle, and Maple Streets. In the summer of 1875, upon his return to Gainesville to retirement after the Civil War, General James Longstreet purchased the hotel from Smith for $6,000 and operated it until 1905[42]. Local advertisements listed twelve public establishments in Gainesville for room and board. Heading the list was the Piedmont Hotel, under the immediate supervision of its owner, the distinguished old veteran and his wife. After fires and neglect, the Piedmont was substantially torn down in 1918.

Longstreet's thirty-four-room Piedmont Hotel[43] was an attractive site for countless distinguished politicians, former soldiers and others to lodge and dine. The standard and popular fare in the dining room was chicken and the Piedmont Hotel is considered the genesis of the chicken industry in North Georgia[44].

Some of the guests of the hotel on two occasions were Woodrow Wilson of Atlanta and his wife, Ellen Louise Axson, raised in Rome, Georgia. They stayed at the hotel and at the home of Ellen's aunt, Louisa Wade, at her house on Bradford-Myrtle Streets during several days preceding and after the birth of two of their three daughters. Margaret was born in Wade's home in 1886, and Jessie was born in 1887 at the hotel[45]. Parents such as the Wilsons frequented Gainesville for births because of the medical reputation of Dr. John Wimbish Oslin (1827-1906)[46], a local obstetrician, and also because the climate was considered more pleasant than some locales in Georgia.

Longstreet's contemporary, Colonel Allen D. Candler was an important local Democratic Party figure. In early 1898, the *Gainesville Eagle* reported Candler's candidacy for the governorship of Georgia. Candler was nicknamed by his opponents as the "one eyed plough boy from Pigeon Roost," in reference to his loss of an eye during the Civil War and birth near the Pigeon Roost gold mine in Lumpkin County in 1834. Candler came to Gainesville in 1870 and established himself as a successful building

contractor and investor. Among his investments were the Gainesville Street Railroad, the Gainesville, Jefferson, and Southern Railroad (later Gainesville Midland Railroad) and the Arlington Hotel, which later became the Hunt Hotel, then the Dixie Hunt Hotel.

With the streetcar system, fancy homes began to be located along those routes. Progressively, the most impressive residences were along South Green, South Bradford, South Main, West Washington, East Washington, East Spring, and North Green Streets to Riverside Drive.

General A. J. Warner, developer of electricity in Gainesville from 1902 to 1908, built a residence on Riverside Drive. His son-in-law, William H. Slack, founded Slack Auto Parts on South Main. The company has been operated by three generations of the Slack family, including William H. Slack, Jr., and his son, Henry Slack III.

The coming of the railroad, electricity, and streetcar line led to location of businesses along South Main, South Bradford, Grove and South Green Streets and the removal of residences. Beginning just prior to 1900, North Green, East Broad, East Spring, West and East Washington Streets attracted newer, more prominent residences. The post-WWII years brought new businesses and expansion of existing businesses along South Main, South

Above: A rough winter day on North Green Street near Green Street Place during the electric streetcar days, c. 1908.

COURTESY OF DAN HUGHS.

Below: Roy Brewer Maness, a Candler Horse Guard commissioned in 1905.

COURTESY OF MARSHALL JUDSON.

Bradford, West and East Washington, East Spring, and East Broad Streets, replacing more fine residences.

WAR: 1898-1918

The Gainesville newspapers reported on March 31, 1898 that "It looks more like war," and within a month local readers were told that President William McKinley would be calling for 60,000 volunteers from state militia, including about 2,000 from Georgia to fight the Spaniards in Cuba. Accordingly the Piedmont Rifles, the local militia unit made up of men from the Gainesville and Athens areas, "have called for forty volunteers to make their company up to seventy-five."

The Spanish-American War and the governor's race both played themselves out by the end of 1898. Peace was reported in sight by August. By October, Candler's race for governor in 1898 was all the talk locally. Victory was accomplished for the local favorite and Teddy Roosevelt, who had made the recent war a "bully feather in his cap," became a national hero.

However, in 1917, the local news regarding the military was not as much about the war in Europe as it was of the returning of local young men who had in June 1916 been

sent to the Mexican border in support of the border squabble between the U.S. and Mexico. The Candler Horse Guards had been called to active duty as Troop F of the Georgia State Guard. Newspaper accounts said that the unit "acquitted itself creditably," but the soldiers were anxious to get back home after a relatively quiet assignment of patrolling the border while regular army troops were busy across the border. In what might be considered an early example of federal aid to

Top, right: World War I introduced the U.S. to world affairs and local boys to far-away places. Shown here is Edwin Fennell Hughes, Sr., U.S. Navy, WWI.

COURTESY OF DAN HUGHS.

Below: Young ladies and "friend" pose at the offices of the Gainesville Eagle on South Main Street, c. 1890s. Note the condition of the street.

COURTESY OF DIXIE RAMSEY & THE RAMSEY COLLECTION.

Bottom, right: Portrait of an artist. Photographer W. J. Ramsey in window of his studio when it was above a Gainesville business operation.

COURTESY OF DIXIE RAMSEY & THE RAMSEY COLLECTION.

a local community, the young men were returned to Gainesville with thirty-two horses and equipment. "They never had horses before," said a news account, "which has always been a considerable hindrance to the organization." Once, they had them they worried about who would pay to keep them up and where that would be done, perhaps illustrating that federal aid frequently has strings attached.

CLEANING UP THE SQUARE

In 1910 the streets of the Square were paved with heavy blue bricks made in Augusta, Georgia, replacing the mud, dust, and filth of the packed dirt streets. These brick pavers still remain under the concrete and asphalt of the Square and other streets. The City's efforts to clean up the Square soon met with an obstacle that had its foundations in a long-standing city/county feud. Repeated requests by the Gainesville City Commissioners for the County to clean up its center circle went unanswered. Finally, in frustration in early 1910, the city sent a work crew to remove "ten or a dozen" shade trees, dig up the trunks, plow the ground, and shape up the area. This activity was soon noticed by the county commissioners who ordered the sheriff to arrest the workers. Responding immediately, the city commissioners bailed the workers out of jail and sent them back to work. In March 1910 the County filed suit for damages against the city. The suit went to trial in July of 1911 and the city lost. The jury did not assess the city any monetary damages but ordered "that the City of Gainesville be perpetually enjoined from further trespassing upon the property described in the petition[47]."

SOLID GROWTH

The booming years from the coming of the rails in the 1870s to the post World War I years owed much to events out in the County and in the surrounding counties beyond, especially toward the southern side of Hall where an especially fine variety of cotton was grown. The upper Piedmont of Georgia in 1920 was still a farm region. Gainesville was important not for

its center of life so much as for its center of commerce and for its serving as the county seat. Within the following half century (1920-1970), the town had become the tail that wagged the dog as the industrial component of "agribusiness" (an unknown term in that era) overwhelmed the row croppers of the turn of the twentieth century. In 1920 there were 2,820 farms in Hall County. Of these, 2,665 raised corn, 2,467 raised cotton, and many of them raised vegetables and livestock for home consumption. In 1920 more than half of

Above: An early twentieth century produce peddler in front of the Gainesville City Hall-Fire Station, which was destroyed in the April 6, 1936 tornado.

COURTESY OF DAN HUGHS.

Below: The Ramsey's home/studio at Prior and Park Streets.

COURTESY OF DIXIE RAMSEY & THE RAMSEY COLLECTION.

Above: The American Legion-Paul E. Bolding Post Meeting Room. This room, located near the Jackson Building, was in use from 1922 to 1936.

Below: A barbecue for the state American Legion convention, held in City Park, 1920s. Note the wooden baseball bleachers in the background.

COURTESY OF ED DUNLAP, JR.

all farmers who were not working their own land were tenant farmers or sharecroppers. Farms were small, only twenty-five percent of Hall farms in 1925 were over one hundred acres in size. Farm labor was a family matter and the size of the family determined how many hands could work the crops. Large households of robust children were great assets. The small hilly farm may account for the fact that slavery was not prominent in North Georgia agriculture.

Factors external to the household, however, often determined the success or failure for farmers. The arrival of the boll weevil in this part of Georgia in 1920 was just such an external factor. That year Hall County and the service area of Gainesville was still overwhelmingly a region of small farmers.

As the nineteenth century ran its course and the twentieth century took hold, Gainesville and Hall County began to undergo more changes. Neighborhoods began to grow up by way of land subdivision and development beyond the Square and the commercial center of town: around Summit Street, along Green, Candler, and Park Streets with City Ice Company on Main Street[48].

The area immediately adjoining the Southern Railroad Depot on Industrial Boulevard at Main and Myrtle Streets became the location of Gainesville Iron Works (1900-1970s), Georgia Chair Company, and Chambers Lumber Company. Davis-Washington Lumber adjoined the Gainesville Midland Railroad at Grove Street. Originally located in Flowery Branch, in 1912, J. B. Edmondson moved the Georgia Chair Company plant to the current location at 456 Industrial Boulevard after a fire in 1922. Three generations of Edmondson-Bagwell owners (Charles Edmondson, Austin Edmondson, and Jimmy and Harry Bagwell) have produced high quality solid wood, primarily oak chairs and tables for schools, churches and offices (and the supremely popular "tote stool" of a million uses) throughout the United States.

WOOD'S MILL NEAR THE "ROCK"

Also, after the location of the railroad depot at the end of Main and Bradford Streets, development proceeded south of the railroad

tracks. That area toward Ridge Road was lowlands, "bogs" and swamps, which produced pesky mosquitoes for many years. Later the area contained Hudson's Brickyard which produced clay brick from 1910 to the 1930s. The flatlands cow pasture area along Chestnut Street in the late 1920s to early 1930s, sometimes referenced as "Mr. Birchfield's pasture," accommodated annual circuses[49] and occasional visiting barnstorming airplanes selling rides. Around 1929 the City of Gainesville began preparation of a dirt field airport on higher ground south and west of Gainesville Mill and east of Chicopee[50]. After the Great Tornado of April 6, 1936, debris from the destruction was dumped in the former swampy low areas south of the Railroad depot. The new dirt airstrip on the ridge became well used in the 1930s[51] and, during WWII, was taken over by the U.S. Navy, which improved it to become a paved, towered, small U.S. Navy radar flight training airport satellite to the central Chamblee-Atlanta airbase.

The Square underwent major revisions after location of the railroads, electricity and streetcar lines with new brick Victorian-styled two-story buildings and paved sidewalks. During this time following the beginning of the twentieth century, a new opera house at East Washington and North Bradford Streets complemented an array of hardware, dry goods, drug, clothing, grocery, and meat retail stores. A number of hotels[52] for visitors and office buildings for doctors and lawyers also sprang up. Several shoe companies were organized locally and for a period they constituted the largest employer outside agriculture in Hall County. One account of local industry during this period lists truss makers, a match factory, the Piedmont Foundry and Machine Shop, a mattress factory, and a brick making factory as well as cotton warehousing[53].

COTTON FARMING

Significant changes developed in labor patterns in the 1920s. The arrival of the boll weevil in the 1920s was followed by at least a decade of bad times for cotton farmers. The drop in markets following World War I reduced prices to six cents per pound.

Aviation joined the auto as an important element of local change. In the rear seat is Johnny Kytle, a pioneer pilot who grew up in the Clermont community.

LEE GILMER MUNICIPAL AIRPORT

The Gainesville Municipal Airport, first commenced in 1929, was a red clay, no sod, muddy-when-wet, dusty-when-dry affair with one small wooden hangar[54] on the southeast edge of the field. A single runway parallel to the railroad tracks was approximately twenty-five hundred feet long[55]. When the US Navy Flight Training improvements were complete it had two four-thousand-foot runways. In early 1947 the Navy returned the airfield to the use of the city.

In a far-sighted progressive move, the City Commission which served from 1972 to 1974 approved the airport Master Plan. The plan outlined improvements to be accomplished in three stages over a period of several years with substantial federal government participation. Under the Master Plan, one runway was extended to five thousand feet with several hundred feet of sod extension. City Manager Ray Keith and City Engineer George Austin were responsible for implementing the plan. Upon a suggestion from Commissioner Henry Ward, an advisory committee[56] was subsequently appointed by Mayor Robert Hamrick. The Citizen Committee which met regularly was without real authority, but made suggestions and responded when consulted by the commissioners. Consistent improvements helped make the airport an up-to-date operation which is the envy of other similar communities[57].

During this period, the fixed base operator was Al Fosnocht, owner of Blue Ridge Aviation, which offered full services and training. In the airport's earlier years, Lee Gilmer was engaged to manage the facility for the City and served as the base operator, providing flight training, fuel, and service. In the 1970s the City dedicated it as "The Lee Gilmer Municipal Airport" in honor of his pioneer and impressive airport management services.

Farmers went deeper into debt to grow more cotton to pay off earlier debts. The increased production drove prices down further. This resulted in the loss of farms and more tenant farming with many leaving the farms for the

textile mills. The cotton market crashed in 1931 on the heels of a forecast of a large crop, falling to 6.7 cents a pound. In Hall County the *Eagle* predicted "five cent cotton for the 1931 crop." Out-of-work former farmers, suffering and desperate for any employment, turned to local welfare offices for help, a sure sign of the extreme conditions of the "Great Depression" of the 1930s. In September 1931 there was a meeting of farmers and businessmen at the Hall County Courthouse to discuss the cotton farmer's plight and to consider a plan to limit cotton planting in an effort to drive prices up, an idea which failed to win local approval. But, nationally the idea had support and, in 1936, led by the Roosevelt Administration, congressional legislation imposed "quotas" on each farm which restricted planting of cotton and other crops.

TEXTILES

With the railroads came the textile mills. Gainesville's first cotton mill dated back to 1879, but the real takeoff of the mills dates to 1898 when the Pacolet Company of South Carolina took notice of the potential of this area's cotton supply and potential labor force. Pacolet dismantled a mill in New England and had it moved to New Holland where it employed fourteen hundred workers. The "Limestone" spring was an ample water source. Boston architects were employed to design a recreation building, church, school, and houses. In 1900 the Vesta Cotton Mills of Charleston, South Carolina came to Gainesville to make a million-dollar investment in Hall County. A year later with the encouragement of a local subscription of over $100,000, a half million-dollar addition was announced for a mill at the junction of the Gainesville, Jefferson, and Southern Railroad and the Southern Railroad. With the success of the local fund-raising campaign the *Atlanta Journal* wrote: "Gainesville will take high rank as a manufacturing center." The *Savannah News* explained that available "white" labor attracted the mill to the Hall location, and proceeded to predict an influx of labor from outside Hall, from Habersham, Dawson, Lumpkin, and Banks Counties.

Since their beginnings late in the nineteenth century, the textile mills had provided the most large scale labor opportunity in the region[58]. Chicopee Mills, dedicated in June of 1927, witnessed the gathering of "one of the largest crowds ever assembled in Gainesville." Senator

Walter F. George was the featured speaker at the celebration of what was called "the world's largest one-story building dedicated to manufacturing purposes." It was the village of two hundred residences which came to be an important feature of Chicopee history. Chicopee was a designed greenbelt environment of uniform brick residences and one-story factories and warehouses, schoolhouses, shops, an infirmary, under-ground utilities, indoor plumbing, street lights on substantial metal posts, connecting lawns and grass, paved sidewalks separated from streets by grass and tree lawns. Trees were liberally planted. It had in-village churches, schools, playgrounds, and a fine baseball field. Workers living in homes across from the plant testified to the positive changes these modern conveniences made in their lives.

In a recent biography of Robert Wood Johnson of Johnson & Johnson, Inc.[59] there is a fine tribute to Johnson's decision to "build the nation's first modern textile mill on a large tract of land on the outskirts of Gainesville, Georgia." When completed "it was a showplace that attracted factory and mill designers from all over the world." It was internationally hailed as the most beautiful "model mill village" in the world.

There were numerous cotton gins and corn grist mills in the area—Hall and other counties—during the 1920-30s. None were operating by the 1950s. The last grist mill was probably Bell's Mill on Little River, three miles from downtown Gainesville on Highway 129, inundated by Lake Lanier in 1957, or Tanner's Mill (near Chestnut Mountain) or Healan Mill (near Lula.) All except Healan and Gilstrap Mill[60] are now lost.

The first labor strike in local history came in the summer of 1935. Seven hundred and fifty workers at Chicopee walked out after the company fired eleven men following their attack on a "clock man." Apparently a time-motion expert, J. H. W. Sneed, had been employed to keep a stopwatch on workers. When threatened by some workers Sneed refused to stop what he was doing, and was taken out and "whipped" by eleven men who were subsequently fired. The walk-out commenced July 15 and ended before August. The company agreed to rehire the eleven men,

to delay the time-motion study, and to allow the purchase of milk and butter from sources other than the company dairy store, an issue apparently festering for some time before the "clock man" incident.

In 1932 Owen Osborne Company, a ladies silk hosiery mill, closed its Philadelphia plant and moved to Gainesville. It constructed a plant on East Spring Street adjoining the property of Pacolet Manufacturing Company. The principle stockholder and chief executive was Leslie Quinlan[61], who purchased a residence at North Green Street and North Street formerly owned by Harvey Newman, Sr.,

Chicopee Manufacturing's officers and staff in 1932.

COURTESY OF THARPE WARD.

Above: The Square looking toward Bradford Street, Gainesville, c. 1912. Note the Opera House at far left at East Washington and Bradford Streets and the steeple of the First Baptist Church in the background. Also, note the bales of cotton in the wagons.

Below: Chicopee Mill, built in the 1930s at 2100 Atlanta Highway, c. 2000.

owner of Newman's Department Store. Quinlan brought with him Roy Judson as interim plant manager. Judson learned to love Gainesville and became a permanent leading citizen. Primarily because of increasing labor relations problems in the Philadelphia-Reading area, many Philadelphia area hosiery mills, as well as other textile plants in the north, moved to the south during the early 1930s.

The George P. Phinx Corporation was one of several manufacturers of silk thread sold to the many hosiery mills in the Philadelphia-Reading area. With the movement of the hosiery mills to the southern states, Phinx recognized that it

would be preferable for silk manufacturing facilities to be nearer these hosiery mills. Led by Leslie Quinlan, Sidney O. Smith, Sr., H. H. Estes, and others in the Gainesville Chamber of Commerce, Phinx was urged to establish a silk manufacturing facility in Gainesville. The resulting Best Manufacturing Company constructed a twenty-thousand-square-foot silk manufacturing plant on Oak Street in 1938.

The manager of the Phinx subsidiary, Best Manufacturing Company, was Jack Reynolds, who moved to Gainesville from Pennsylvania. In 1938 Eugene Bobo, upon his graduation from the Clemson College School of Engineering, moved to Gainesville from Lauren, South Carolina, and took a job with "the silk mill." He later became general manager of the Best plant on Oak Street. Lake Terrell and Bobo worked at Best until joining the United States Army in World War II. On December 8, 1941, the day following the Japanese bombing of Pearl Harbor in Hawaii, Owen Osborne and Best Manufacturing Company received telegrams from the United States government terminating all manufacture of silk and nylon fiber for civilian consumer products. Immediately, Owen Osborne received requests from the U.S. Army to convert their machines to the manufacture of nylon parachutes for the military[62].

The relations between the United States and Imperial Japan had been deteriorating during the early 1930s. By the late 1930s the government feared an expanded war in the Orient and a cut off of the importing of silk supplies from across the Pacific. The government feared the reduction of textile manufacturing would cause unemployment in the United States which relied on silk from the Far East. But at the same time, female consumers of stockings had a preference for silk and a bias and aversion to nylon stockings.

By 1940, urged by the federal government, Best had bought nylon processing machines and began processing nylon as well as silk. Later, Bobo and another experimenter at Best, in secrecy on personal time, developed a new machine process to manufacture "stretch" yarn and "seamless" hosiery which they patented. This process became an industry nylon standard. The stretch yarn process reduced the number of sizes needed to be manufactured from fourteen to four and the "stretch" hosiery was better able to fit legs.

Above: The Gainesville "Square," c. 1950. Note the large trees interspersed with the underground utility wiring light posts purchased from Chicopee Mills. The 1906 First Methodist Church can be seen on the left corner and the Jackson Building, First Baptist Church, and the Federal Building can be seen in the background on the right. Businesses visible around the Square in this photograph include Roses 5 10 25¢, Hulsey's, Citizens Bank, Imperial Drug, Piedmont Drug, The Leader, the Hub, Jake Sacks, and Gainesville National Bank.
COURTESY OF THARPE WARD.

Left: A photo of the New Holland Mill (Pacolet Manufacturing) and Company Store from a 1915 postcard.

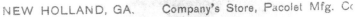

NEW HOLLAND, GA.   Company's Store, Pacolet Mfg. Co

Above: New Holland Mill Village, built around 1900, c. 2000.

Below: Gainesville Mill and residences from a 1910 postcard.

By 1946 Owen Osborne and similar hosiery mills converted to the DuPont nylon product and to seamless stockings.

The textile mills were central to the local economy even by the end of the 1920s. Pacolet at New Holland used 60,000 spindles, employed 850 workers, and processed 20,000 bales of cotton per year. Gainesville Cotton Mill with 40,000 spindles employed 600 workers and processed 9,000 bales per year; Chicopee, the new kid in town, used 40,000 spindles, employed 500 workers and processed 10,000 bales per year, while Owen Osborne and Best were strong contributors to the employment economy.

WAY OF LIFE:
THE EARLY 1900s

The "movies" were the premier form of mass entertainment during the 1920s. For most of those years they were silent, except for the music provided by a piano or organ playing near the screen. In 1924 the Alamo Theatre in Gainesville was showing films at 1, 3, 5, 7, and 9 p.m. daily. The tickets were 25 cents for children and 50 cents for adults. Douglas Fairbanks starred in *Don Q, Son of Zorro* shown at the State Theater on East Washington Street across from the Jackson Building. Old-time favorites of the silent

screen included Ken Maynard, Clara Bow, Tarzan, and Billy Dove, all of whom had movies showing locally in the spring of 1928. Finally a year later in May of 1929 the State offered *Trial Marriage*, at long last a movie one could "see and hear in *sound*."

Gone With the Wind finally made it to local movie houses in March of 1940. It played at the Royal Theatre on South Main Street from March 25-30 with three shows daily. Fans were urged to buy advanced tickets to avoid the rush. Ticket buyers faced staggering $1.10

reserve seat price and seventy-five cents tickets for general admission.

The feeling of "prosperity" via easy payment purchases came to Gainesville and Hall County before the middle of the decade. As Christmas sales campaigns for 1925 the power company advocated "Holiday Gifts with Everyday Uses" in large newspaper ads. These included electric coffeemakers for $4.95; heating pads for $5.75; irons for $1 down and $1 per month; heaters for $6.50; waffle irons for $15 to $18; Radiola IIIA

Top, left: Tanner's Mill near Chestnut Mountain. The mill was destroyed by a fire around 1990.

Below: A postcard of Washington Street on the north side of the Square in Gainesville, c. 1910. Note the streetcar, streetcar tracks, and the old Opera House (right) in the background.

GAINESVILLE, GA.   View on Washington Street

Confederate
Statues
in Bronze

❧

We furnish
Statues for
ALL KINDS
of Monuments

❧

Write Us For

Prices,
Designs,
etc.

American Bronze Foundry Co.
3rd and Woodland Ave. • • Chicago, Ill.

Above: An advertisement from the American Bronze Foundry Company, Chicago, Illinois, for "Confederate Statues in Bronze," c. 1905.

COURTESY OF DIXIE RAMSEY & THE RAMSEY COLLECTION.

Right: The local phone system was well established by 1900 and these "central ladies" kept communications going.

COURTESY OF DIXIE RAMSEY & THE RAMSEY COLLECTION.

radios for $49.50 to $67.50 (small down payments and monthly terms); and toasters for $6.00. A chart listed family members (mother, father, brother, sister, grandparents, etc.) and suggested gifts for each member.

Pilgrim-Estes Furniture Company on North Bradford at Brenau Avenue had a wide range of Christmas offerings for the home with "easy credit terms." Leather rockers were $30, lamps $15, spinet desks $25. A three-piece bedroom suite was offered for $98, living room suit for $169 and a 10 piece dining room outfit for $150. Hoosier cabinets were available for $5 down. Jay's Department Store at 11 Washington Street on the Square

was selling men's work shirts for 49 cents, pants 98 cents, and housedresses for 99 cents. Kelly Chevrolet offered a new Chevy Coach for $595 in the summer of 1927.

THE STATUE

Starting in the 1900s an organization of well connected members of the local United Daughters of the Confederacy (UDC) began a relentless campaign to have erected a memorial to the Confederacy honoring Hall County veterans of the Civil War, as many other towns had done. The widow of General James Longstreet was one of the leaders of the effort. The Statue Committee consisted of Mrs. C. C. Sanders, chair; Mrs. J. C. Dorsey, treasurer; Mrs. Aaron Whelchel; Mrs. A. W. Van Hoose; Mrs. George P. Estes; and Nell Robert Murphy. With $2,500 to spend, the UDC opted, perhaps prudently and wisely, to purchase a mass-produced bronze statue of a late ninteenth century Spanish-American War-era soldier then in-stock and being marketed to similar memorial groups by the American Bronze Foundry Company of Chicago[63]. The statue labeled "At Ready" was purchased. In 1909, it was mounted atop an elaborately carved marble base donated by Colonel Sam Tate, owner of the Tate Marble Company. The transport of the heavy piece of marble base by rail from Tate to Gainesville and then by team of mules pulling the multiple stones (one weighing over ten tons) on a special wide wheeled wagon up Main Street from the Railroad Depot was quite a feat.

Locally the statue became nicknamed "Ole Joe," and was dedicated to "defending our states rights whenever they might be threatened." Gainesville thus joined other cities such as Charlottesville and Farmville, Virginia; Oxford; Lexington; Louisburg; Tarboro; Fayetteville; Edenton and Shelby, North Carolina; Parkersville, West Virginia; and Raymond, Mississippi with one of these identical statues. Tarboro, North Carolina, and Raymond, Mississippi, statues are slightly different in that the arms and rifle are down at the "at rest" position.

The 1910 County lawsuit against the City contained a paragraph about the statue. Referring to the County Commission, the petition read:

> Your petitioners show that a few years ago the County gave permission temporarily to an organization of ladies known as Daughters of the Confederacy to erect a monument on the center of said Square, and in the center of the said circle, with the express understanding that said ladies should remove said monument at any time when requested by the authorities representing the said County, a copy of said agreement is hereto attached and marked exhibit A.

However, court records fail to reveal a copy of the referenced agreement and despite research none has been discovered. The statue remains today as the most prominent and treasured symbol of historic downtown Gainesville.

THE GUBERNATORIAL ELECTION OF 1912

In the spring of 1912, Woodrow Wilson, New Jersey Governor, attempted to win the Democratic presidential nomination. This was of local interest because the governor had grown up in Augusta, practiced law briefly in Atlanta and, most importantly, his two daughters had been born in Gainesville.

Governor Woodrow Wilson was scheduled to address the voters of Hall County in early April, but when his train was delayed for several hours the handful of admirers who went down to the depot to greet him got only

brief comments from the rear platform of the train. When the Democratic primary was held in May, Alabama Congressman Oscar Wilder Underwood carried Hall with 1,328 to Wilson's 1,068 votes. In explaining the Underwood victory over the locally connected Wilson, the editors of the *Gainesville News* marked it up to a desire to support "a winner." In April 1912, Wilson won his party's nomination in a heated, lengthy convention and Gainesville was admonished by the *News* to "get busy now for Wilson. We don't want Taftism or Bulli Mooseism."

In Hall County the vote was Woodrow Wilson, 1,145; Theodore Roosevelt, 376; and William Howard Taft 116.

Ole Joe "at ready" on the Square since 1909, witness to it all.

COURTESY OF GEORGE EVANS. WATERCOLOR, 2000. LIMITED EDITION PRINT. SIZE 6 X 15 INCHES. AVAILABLE FROM THE HALL COUNTY HISTORICAL SOCIETY.

CHAPTER 2 ENDNOTES

[1] A. D. Candler, Gainesville, president; W. C. Howard, Atlanta, secretary.

[2] White County Historical Society. *A History of White County 1857-1890*. Inter-Collegiate Press, 1981. pp 6; 9-10; 52-53.

[3] Ibid. pp. 6; 52-53.

[4] Frequently referred to as the copper mine dating from before 1900. Amerson. *I Remember Dahlonega*, Vol. 2, Dahlonega, second printing. Chestatee Publications, 1998. Chapter 4 "Early Hydroelectric Power in Lumpkin County," pp. 13-20; Amerson, Chapter 9 "Grand Reunions," p. 63.

[5] Amerson, Chapter 4, p. 19.

[6] Great grandfather of Judge Sidney Oslin Smith, Jr., and Charters Smith Embry.

[7] Amerson, Chapter 5, "The Railroad that Almost Came to Dahlonega," p. 23.

[8] Ibid. pp. 21-28.

[9] Ibid. p. 23.

[10] Ibid. p. 23.

[11] Ibid. pp. 21-28

[12] Ibid.

[13] Ibid.

[14] Wade H. Wright. *History of the Georgia Power Company, 1855-1956*. Atlanta: Foote and Davies, 1957. pp. 110-111; Amerson. Chapter 5, pp. 26-28

[15] Wright, pp. 110-111. Amerson, Chapter 4, p. 18.

[16] Wright, pp. 110-111. Amerson, Chapter 4, pp. 17-20.

[17] The town's name was based on the Indian name *Anaguluskee*, meaning "Blossoming Creek."

[18] Wright, pp. 110-111. Amerson, Chapter 4, pp. 17-20.

[19] Ibid.

[20] Amerson, Chapter 4, p. 17.

[21] Wright, p. 111.

[22] Ibid.

[23] Amerson, Chapter 5, p. 23.

[24] Wright, p. 111.

[25] Amerson, Chapter 5, pp. 25-26.

[26] Amerson, Chapter 5, pp. 25-28.

[27] Amerson, Chapter 5, p. 27.

[28] Amerson, Chapter 7, p. 27.

[29] Ibid.

[30] Ibid.

[31] Amerson, Chapter 5. While newspapers of July 1900 reported announcement of Colonel Price to transfer his line to the Warner group, we have found no record of a deed or contract of conveyance from the Price group to the Warner group.

[32] In the transfer agreement recorded in Hall County Deed Records Book 13, Page 115, the route was described "from a site near the Southern Railroad Depot, across Broad (near the present chicken statue) and West Washington Streets to and across the Chattahoochee River and then along the old roadbed of the Gainesville and Dahlonega Railroad to 'New Bridge' on the Chattahoochee River in Lumpkin County."

[33] Hall County Deed Records Book 13, Page 115; Amerson, Chapter 5, pp. 26-28.

[34] Wright, p. 111, Hall County Deed Records Book 13, Page 115.

[35] Hall County Deed Records Book 13, Page 115.

[36] Some Gainesvillians remember the rugged dirt road (Woods Mill Road) that began at Oak Street and the present location of the Gainesville Middle School and traversed along the hillside edge of the Gainesville Golf Course of 1930-50 through the valley which Black's Branch followed from the end of West Washington Street to the Chattahoochee River. This road connected Oak Street and the West Washington Street and Dawsonville Highway area with Thompson Bridge Road at the bridge.

This road was covered by the waters of Lake Lanier in 1958. It led to a condemnation lawsuit by the City of Gainesville against the U.S. Corps of Engineers in the U.S. District Court. The City of Gainesville was awarded some $2.3 million as compensatory damages for its alleged plans to replace that road with the road connecting West Washington Street with Thompson Bridge Road on higher land above the lake. At that time there were no residences along the route of the proposed replacement road. Although discussed for years and a City plan for the road announced and building permits denied along the route, the City failed to locate and acquire land for the road and the area became congested with the present residences along the extension of Dixon Drive, Piedmont Road, and Mountain View Drive. Now that area of residences is immersed in controversy involving the excessive traffic impacting the streets of those neighborhoods and the city-DOT threat of the long-planned extension of Pearl Nix Parkway across Dixon Drive through the thirty-acre property formerly occupied by Dr. Hartwell Joiner and connecting to Enota Drive and thence Thompson Bridge, Riverside Drive, Cleveland Road, Downey Street, and Martin Luther King, Jr. Boulevard to New Holland. Nobody seems to know what the City did with the funds received from that court litigation or the City's formalized plans to construct that route on higher ground between West Washington Street and Thompson Bridge Road.

[37] Amerson, p. 28.

[38] This devastating fire destroyed all of Longstreet's papers and his military memorabilia.

[39] *The Quarterly Journal of Military History*, Volume 11, Number 2, Winter 1999, p. 62.

[40] During development of Longstreet Hills in 1938 by W. L. Norton, Sr., he donated land to the City for widening of the street around the 1932 City Swimming Pool, named Longstreet Circle, and gave a lot adjoining the City water tower on the highest point in North Gainesville to the local chapter of the United Daughters of the Confederacy for a memorial area to honor General James Longstreet. The lot adjoining the water tower and facing Longstreet Circle back to Park Hill Drive has been the residence of JoAnn and Robert Adams since 1951. Across the street from that homeplace site, the W. L. Norton family resided at 960 Longstreet Circle from 1938-88.

[41] A name frequently applied because it was at the threshold of the mountains.

[42] Jeffry D. Wert, *General James Longstreet: The Confederacy's Most Controversial Soldier*, New York: Simon & Schuster, 1993, p. 417.

[43] Now being restored by The Longstreet Society, Gainesville-Hall Trust for Historic Preservation and the Hall County Historical Society as a museum with civic community uses and headquarters for the Longstreet-Wilson Center for Peace and Reconciliation, Inc. In the spirit of the philosophy of General Longstreet and President Woodrow Wilson, the civic center will foster understanding, friendship, and respect among the ethnic and cultural diversity in the community.

[44] Statement in the memorandum history of Georgia poultry industry by Georgia Poultry Federation.

[45] According to letters written by Ellen Wilson describing the hotel and pointing out the birth room on post cards of the hotel. *My Aunt Louisa and Woodrow Wilson* by Margaret Axson Elliott (a colorful description of Gainesville of the 1890s).

[46] Great-grandfather of Sidney O. (Oslin) Smith, Jr. (b. 1923), lawyer, Superior Court judge, and U.S. District judge, and Charters Smith Embry (b. 1919), Gainesville.

[47] See the *County of Hall, State of Georgia v. City of Gainesville Georgia*, Hall Superior Court July Term 1910.

[48] Carl B. Romberg moved to Gainesville from Texas during WWI and established the City Ice Company, which manufactured and delivered block ice to homes and businesses. Ice pickup was also available at the plant on South Main and South Bradford Streets at Church Street (now Jesse Jewell Parkway). With the development of the poultry industry, City Ice Company blew wholesale ice shavings into large trucks for preservation of processed fresh poultry during interstate deliveries. Romberg's brother, Conrad, joined the business in the late 1920s and, in the 1970s-80s, his two sons, George and Carl II, and a grandson, Chris, became successors to the ice, cold storage, and restaurant equipment businesses. In the 1930s, along with George Ashford, father-in-law of Conrad Romberg, Carl Romberg purchased City Plumbing and Electric on North Bradford Street which likewise became prominent.

[49] Three ring Downey Brothers, Cole Brothers, Ringling Brothers and others. They unloaded equipment and animals from a special train located on tracks just north of Southern Railroad Depot and moved out onto Chestnut Street. This is the approximate location of present Warren-Featherbone Plant, ConAgra Mill, Hall County Recycling Center, and the former West Lumber Company.

[50] With only one small hangar available in the late 1930s, flyer Dean Parks built a wood slab "T-Hangar" on his property, well off the field boundary, to house a Taylor Cub airplane (later named Piper Cub) purchased in the late 1930s by auto dealer Frank DeLong, Sr., for use by his three teenage sons, Frank, Jr., Jim, and Harold. During the 1930s and until the bombing of Pearl Harbor in December 1941, the field was used mostly for weekend flying, visiting planes and occasional air shows by visitors. Mostly the planes were such as Waco bi-planes with open cockpits, small cubs, Aeroncas, and Taylorcrafts. Local pilots at the time included Boyd Hughes, Doc Stowe, Lee Gilmer, Frank, Jim, and Harold DeLong, Paul Plaginos, George Rutherford, R. I. Tyner and Hugh Minor.

[51] James DeLong.

[52] Hunt Hotel on lot #1 at the corner of Main and Spring Streets (now Hunt Tower); Princeton Hotel at North Main and West Washington Streets. Wheeler Hotel at North Main-Oak Streets (now Hall County Library System headquarters).

[53] L. R. Sams had a cotton warehouse through WWII on South Main Street near Summit Street on the south and College Avenue on the north. Ralph Cleveland, buyer for Pacolet Manufacturing Company and other textile mills, had a cotton warehouse on Grove Street.

[54] James DeLong

[55] James DeLong

[56] Including, James DeLong, chairman; Jack McKibbon, David Rankin, Bob Andrews, Paul (Pete) Cochran, Hiram Thompson, Neal Ferguson, Al Fosnocht, and George Austin, and Colonel Ray Keith (city manager) appointed by Mayor Henry Ward.

[57] The detailed, comprehensive written Master Plan (prepared under the assistance of Environ Plans, Inc., FAA, and DOT) continues to impress federal and state regulators dealing with Gainesville on the Airport.

[58] Both New Holland Mill and Gainesville Mill constructed appealing village streets and rental residences for rental to workers. Workers were attracted to these mills and company-provided homes from wide distances of more rural areas. In the 1950s, the mill corporations sold the homes to occupants as preferred purchases. Along with the New Holland Village and Gainesville Mill Village of company-built residences, the three "mill villages" are now historic reminders of a progressive textile industry.

Many believe that these "Mill Villages" and Chicopee Village are distinguished historical residential neighborhoods which should be designated historic districts on the National Register of Historic Places and protected as to environmental and architectural character and property values by a local Historic Preservation Ordinance pursuant to the Georgia Historic Preservation Act.

[59] Foster, Lawrence G. *Robert Wood Johnson: The Gentleman Rebel.* Lillian Press, November 1999.

[60] Healan Mill is owned by the Healan family. Currently there is a movement by the Hall County Historical Society and the Gainesville-Hall Trust for Historic Preservation to get the state/county and/or private interests to acquire Healan Mill and several surrounding acres for a local park. Gilstrap Mill, owned by Don Park, is located on Gilstrap Mill Road off of Mt. Vernon Road in North Hall County.

[61] In 1963, Leslie F. Quinlan, a consistent, willing business and civic leader in several roles, contributed initial capital funds to the long existing Gainesville Art Association to establish the Art Center which now bears his name. One daughter, Edith, a sophomore at Gainesville High School in 1933, remained a lifetime in Gainesville and became the wife of David Rankin, a business leader, and city commissioner.

[62] Nylon had been developed by the DuPont Company in the early 1930s and for several years had been urging hosiery mills to convert from silk to nylon without great success until intervention by the government in the late 1930s to urge hosiery mills to phase out silk and manufacture more nylon products.

[63] Several other cities have bronze statues of the same or similar mold of the American Bronze Foundry Company purchased during the same period in the early 1900s.

The restoration in progress of the remaining six rooms of the Historic Longstreet Piedmont Hotel, 2000.

COURTESY OF W. L. NORTON, JR.

CHAPTER III

UP TO DATE

Although liquor was banned by city ordinance at the turn of the century, open bars remained for several years on the Square on Main and Washington Streets between Bradford and Main Streets and perhaps other locations. Many other things remained the same. But with the downtown brick-paved streets in 1910 came the construction by Felix Walton Jackson of a five-story "skyscraper" just off the Square on East Washington Street. It is told that a farmer from across the Blue Ridge Mountains packed up his family and made the long wagon journey to Gainesville just to see the soaring Jackson Building and its marvelous elevator. People also came from many miles just to see that mechanical marvel, the elevator. For years it was the tallest building between Atlanta and Greenville, South Carolina. This wonderful historical structure was built by Levi Prater.

In 1919 the Jackson Building was sold to brothers, J. M. Parks and B. A. Parks and to Judge A. C. Wheeler. J. M. Parks, and B. A. Parks owned J. M. Parks & Son, retail men's store. At the death of Judge Wheeler in 1961, the Parks family purchased his interest and in 1980 sold it to the City of Gainesville, who subsequently sold it to others.

Continuing commercial development of downtown Gainesville, Felix Walton Jackson, Jr., purchased the Bailey Building, a stately Victorian former residence of Dr. West, which was severely damaged later by the 1936 tornado. In 1937 Jackson constructed retail stores with white marble facades at North Green and East Washington Streets across from the Jackson Building and the 1911 Post Office.

Young folks of Lula enjoy a ride in an "EMF" auto, c. 1913.

COURTESY OF IRIS FRY.

LEVI PRATER & THE JACKSON BUILDING

Levi Prater moved from Toccoa to Gainesville in his early teens to seek gainful employment. Working in construction, amazingly Prater acquired the reputation of a "Master Builder" of a variety of commercial and residential properties in Gainesville, Toccoa, and Atlanta between 1910-1946. His Gainesville heirs were daughter Belle Prater, who married H. A. Terrell (parents of Colonel Harold Terrell) and daughter Dot, who married Charles Mauldin.

Prater had little formal education. His mastery of carpentry, building skills, reading and understanding blue prints, preliminary drafting designs, and understanding structural demands came only from experience, observation and study. He has been recognized in a project of the Historic Preservation Division of the Georgia Department of Natural Resources, entitled "Architects and Builders in Georgia Research Project." The project established individual files of information on the lives and works of those individuals in Georgia prior to 1940 who designed and built structures which were considered outstanding.

In Gainesville, Colonel H. H. Dean, a lawyer and property owner, commissioned Prater for building construction work both in Gainesville and Atlanta. One of the Atlanta projects was the J. P. Allen store on Whitehall Street. General Sandy Beaver commissioned Prater for major construction projects at Riverside Military Academy at the campus in both Gainesville and Hollywood, Florida. Several of Gainesville's early major structures are the result of Levi Prater's work. Some of these are: Candler Street School at 525 Candler Street (1906); 781 North Green Street; 393 North Green Street[1]; 466 North Green Street[2]; 829 Green Street Circle[3]; 819 Thompson Bridge Road; 1735 Riverside Drive[4]; 1531 Park Hill Drive; and 977 Cherokee Road (Longstreet Hills)[5]. He also built the Jackson Building (1910); the Coca-Cola Building on West Academy Street (1946); New Holland Mills Village School Building; New Holland Mills Village Community Center (the gymnasium, and swimming pool); the Gainesville Mill Village School and clinic buildings; Concord Baptist Church, Clermont; and First Baptist Church, Toccoa.

None of the structures by Levi Prater which were in the path of the Great Tornado of 1936, suffered structural damage beyond broken windows. The Jackson Building and others withstood the full force of the terrible storm, thus demonstrating the quality and character of construction by Levi Prater.

Above: The Jackson Building on East Washington Street, built by Levi Prater, was completed in 1909-1910.
COURTESY OF WILLIAM L. NORTON, JR.

Bottom, left: The Matthews-Norton House, built by Levi Prater, 393 North Green Street, Green Street Historic District.
COURTESY OF WILLIAM L. NORTON, JR.

Bottom, right: The Congressman B. Frank Whelchel House at 977 Cherokee Road was the last project built by Levi Prater and completed in 1947.
COURTESY OF WILLIAM L. NORTON, JR.

THE AUTOMOBILE

From their introduction early in the twentieth century, the automobile, mixed with horse and mule wagons, became more and more a common sight around the Square.

It is not possible to determine the exact sequence or extent of auto dealerships in Gainesville. During the early days of auto manufacturing there were many hundreds of manufacturers scattered over the U.S. In Toccoa, Georgia, one was started, but failed. Since dealers sold only two or so automobiles per year prior to the 1930s, the ownership of dealers frequently changed.

Swift Motor Company of Gainesville announced in April 1923 that "you can buy and pay for a Ford car out of your weekly earnings on the Ford Weekly Purchase Plan." In cooperation with the First National Bank of Gainesville, it cost $5 to enroll and as the account was added to "in a short time your deposits plus interest will be sufficient to obtain delivery of your car." The Ford automobile changed courtship habits, visitations, business communications, travel, education, job opportunities, and such institutions as schools and churches which, via the automobile, became more and more consolidated, impacting former community values.

Advertising in the local newspapers attested to the growth of Gainesville as a trade center for nationally distributed products. The automobile industry played a large part in that growing role. In late 1914 the Gainesville Auto Company offered an advertisement which spoke to the odd juncture of the modern and the traditional. In addition to having for sale Studebaker, Maxwell, and Overland automobiles, they offered an "almost new" Columbus Buggy, a good horse and a set of harnesses, along with a colt.

On the other hand, the local Bagwell family, long associated with the manufacture and sales of "high grade buggies and wagons," acknowledged the new competition in the establishment of the Bagwell Buick Motor Company, and kept their hands on the traditional trade as well. Some of their initial customers were Newman, Frierson and McEver Department Store, W. B. Spain, and Jack Hancock.

By some accounts, Will Summers, an early auto dealer, was the first automobile owner. But the first official state record in late 1910 of an automobile registered in Hall County names P. H. Morton of Gainesville as holder of state registration number 416. Other registrants listed included: Dr. R. L. Neal, number 1435; J. B. Thompson, number 1864; Dr. Latimer Rudolph, number 1865; Dr. E. P. Ham [father of Mrs. Heyward (Ernestine) Hosch, Sr. and Mrs. E. H. (Hilda) Kimbrough], number 2706; W. A. Roper number 2889; and F. B. Simmons' number 2890. By 1912 there were apparently enough cars in Hall County

Above: The automobile changes Gainesville. This photo is of the Motor Inn, a Gulf station on West Street at Maple Street, behind the Arlington (Hunt) Hotel, looking toward the Square.
COURTESY OF DAN HUGHS.

Below: Herbert Bell and his crew at Bell's Cleaners on East Washington Street across from the Jackson Building, c. 1935.
COURTESY OF HERBERT BELL.

Frank W. DeLong, Sr.'s automobile business on South Main Street, c.1921. DeLong sold tires and auto supplies.

COURTESY OF JIM DELONG.

that the *Gainesville News* suggested that the city should "give attention to allowing children to drive automobiles," noting at the same time that children "under 12 are not yet strong enough nor do they have enough judgement to control their mounts."

Those who heretofore were associated with traditional professions and businesses were finding the new products good investments. E. B. Dunlap, H. H. and C. T. Estes as "Dunlap and Estes" were appointed the local sales agents for Hupmobile and Dodge Brothers automobiles in 1915.

In 1928 the main Atlanta to New York concrete paved U.S. 23 highway was completed through Gainesville passing down Broad Street by the City Hall and County Courthouse one block from the Square. By the end of the 1920s highway building reached ten thousand miles per year on the national level. The progress was slower in Hall County despite the fact that Gainesville Ninth District Congressman Thomas Bell, beginning 1905, fostered federal aid to road development. In 1906 he was the first member of Congress to introduce a bill to provide federal funds for road building. His bill failed to be enacted, but a subsequent act borrowed heavily from Bell's proposal.

In the 1920s, the cars' reliability was poor. They broke down frequently and few could

repair them. Roads were dirt, muddy and difficult to traverse. The noise and smoke scared animals and people. Many cars were deliberately burned because they scared teams of mules and horses pulling carriages and wagons. In the 1920s Will Summers was an auto dealer of several "makes." Edward Thomas (Ned) Parks, Sr., the grandfather of Curtis Parks, Jr. (b. 1930), was a partner of Will Summers in auto dealerships and other retail businesses. Ned Parks, and his two young sons, Curtis Parks, Sr. and Ed Parks, Jr. went to Atlanta in the 1920s to pick up three new Maxwell automobiles. On the way back, one broke down near Suwanee and another near Buford. They abandoned the two automobiles, drove the other back to Gainesville and returned the next day to find the two cars burned. In 1937 Curtis Parks, Sr. carried his son Curtis Parks, Jr. to Will Summers' house and barn to see the first automobile of Will Summers. It was much similar to a wagon or carriage, very small wheels, similar to bicycle wheels and tires. It had a lever/pole as a driving guide instead of a steering wheel.

There was a series of owners of Ford dealerships before Roy Otwell (Cumming) sold Gainesville Ford Company to O. B. Leverette during WWII. After WWII in 1957, the first Gainesville owner of the much-ballyhooed Ford Thunderbird, ordered well in advance of production, was young Dr. Rafe Banks, Jr., who said he always admired sports cars but would not buy one until an American manufacturer developed a viable entry.

Frank DeLong, Sr., auto dealer, 1920s-1960s, frequently commented that he made his first connection with the vehicle business as a teenager before WWI painting stripes on hoops of wheels at Bagwell Wagon and Carriage Manufacturing Company on Athens Street (between Broad Street and College Avenue). He later worked for Merck & Elliott Buick dealership before WWI at North Green Street (the location became the Gainesville Coca-Cola bottling plant in the 1920s, and is now the site of SunTrust Bank). The Buick (and Pontiac) dealership was purchased by Frank DeLong in the 1930s. He also, from 1938 to 1950, owned Firestone Tire and Cycles dealerships on South

Main Street. In 1947 DeLong Buick-GMC and Jacobs Olds-Cadillac built adjoining buildings at East Spring and East Broad Streets on a former residential property severely damaged by the 1936 tornado[6]. These dealerships continued at that location until the 1980s. Others had careers in the auto business: Mark McConnell, who sold Lincoln Zephyrs and used cars starting in the 1930s off East Spring Street; C. V. Nalley, a Dodge dealer on East Spring Street between Green and Bradford Streets; D. T. Pethel, who sold Pontiacs and used cars on Main Street; John Martin, a Chevrolet dealer on South Main Street; Sawyer & Womack, Dodge dealers purchased from C. V. Nalley, Jr.; Milton Martin, dealer of Toyotas and used vehicles at East Spring Street, later at Browns Bridge Road; Moss Robertson, a Cadillac-Olds dealer on Browns Bridge Road; Jim Hardman, a Buick-Pontiac-GMC dealership on Browns Bridge Road; and Green Ford on Browns Bridge Road.

With the increase in the number of mechanized vehicles, the use of wagons and carriages correspondingly declined. The wagon manufacturer located on Oak Street and one at Main Street and the Bagwell Wagon and Carriage Manufacturing Company on the east side of Athens Street near College Avenue went

On the Southeast corner of the Public Square of the Queen City of the Mountains is located the best known Bargain Store in the South.

| COME AND SEE IF IT IS TRUE |

The Store that Made Gainesville Famous as a Bargain Center

D. D. JACKSON
Sole Owner

Telephone 481 :-: Gainesville, Ga.

out of business about 1950. Next door to the Bagwell Wagon and Carriage Manufacturing firm on Athens Street was a livery stable owned by the Bagwell Brothers that continued until the 1950s. The federal-city urban renewal program of the 1960s removed those facilities and redeveloped the Athens Street-College Avenue block and other blocks, along Athens Street to Summit and Myrtle Streets, in an area at one time generally owned and operated by blacks.

NEW BUSINESSES IN THE TWENTIETH CENTURY

By the 1920s the Square found itself an oasis for travelers looking for accommodations and ready to spend money. Gas stations, mechanic shops, hotels, restaurants, and retail stores sprang up and their success helped to cushion the depression years of the later 1930s.

In the years prior to WWI, the purchasing power of the dollar was impressive. W. A. Roper, local Ford agent, advertised Model T Fords for $690 at factory. For roughly the price of a new Model T one could buy twenty-seven acres of orchard land with a stream near the north city limits of Gainesville ($675). For $2,250 one could buy a house and lot on Green Street Circle. A five room house and lot was available on Academy Street for $2,000. By the late 1930s, lots off Riverside Drive—Thompson Bridge Road, developed by W. A. Roper, and Longstreet Hills, developed by W. L. Norton, Sr.,

Above: J. Marvin Bell's station at the corner of Main and Broad Streets. Virginia Souther's uncle, J. Marvin Bell, is at the reins, c. 1920s.
COURTESY OF VIRGINIA SOUTHER.

Below: The D. D. Jackson Company (East Spring-South Bradford Streets) appealed to a wider public as automobiles made trips to town easier and more frequent, c. pre-1930s. Later occupied by Gallant-Belk to the late 1970s when the Georgia Mountains Center was built and South Bradford Street was closed.

were in the $1,500 range and houses and lots through WWII were $4,500-6,000.

Cotton was selling for eight to nine cents per pound in the fall of 1914 when Hall County folks joined the "Buy a Bale of Cotton" movement which had started with the Atlanta newspapers. The scheme urged individuals and businesses to buy one or more bales of cotton at ten cents per pound, i.e., over market price, in an effort to stimulate prices and encourage production and thus help farmers and the important local mill operations. A bale, at

500 pounds, would generate $50 and local businesses received a little free publicity with their cotton purchases. The Piedmont Hotel proudly displayed its bale gaily decorated with American flags in the lobby.

In those prosperous days new names and companies that would survive through the remainder of the century were establishing themselves locally. In July 1916 the Georgia Railroad and Power Company (Georgia Power), headed by A. J. Warner, acquired the property of the North Georgia Electric Company and Gainesville Electric Railway Company for $190,000. The sale included the power station at Dunlap Dam, Lake Warner and the streetcar line. In April of 1917 Colonel Sandy Beaver, previously a teacher and superintendent at Riverside Military Academy on the Chattahoochee River, acquired the Academy (organized in 1907), formerly owned by Dr. H. J. Pearce, owner of Brenau College, for $11,000 according to newspaper reports. Under Sandy Beaver's dynamic academic and business leadership, it became a successful, widely known institution and, with Brenau College, attained respect and renown for the institution and Gainesville far beyond the local area and Georgia.

The events around the Square in Gainesville were recorded in the newspapers, businesses in

town advertised their wares, big churches boasted of their attendance numbers, rails and roads converged in town, and "politickin'" and the offices of government focused around the courthouse. However, life for the most part was still the farm and family life near Tadmore, Gillsville, Murrayville, Klondike, and Lula and on small, hand-cultivated patches of corn and cotton on farms out in the County, not a lot different from the Hall County of 1870, fifty years before.

The Dixie Hunt Hotel opened in late April 1926, replacing the Hunt, formerly Arlington, just off the Square. Governor Clifford Walker came to town for the lavish dedication ceremonies for the opening of the half million dollar hostelry, part of the Dixie chain of hotels. It had three stories and 125 guest rooms, 75 with baths. The style was Spanish with stucco exterior and tile details with an iron porch over the Main Street sidewalk. A central dining room could accommodate a hundred people, just the ticket for the growing number of civic organizations around town. The hotel was heavily damaged by the tornado of April 1936 and reconstructed as a concrete-steel "cyclone and fire proof" five story building in 1938 and converted to the prestigious Hunt Tower office building in 1981.

For the local male population, Gainesville boasted the Ideal Billiard Parlor at Main and Broad Streets, which was managed by D. G. Jacobs. A testimonial typical of the advertising of the day proclaimed that "medical experts agree that billiards and pool are splendid exercise and good for the digestion." Women, however, were seeing to their relatively new right to vote by participation in the local chapter of the League of Women Voters, chaired by Allie Maxwell. The "Progressive Arts Club" offered a taste of higher culture with music and readings as other proper outlets for women.

BASEBALL, RADIO, DEPRESSION & HOPE

Summer time brought baseball. In the summer of 1922 a crowd of more than three thousand enjoyed what some allege was "perhaps the greatest (ballgame) ever played in Gainesville." It was a contest between Buford and Tate and sponsored locally by the American Legion, which also supported many carnivals, circuses, and other events to the beginning of WWII. Buford and Tate were touted as "the two strongest baseball aggregations in the state of Georgia." The owner and editor of the *News*, Albert Hardy, Sr., urged his readers to "crank up the fliver,

Left: Local players for Osborne Mill baseball team: Doc Skelton (left) and Herbert Judson, 1935.
COURTESY OF MARSHALL JUDSON.

Below: A birthday gathering at the residence of Ed Roper on East Spring Street, c. 1933. Sidney O. Smith, Jr., (left) and William L. Norton, Jr., (right) are seated next to Eula Mae Grigg (Pearce), who is seated on the fourth step, fourth from the right. Others identified in this picture: Evelyn Smith (Hancock), Eddie Kimbrough, Johnny Blodgett, Marion Roper, Olive Price Charters (McKeever), Susan Pearce, Millicent Hosch, Carolyn Plexico, Frances Wheeler (McBrayer), Martha Frances Laws, Laura Griffin (Fuller), Betty Phillips, Jim Fuller, Carolyn Smith, Elizabeth Smith, Mary Ruth Elrod, Eddie Fish, Jim Smith, Jack Hulsey, Harry Grimes, and Joe Jones. Frances Moore (Nalley) is seated on the far left, and Margaret Roper is seated on the far right. Can you put the names with the faces?
COURTESY OF DIXIE RAMSEY & THE RAMSEY COLLECTION.

Oakwood High graduates in 1936.

step on the gas, leave the boll weevil, the unpaid bills, and the strike for somebody else to worry about for an afternoon and come to the game." Buford carried the day two to one.

Through the 1930s local and area textile and other mills fielded baseball teams in "industrial," "textile," or "sandlot" leagues[7]. Good players and managers who worked in the mills, plus some youngsters competed vigorously in the summer afternoons. Gainesville Mill, New Holland, and Chicopee had good playing fields and grandstands. Also, a wooden grandstand was located at Gainesville City Park. Several hundred spectators regularly attended each event. Late summer and early fall featured championship games regionally and nationally.

Each town and region produced fine talent who became local legends. Some of these rose to baseball heights. During the 1920s two local Hall County young men, Ivy and Red Wingo, made names for themselves. Ivy caught for the St. Louis Browns and later the Cincinnati Reds while Red played for the Toronto Leafs of the International League. In 1923 there was talk that the Detroit Americans were willing to pay Toronto $100,000 for Red. Ivy and Red were described as being "raised in Wilson's district three miles from Gainesville."

Radio captured the nation in the 1920s. Before the widespread commercialization of broadcasting it was the individual tinkerers who introduced this revolutionary device in communities around the country via the homemade crystal sets. In 1922 Gainesville's Master Lambert Williams, son of J. L.

Williams was reported to have "built his own radio." An enthusiastic radio fan, he was able to pick up many broadcast stations throughout the country.

The great stock market crash of October 1929 got no headlines in the local papers. As late as October 16 the only front page item on the economy reported a "Record Building Year for the Queen City as Activity Continues in all Sections." There was, however, a hint of recent economic difficulties in an ad from Frierson-McEver Company at the end of the month: "Although business conditions generally were not so good during October, we are very happy to state that our sales during October were the biggest of any October since the firm was organized."

Behind the headlines and cheerful optimism of merchants, however, there was a depression which had been building on the farms of the County for almost a decade before the market crash. The boll weevil, row crops not properly rotated, declining purchasing power, and reduced demand for cotton products, and low prices for cotton combined for effect. Nationally some 2,000 banks failed in 1928, some in North Georgia—one in Clermont, two in Cleveland, one in Maysville, and one in Gainesville. Surely these failures were signals for the 1929 crash and the 1930s Depression. Folks began to lose their farms to foreclosure, there were few tenant farming opportunities, and jobs in the mills diminished and many lost jobs.

Some optimism in 1930 began with suggestions and hopeful predictions. "Poultry on the farm means fine income" promised an article which suggested a goal of one hundred purebred hens on every farm in Hall County.

RECOVERY

In March 1933, following Roosevelt's "Bank Holiday," Citizens Bank and First National Bank of Gainesville were quickly reopened to unrestricted transactions, while conservators were appointed to manage the community's Gainesville National Bank.

While Roosevelt's action to assure orderly regulation of the banking world clearly put government in the business of business, the

Gainesville Chamber of Commerce pledged "wholehearted support and complete confidence in FDR's ability to meet the present acute economic crisis." The Gainesville National Bank quickly reorganized and recovered and the three banks prospered and expanded through the 1970s and '80s when new banks appeared[8].

Edgar B. Dunlap, Sr., an early FDR man, was appointed by the president to be attorney for the Atlanta Regional Office of the Reconstruction Finance Corporation and local merchants soon were cooperating with the National Recovery Plan, posting "We Do Our Part" signs in their windows. Young men came to north Georgia Civilian Conservation Corps (CCC) camps to work under military type conditions. By 1934 farmers were being required to plow under their cotton and other crops which exceeded their allotment pursuant to "crops control" legislation.

THE GREAT TORNADO

Gainesville's greatest tragedy punctuated the decade. On Monday, April 6, 1936 at 8:27 a.m., a devastating category F5 tornado decimated more than one half of the Square and for a mile or so east and west.

Gainesville became "a city laid waste." A book of the same name by W. M. Brice, "a lifetime resident" and Gainesville correspondent for the *Atlanta Journal* and the Associated Press, provides more than 120 pages of photographs, commentary, and details of the tornadic devastation that struck that morning[9].

The storm originated from two separate large black clouds west of Shallowford Road that gradually moved and merged together as twin funnels which dominated the sky. They moved eastward between West Broad Street and Dawsonville Highway, the storm centering virtually over the Square and Washington and Myrtle Streets to New Holland; all in three to five minutes. Wind force was estimated at seven hundred miles per hour. The tornado cut a path of destruction eight miles long and in some places a mile wide. Almost a thousand buildings were destroyed or damaged and property losses were estimated at $16 million. *A City Laid Waste* records that deaths reached 162,

THE TORNADOES OF 1903 & 1998

Two other tornadoes devastated Gainesville in the twentieth century. On January 1, 1903, a tornado tore through Gainesville and New Holland. A total of 106 people were killed, 40 of them at one of the cotton mills, and 300 were injured, still recorded as one of our nation's worst storm casualties. No photographs of the tornado exist and information is meager, but damage was said to total $750,000.

The first day of spring, March 20, 1998, another killer F3 tornado swept through northeast Hall County. The violent storm arrived just before 7:00 a.m. without warning; it did not show up on radar and no one was prepared for the damage to property or lives. It tore a path one half-mile wide and 10 miles long, killing 12 and injuring 80. Forty-one houses, 29 mobile homes, and 8 commercial chicken houses were destroyed. As many as 100,000 chickens and 40 head of cattle were killed. One-third of Lanier Elementary School was destroyed; had the tornado struck 45 minutes later, 600 children would have been at the school. Property damage was estimated at $13.5 million, but thankfully, the mortality rate was much lower than it could have been at a different time of day.

Other "minor" tornadoes have hit Gainesville. One in 1972 started over Lake Lanier and crossed Mountain View Drive, Thompson Bridge Road and Riverside Drive hitting several houses and uprooting trees in a two-hundred-yard path. Some speculate that the lake and proximity of the mountains to the lake encourage tornadoes, but others point out that the lake was not created until after the tornadoes of 1903 and 1936.

injuries 950, and 8 bodies were never recovered. Subsequently the death count rose to 216 as numbers came in from outlying areas in Hall County[10]. The collapse of the Cooper Pants Factory at Broad and Maple Streets produced seventy employee deaths, the largest death toll to date in a single building for any United States tornado. Everyone in Hall County was affected by loss or injury. The noise was described as

The destruction at Gainesville Midland on Spring Street after the tornado that struck in 1936. The location of the rail cars and station is now the Arts Council headquarters.

being like a combination of many simultaneous freight trains. Immediately after, the rain came in torrents for more than a day. In the year 2000, there are still many in Hall County who remember that event first-hand. They lost members of their family, friends, school chums, homes, churches, stores, or other property. They remember exactly where they were and what they were doing when it hit. Thousands of photographs were spread across the pages of newspapers all around the country. Carl Lawson had finished Gainesville High School and was in Los Angeles, California, studying radio technology in the spring of 1936. At about noon the Monday morning that the tornado hit his hometown he walked past a newspaper stand. In lurid headlines he read "Gainesville, Georgia Hit By Tornado." It was national news of the first order[11].

Colonel John Beaver, Riverside Military Academy, at 9:00 a.m. from the only operating telephone at the Southern Railroad Depot, called Governor Eugene Talmadge. Immediately, the Georgia National Guard was ordered to help the City government maintain order, help recover bodies, attend to injured, and assist fire relief, transportation, communications, and clean-up activities. His father, General Sandy Beaver, owner of Riverside Military Academy, was a

University of Georgia classmate of Talmadge and chief of staff and commander of the Georgia National Guard. Martial law was declared and the U.S. Army took command of the catastrophe. Riverside Military Academy officers and cadets and North Georgia College faculty, cadets, and students assisted for several days.

After visiting for a few days in Warm Springs on April 6, President Franklin Roosevelt, returning to Washington, D.C., stopped the train at Southern Railroad Depot on April 9 and received the mayor, city officials, and local leaders in his rail car. President Roosevelt offered to replace the heavily damaged County Courthouse and City Hall, housing, and offered other assistance. He proposed the appointment of the U.S. Corps of Engineers to coordinate all federal, state, and private agencies and the planning of recovery and reconstruction. Lieutenant Colonel Brehon B. Somervell, who served as a four-star general in charge of U.S. Army supply during WWII, was appointed to head the army team. He headquartered in the newly-completed Federal Building and United States Courthouse on East Spring Street.

Somervell and his team of architects and engineers recommended the removal of all of the substantially demolished buildings on the block of the 1885 Hall County Courthouse at East Spring, South Bradford, South Green, and Broad Streets and that the new County Courthouse should be the sole structure on that block. Likewise, the City Hall should be the only structure in the next block. He and his planners proposed a "Civic Center" composed successively of a Federal Building (with a United States Courthouse and Post Office) on

Above: Convicts clearing rubble just off the Square after the 1936 tornado.

Below: A farmer in South Carolina found this fragment of the University of Georgia diploma of Edgar B. Dunlap, Sr. in his field the day after the tornado in 1936. After April 1936 others reported identified papers from as far away as Greenville, South Carolina.

COURTESY OF ED DUNLAP, JR.

one block; a County Courthouse on the next block; and a City Hall on next block. The new white Georgia marble Courthouse and City Hall "Civic Center" was completed by the Public Works Administration (PWA) and dedicated by President Roosevelt in March 1938 from a platform and podium especially constructed for President Roosevelt on the sidewalk edge of the new County Courthouse lawn on Broad Street. The many thousands who attended witnessed the unveiling of the "Roosevelt Memorial Monument" on Broad Street between the new County Courthouse and City Hall.

Thus, for many years, Gainesville was distinguished by a three block Civic Center of three levels of governments surrounded by lawns of grass and shrubbery[12].

The housing promised by President Roosevelt to replace the many residences razed by the tornado produced the so-called "New Town" off Myrtle and Athens Streets and the "Government Houses" facing Ivy Terrace Park[13] at the end of North Street (now North Avenue) and North Main Street. Both were constructed by the Works Progress Administration (WPA) by 1938.

Immediately after the storm, the 1906 First Methodist Church building at Green and Academy became the morgue, command and communications center of the City government and Red Cross. A short wave radio station was set up by Reverend Henshelwood, pastor of the tornado-destroyed Grace Episcopal Church, at his home on Park

Street. That radio station and other ham radio operators provided communication for several days until Southern Bell Telephone established new lines.

Boy Scouts from Troops 16 and 26 delivered on bicycles Western Union and Postal Telegraph telegrams from Southern Railroad Depot throughout the community, including Riverside Military Academy, Brenau College, and the outskirts of Gainesville.

A soup kitchen and a blankets and clothes distribution center were set up by the Red Cross on the Square serviced by local citizens including local high school and grammar school students. A central food, clothes, and blanket center was set up at the Coca-Cola

Above: The aftermath of the Tornado of April 6, 1936. Note the vehicle advertising the phone number "9176" of Moore's Service Station. This car was probably located at the wreckage of St. Paul Methodist Church on Grove Street. The photo was taken looking down Grove Street. Spring Street is to the left of the photo. The two-story building with a canopy above the first floor is the Gainesville Midland Railroad Station, with the railroad cars adjoining to the right. The Carter Grocery Co. and Main Street School in the left center background.
COURTESY OF THE HALL COUNTY HISTORICAL SOCIETY.

Bottom, left: Lost now to the public eye in "front" of the Courthouse is the 1938 monument to President Roosevelt, for his support following the 1936 tornado.
COURTESY OF RICHARD STONE.

Bottom, right: The podium, constructed locally, used by President Franklin D. Roosevelt in March 1938 upon dedication of the 1938 Courthouse and City Hall and Roosevelt Monument. Note the bronze arm supports installed to assist Roosevelt in standing during his speech. Used by countless dignitaries including President Lyndon Johnson. Preserved and protected by the students at Gainesville High School since 1938.
COURTESY OF WILLIAM L. NORTON, JR.

Above: The Walton Jackson, Jr. shops on North Green Street were built in 1938.

COURTESY OF WILLIAM L. NORTON, JR.

Below: Places like Bell's Mill were popular recreation sites in the 1930s before the proliferation of state and commercial recreation areas.

COURTESY OF HERBERT BELL.

Bell's Mill Appeals as an Ideal Spot For Pleasure-seekers

bottling plant[14]. Truck loads of potatoes and cabbages were dumped on the sidewalks on Spring Street at the Federal Building. Fresh, clean drinking water was brought in new unused gasoline fuel trucks from Atlanta, and elsewhere to Gainesville and dispensed day and night by local Boy Scouts of Troops 16 and 26 along the streets to pails and buckets brought by residents to the trucks. The newly-fashioned New Deal agencies of relief poured assistance into the community.

On the other hand, Roosevelt's New Deal programs did not bring as much to Georgia as they might have due to the obstructionist actions on the part of Governor Eugene Talmadge (1933-1937). Eurith D. Rivers, a Democrat who succeeded Talmadge as governor, brought Georgia into sync with the New Deal with an enthusiasm that brought help to Hall County. In 1939 the State Welfare Department distributed more than $30,000 in food and clothing to indigents in Hall. More than two thousand payments averaging $6.20 per month were paid out to jobless individuals in Hall County from July through October that year.

There are some today who recall fondly job opportunities which came by way of the PWA and the WPA. Glenn Whitmire remembers wages of $2 per day for working with the PWA on paving of Cleveland Highway. The Reconstruction Finance Corporation (RFC) made over $1.3 million in local loans for rebuilding. The American Red Cross played a vital role in the days and weeks following the storm[15]. Individuals and businesses unharmed by the winds came to the aid of their fellow townspeople and the community paid tribute in a multitude of ways to those killed. White and black citizens joined together in a memorial service at St. John Baptist Church on May 10 where ministers from black and white churches held special services with more than one thousand people in attendance. As usual, merchants quickly set out to rebuild better than before and many businesses survived[16].

THE WONDERFUL SQUARE

The Square was again relandscaped after the Great Tornado when trees were severely damaged, but "Ole Joe" resisted the storm unscathed. Prior to 1900, granite posts about five feet tall were installed surrounding the circle of the Square. These posts were connected by heavy iron chains, to which wagons and animals were hitched. The posts and chains remained until the 1936 tornado, after which they were removed. Some were acquired by local residents as historical treasures.

After WWII, the City purchased from Chicopee silver-painted metal electric light posts which were installed around the Square and one block each way, and Southern Bell and Georgia Power were persuaded to install utilities underground, a process completed in

HISTORIC GAINESVILLE & HALL COUNTY

62

the 1950s. The beautification action was greatly praised by an appreciative public. Later, the utility companies persuaded the City to abandon the uniform beautification program and again allow the visual pollution of unsightly poles and wires[17].

During the period preceding WWII, Gainesville began to benefit from a number of Jewish merchants locating retail businesses on the Square. These merchants provided essential goods, economically priced and cordially sold. Prominent among these highly regarded Jewish families were the Sacks, owners of Jake Sacks, a men's clothing store at 14 South Bradford Street; and the Millners, owners of Millner's, a ladies ready-to-wear clothing store on East Spring Street. Gem Jewelry was originated in 1937 at East Washington Street by Mose Eplan, father-in-law of Marvin Orenstein. Gem Jewelry was a tenant in a small area in front of Bell's Cleaners[18]. In 1945 Gem Jewelry moved to East Spring Street on the south side of the Square and, in 1958, to South Bradford Street on the east side of the Square. Additional prominent families were the Mintzs, owners of Lewis Mintz Jewelry on East Washington Street; the Shapiros, who owned a grocery store and a radio repair shop; and the Schrages, owners of Saul's, ladies ready-to-wear clothing store on East Spring Street.

THE POULTRY INDUSTRY

An economic result of the Great Tornado of 1936 was the commercialization of the former backyard "raising" of chickens. The tornado damaged part of the building of Jewell-Loudermilk Feed Store just three blocks off the Square on Grove Street. Having no place to keep baby chicks on hand and receiving more regularly by railroad, Jesse Jewell contacted farmers to accept his chicks and feed without payment. Jewell agreed he would take the fully grown chicks when marketable sixteen weeks or so later and sell them and share any profits. Thus, "contract grow-out programs" began in Georgia, and during the late 1930s and WWII years, Georgia's great poultry industry began at Jewell-Loudermilk Feed and Seed Warehouse. Young Jesse Jewell had sought merely to expand the family business there by including poultry. By January 1941 the J. D. Jewell Company at 322 South Maple Street took out a large advertisement in the *Eagle* with a photo showing its loading dock and offering "Baby Chicks, Broilers, Friers, Hens, Feeds and Fertilizers."

On the eve of World War II the poultry industry was on the verge of taking off. In 1929 farmers in Hall County raised 106,410 chickens valued at $174,443, but by 1939 farmers sold 1.5 million birds at $750,000. That year poultry became the County's highest valued crop, overtaking cotton. By 1950 Hall County poultry values rose to $5,227,531 and the number of chicken farmers rose from 57 to 975. By 1950 Gainesville's poultry industry processed $71 million worth of broilers and employed 1,200. The farmers in the County,

The Gainesville Daily Times *news (right) and advertising (left) staff in 1947. Editor Sylvan Meyer (middle right in bow tie) became a distinctive voice of conscience for a community increasingly facing change. Managing Editor Lou Fockele can be seen in the lower right.*

together with the multitudes of auxiliary operations, made the chicken a fitting symbol for opportunity.

Jewell's visionary and aggressive leadership efforts resulted in his operations ultimately having Georgia's first broiler processing plant. Jewell's facilities included ancillary divisions, a feed manufacturing mill, a chicken hatchery, and a chicken freezing facility, and a system to market further-processed breaded and cooked parts of chickens and chicken pies. His corporation conceived and copyrighted the terms "Chicken Burgoo," "Drummettes," and "Chick-filet." He started a by-products rendering plant, necessary to dispose of chicken waste (feathers, offal, feet, heads) and for environmental concerns and ancillary rendered product revenue. By grinding and cooking chicken waste at ultra-high temperatures in specially designed vats, later via leading-edge continuous cook processing, these waste parts of chickens were converted into high quality, valuable meal (ninety-four percent protein) that is added to other grains to formulate animal feeds. The by-products rendering plant was first located in the city on city sewage, but after WWII, for environmental reasons, Jewell bought approximately fifteen hundred or so acres off Highway 129, east of Pendergrass in Jackson County. In the 1960s, Jewell constructed a major rendering plant at Pendergrass for disposal, processing and cooking of by-products of J. D. Jewell, Inc. and additional waste products obtained from many other processing plants within a wide radius of Gainesville. After WWII, the Gainesville Airport processing plant, including its further-processing plant, and research department, the feed mill and hatcheries, and the Pendergrass by-products rendering plant became the country's largest integrated poultry producing enterprise and Gainesville's largest employer of over eleven hundred employees.

In the 1960s Jesse Jewell sold his stock to a New York group led by director Carl Chandler and J. D. Jewell, Inc. became a public company. Shortly thereafter Jesse Jewell was stricken, but continued for several years as a director and consultant.

It is imperative that poultry by-products be processed for environmental purposes because it cannot be buried or burned or otherwise disposed successfully. The rendered meal product is a valuable additive ingredient to all types of feeds. Interstate Highway 85 was constructed through the rural property near Pendergrass, placing the by-products plant very near the Highway 129 interchange. Despite state-of-the-art cooking and "scrubbing equipment" to minimize odor, property owners at the interchange and the Jefferson community objected brought a series of lawsuits alleging "nuisance." Jewell prevailed in the lawsuits, but the constant litigation was financially devastating and the company was liquidated in 1972.

Today the original site at Grove Street, just off the Square, is mostly covered by the divided four-lane street known as Jesse Jewell Parkway[19].

Other poultry enterprises developed in Hall County. During WWII, Tom Paris, Sr., organized Piedmont Poultry processing plant and John and Lula Mae Martin[20] and William Ellison formed Marell Farms processing plant.

Many WWII veterans became feed dealers, transportation owners, grow-out managers, poultry growers, and processors. Marvin McKibbon moved a plant from Griffin, Georgia, and established Mar-Jac Processing Company with this brother Jack McKibbon, Sr., who was a long-time Piggly Wiggly operator and owned Avion Restaurant and Holiday Inn.

Veterans returning from service in 1945-46 were surprised to see chicken houses all over North Georgia on small farms and behind

An old coaster/paperweight bearing the J. D. Jewell logo, c. 1960.

residences. Painted houses (some of which before the War had never been painted), and green grass on front lawns which had previously been dirt brushed by residents with straw brooms were noticeable changes. Chicken litter spread on former cotton acreage transformed bleak terrain into green pasture and gardens, and evidence of prosperity. Some poultry growers worked during the day at cotton mills or other industrial plants. The cash crop of poultry-growing for processing plants provided resources for spending. The new wealth of many of the residents, so obvious to returning veterans, was undoubtedly the greatest change that had come about during the first half of the twentieth century.

Ralph Cleveland formed Gainesville Milling Company (GMC) on Davis Street. Cleveland merged with Martin Feed Company (at Main Street and Industrial Boulevard) and together Cleveland-Martin had a large poultry feed and grow-out program. GMC became one of the largest independent feed manufacturing mills in the region. He was not affiliated with any of the large field grain companies, such as Ralston-Purina, Pillsbury, McMillan Quality Mix, Wayne Feeds, ConAgra, Provico, or Swift.

Organized in 1954, the Georgia Poultry Federation, always headquartered in Gainesville, became the most prominent, respected, influential, and effective poultry organization in the United States. By 1960 Gainesville had become the "Poultry Capital of the World." Representing all segments of the poultry industry throughout the state, the Federation hosted many important regular meetings, conferences, educational and leadership seminars, and federal and state legislative activities. The Federation created *The Poultry Times*, the leading poultry news source, later sold to *The Times*.

With Abit Massey serving as executive director (1960 to present) and W. L. Norton, Jr. as attorney (1957-71), the Federation headquarters building was constructed in Gainesville in the 1960s. Past Federation presidents who lived in Hall County include Joe Tankersley (1952-54), Max Ward (1961-62), Ray Burch (1966-67), James Evans (1970-71), Homer Wilson (1972-73), Elton Maddox (1993-94), and Johnny Burkett (1996-97).

Those with Hall County offices included Hulan Hall (1959-60), Fred Coats (1967-68), Lee Arrendale (1975-76), George Deadwyler (1981-82), Lawton Wofford (1988-89), Doug Carnes (1989-90), and Peter Martin (1994-95).

In the 1960s Hall County became the headquarters for the Georgia Poultry Processors Association, the Georgia Poultry Improvement Association, the Georgia Poultry Diagnostic Laboratory Network, the national Food & Poultry Distributors Association, and two national publications—*Poultry Times* and *Poultry & Egg Marketing*.

In the 1930s and '40s, during the Great Depression, many rural housewives washed feed bags and converted them into garments for their families. In the 1950s poultry feed began to be manufactured in Gainesville rather than arriving by rail and trucks in cotton bags. By the 1960s at least one business in Gainesville purchased used bags for recycling by washing and selling them for conversion into other uses. Feed mills Pillsbury, Purina, Master-Mix (MacMillian Company), and Wayne, all headquartered in the Midwest, established feed mills in Gainesville. Feed began to be delivered in bulk to grow-out houses. Local grow-out programs supported by feed dealers began expanding by establishing their own mix-mills using feed and vitamin concentrates and grains,

Legendary poultry pioneer Jesse Jewell (left), Dago Barron, and a porky friend, c. 1960. This photo hangs in Johnny's Barbecue which is next door to the Big Bear Café (1930s-70s) on Cleveland Highway. Barron owned the Big Bear Café
COURTESY BIG BEAR RESTAURANT.

The Piedmont Drug Store on Bradford Street was owned by John Woodcock, Sr. (on the right at the head of the table) in the 1940s. This photo shows a Christmas dinner for employees and family. Harriet Woodcock, the store's bookkeeper and John Woodcock's daughter, is seated fourth on the right from her father. Specializing in customer service, John Woodcock told the employees "If they ask for a horse and buggy, don't say you don't have it. Go and look," (From The Times, "A Story of Faith," March 3, 1996, p. E1.). Dinner guests include (clockwise from lower left) Mr. Parker, unknown, Harold Kemp, Mrs. Bud Cagle, unknown, Mrs. Pierce Chapman, unknown, unknown, P. F. Brown, unknown, Dr. McDermott and Dr. John Woodcock (both at the table head), Pierce Chapman, unknown, Dr. T. F. Hardaman, Harriet Woodcock, Paul Clark, Bud Cagle, unknown, unknown, unknown, and unknown.

or starting larger mills to manufacture feeds from basic grain ingredients.

Subsequently, Cargill (1960s), one of the world's largest grain producers, established a substantial soybean oil plant in Gainesville at Ridge Road and E. E. Butler Parkway.

As the major feed companies began acquiring processing plants in the early 1960s, the local independent feed dealers organized the Georgia Poultry Exchange, an auction marketing procedure. Birds in the field ready for sale were inspected weekly and evaluated by weight and condition by employees of the Exchange, described and listed for sale and auctioned within a week. The auction was conducted from Gainesville by electronic and telephonic means over wide areas where the processing plants (purchasers) were located. As the major national feed companies expanded to acquire processing plants, the independent feed dealers with large grow-out operators began leaving the live poultry auction marketing program to purchase or merge with processing plants. In January 1960 Mar-Jac was acquired by several feed dealers who had been some of the initial organizers of the Georgia Poultry Exchange. The new owners were A. C. Smith and Mark Heard, Jr., of Forsyth County; Bruce and Wilson (Alton Bruce and Homer Wilson)[21]; and C.W.T. Feed Company (John Cromartie, Max Ward, and Joe Tankersley). Georgia Broilers Company on Industrial Boulevard was merged with Arrendale Brothers Feed Company

in Habersham County and became Fieldale, Inc. headed by Joe Hatfield and Tom and Lee Arrendale. Tom Folger Feed Company, Hall and Lumpkin Counties, likewise left the Poultry Exchange and merged with Marell Farms Processing Company (Lula Mae Martin and William Ellison). Loyd Strickland was a feed dealer who left the broiler growing business in the 1960s to concentrate on egg marketing (Crystal Farms). Another former broiler dealer Lathem and Ramsey (Bob Lathem and Wilbur Ramsey) became a significant egg producer.

Thus, sparked by leadership of Jesse Jewell beginning in 1936, in less than thirty years the poultry business in Georgia replaced cotton as Georgia's largest agricultural crop and brought prosperity to North Georgia and many counties, the likes of which so many Georgians had never enjoyed.

WWII & POST-WAR YEARS

Paratroopers training at an Army camp near Toccoa, and Navy Air Station personnel at Gainesville Airport, frequented the City during 1942-45. Civil defense rumors and notices of enemy aerial attacks and threatened invasions of the Atlantic coast precipitated "blackouts" which became routine during 1942-44. There was an air of excitement as if the Gainesville Square was the center of the universe.

In late 1940 almost five thousand men were registered for the military draft in Hall County and more than two dozen volunteered for service in November. In January 1941 the first local draftees left for the service. They had a big send-off at the Southern Depot, the Gainesville High School band providing the appropriate fanfares.

Within the year the community was well into the unusual routines of war time America. Two hundred tons of rubber were to be salvaged in Hall County for the war effort, local Boy Scout troops being the mainstays of such drives. Ration books for goods and gasoline became a fixture. Locals were reminded by the newspaper that "Sugar Stamp #5 became valid June 28" and was good for two pounds of sugar through July 25. John H. Hosch, president of Citizens Bank, was general chairman of the Hall County War Bond drive with a 1942 goal of $105,700.

The December 11 edition of the *Gainesville Eagle* carried details of the entry of the United States into World War II against Japan after the sneak attack on Pearl Harbor, December 7, 1941, FDR's "Day Which Will Live in Infamy." The *Eagle* observed that "the County has thus far escaped casualties in the Jap fight," but the Christmas day issue provided what amounted to a sad "correction." Eugene Blanchard, age twenty-four, son of Mr. and Mrs. D. W. Blanchard of 713 Pine Street, had died on the *USS Oklahoma* during the attack on Pearl Harbor. Another Hall County resident, Henry T. Woodliff, was in Pearl Harbor with the Corps of Engineers at one of the airports bombed by the Japanese.

Hall County had experienced war.

The D-Day invasion of France, June 6, 1944, passed without any special notice in Hall County, but by June 8 the news seemed to have normal routines at a standstill. "Practically every business house and office in Gainesville was open, but things were not normal" as everyone came in late, having tarried at home listening to the news on the radio.

D-Day did not halt the War in Europe. The march toward Hitler's Berlin took agonizing months before the German surrender in early May 1945. Local news items continued to report casualties from events now famous to history; the Battle of the Bulge (December 16-26, 1944) and the Rhine Bridge at Remagen (March 7, 1945).

On the homefront the commander-in-chief fell to the strain of his years in office and physical decline. President Roosevelt's funeral train passed through Gainesville on its way from Warm Springs in April 1945. A crowd estimated at more than five thousand stood along the tracks to pay homage to the fallen war-time leader and, for many, hero of the New Deal.

The war with Germany was over in May, but the U.S. still faced Japan in the Pacific. Young men who had survived North Africa, Italy, Sicily, D-Day, and the bloody months beyond were now hearing talk of being sent to join the Pacific forces for the bloody onslaught, island by island, to Japan, a daunting prospect. Based on the "kamikaze" actions of Japanese pilots and soldiers, in early 1945, in island-taking invasions, such

Top: Twin brothers Harold and Harodlee Latimer were examples of Hall County's youth gone to war.
COURTESY OF JACK LATIMER.

Middle: The Brothers DeLong (from left to right): Frank, Jr. (GHS 1936), Harold (GHS 1940), and Jim (GHS 1938).
COURTESY OF JIM DELONG.

Bottom: A. R. (Dick) Kenyon, U.S. Army, serving in Italy. Kenyon, a lawyer, would later serve Hall County as Superior Court judge.
COURTESY OF MRS. A. R. KENYON.

CHAPTER III

Top, left: A youthful John Souther before his WWII adventures in faraway places and attainment of the rank of lieutenant colonel in the U.S. Army. Souther served in North Africa, France, and Italy and earned a Silver Star. Other Silver Star recipients during World War II include Captain John W. Jacobs, Jr., who earned his star as well as a cluster while serving in Germany, and Lieutenant Colonel Wilbur Ramsey, who earned his while serving in the South Pacific.

Top, right: James T. "Tee" Moon of Lula was in the medical corps at the time this photo was taken in 1943.

Below: Brothers Ed (GHS 1941) and James (GHS 1936) Dunlap in WWII U.S. Army uniforms. Their father, E. B. Dunlap, Sr., was a veteran of WWI.

as Tarawa, Iwo Jima, and Okinawa, both sides experienced staggering casualties. The American high command calculated that it might take another year, or three or five to defeat Japan at an estimated cost of over a million American casualties and similar numbers of Japanese soldiers, sailors, and civilians. Many Hall County young men were in several Pacific areas preparing for the invasion of Japan, or in Europe or the United States awaiting shipment to the Pacific. However, in two months, it was over.

Truman had ordered the use of the atomic bomb, successfully tested one month before in July 1945 in New Mexico. Hundreds of thousands of American and Japanese servicemen and their families were spared the bloodbath of an invasion of mainland Japan. Locally a newspaper reported: "Youngsters Go Wild, Oldsters Go to Church as Victory Over Japan is Announced."

CHANGES IN THE CITY & COUNTY

Downtown, during the 1930s and '40s the school system conducted Halloween Carnivals on the four streets surrounding the Square. Funeral burial tents housed individual features such as fortune tellers, horror scenes, storytellers, music, hot dogs, lemonade, hot chocolate, and other harmless forms of entertainment for elementary and high school students and families.

During the 1940s to the mid-1950s, the Square was frequented each noon hour by students from the Gainesville High School[22], just one block away. Many seemed to prefer skipping the school cafeteria and choosing a "slaw dog" and a Coca-Cola at one of the Square's drug store lunch counters. Previous to WWII, no school cafeteria existed at Gainesville High School, Candler Street School and Main Street School.

Students went home for lunch, brought their lunches with them, or ate on the Square.

In post-war years, Tadmore School, a 32-by-60-foot frame structure built in 1925, experienced a number of expansions and additions as growing numbers forced three classes to meet in the auditorium. In 1947 and 1949, classroom additions helped. The first school lunch room in Hall County was constructed at Tadmore School entirely by community volunteers using donated materials. Daily, 240 hot meals were provided in two to three shifts under the supervision of Mrs. J. F. Butterworth and her staff—Mrs. Allen Smith, Mrs. Dorsey Peck, and Mrs. A. N. Head.

Across the County in the post-war years the tradition of a large number of small schools was fading. The number of County schools shrank as the County School System consolidated with the creation of East Hall and North Hall High Schools and South Hall, which became Johnson High in the 1970s. West Hall High School was opened in the late 1980s[23]. All over the County new, modern elementary and middle schools sprang up with the expanding population.

In the spring of 1954 a Supreme Court decision had declared racially segregated public education to be unconstitutional. In Georgia there was talk of the "privatization" of public schools and the end of compulsory education. Locally there were public debates, but in November, Hall County rejected Georgia school privatization in favor of school integration by a vote of 2733 to 1723, as did the entire state.

In the summer of '41, Henry Estes, president of the Chamber of Commerce, and A. F. Dean, publisher of the *Gainesville Eagle*, joined with Charles Smithgall and Charles Thurmond to apply for FCC permission to open Gainesville's first radio station, WGGA. By July the tower was up and by the fall a full schedule was being broadcast under the direction of Gainesville native and veteran, widely known Atlanta radio official, Charles Smithgall. Early programming was largely confined to music, farm reports and news. The famous soap operas and adventure serials of the era were not yet a part of the local mix.

In 1947, Smithgall acquired the *Gainesville Eagle* from Austin Dean and established the

Gainesville Daily Times, a regional daily, later *The Daily Times*. Since 1972 it has been known as *The Times*[24], which moved to its current location, Green Street, in 1970. In 1981 it was sold to Gannett Company which also uses the state-of-the-art, modern plant to publish *USA Today* for southern states. He attracted an excellent newspaper management staff who later consistently received numerous state and national media awards (Editor Sylvan Meyer and Publisher Lou Fockele became legendary newspaper leaders). Smithgall's Southland Publishing Company also published the *Georgia Poultry Times* (later *Poultry Times* and other regional editions) which, under the leadership of John Yarbrough as editor and publisher, became the fabulously successful and prominent poultry news publication.

THE POST-WAR SQUARE

After WWII in August 1945 the Square exploded with activity. During the next ten years the Square reached a zenith. Automobiles refilled the parking spaces. Elaborately staged poultry parades, complete with beauty queen filled floats, musical events, and circus parades were regular affairs. People packed the sidewalks to shop or just be part of the scene. In a short radius from the Square were vast assortments of establishments of every description including: three hotels[25], hardware stores[26], gasoline filling stations[27], tire dealers[28],

Above: Three generations of war veterans (from left to right): William L. Norton, Sr. (Army, 1917-19); William L. Norton III (Navy, 1975-79); and William L. Norton, Jr., (Army, 1942-46).

COURTESY OF W. L. NORTON, JR.

Below: The teenage "Pirkle sisters" when the Ringling Brothers Circus made Gainesville a stop on their tours in the early 1920s.

BLACK NEWSPAPERS IN HALL COUNTY

A locally produced and published black newspaper, the *Gainesville Messenger* appeared in Gainesville early in 1904 and was recognized by the editor of the *Eagle* in the January 21, 1904 issue: "The colored people of Gainesville now have a local newspaper of their own...with editorial and local matters of interest to the race." The Reverend J. D. Lovejoy headed the business side of the paper while Professor C. E. Williams served as editor and B. Neal, general agent. The *Eagle* said that "the editorial and news matter is up-to-date, bright and excellently prepared. The colored people are to be commended and congratulated on such a good paper." At this writing no extant copy of the *Messenger* has been located.

a Greyhound Bus station, a railroad station[29], taxi services[30], drug stores with soda fountains[31], clothing stores[32], department stores[33], three banks[34], meat markets[35], grocery stores[36], pool and billiards rooms[37], Gainesville High School (West Washington-Grove), newspapers[38], two radio stations[39], three movie picture theaters[40], photo studios[41], several funeral directors[42], the U.S. Post Office, Federal Building, City Hall, and Courthouse, several restaurants[43], furniture stores[44], several jewelry stores[45], five and dime stores[46], Georgia State Patrol Headquarters, Georgia Power Company, Southern Bell Telephone Company, four churches[47], auto dealers[48], some wholesale enterprises[49], barbershops[50], shoe repair shops[51], and many other establishments[52] along with offices for doctors[53], lawyers[54], and other professionals[55]. Hospitals soon followed[56]. Just off the Square were bakeries[57], laundry, and dry cleaners[58].

Three blocks off the Square on Athens Street (now E. E. Butler Parkway), several black businessmen flourished, respected by all the community. Dr. Wright, a druggist not a medical doctor, operated a drug and sundry store in the 1920-30s. The store, located in a two-story brick building was later operated by Dr. Walter Chamblee, not a medical doctor, on the east side of Athens Street at the corner of West Summit[59]. Above Chamblee's store was the Odd Fellow's Hall, a meeting place for this secret order operated by private investors and was a meeting room for many black civic groups, including the Men's Progressive Club. It later housed the Masonic Order. Greenlee Funeral Home was next to Chamblee's. On the other side of Chamblee's building was the Ernest Burns Barbershop (1930-70s) and upstairs were Dr. E. E. Butler's office, the Atlanta Life Insurance Company, and Dr. E. M. Whelchel, a dentist.

Roxy Theater was located next door in a separate building operated from the 1950s to the 1970s, first by Martin Theaters, then by Paul Plaginos' family who operated State, Royal and Ritz near the Square.

Opposite Chamblee's, on the west side of Athens Street, Rena Bush's Restaurant was located in a two-story building. Rena worked at the hospital during the day and the restaurant at night. Her husband, Pete Harrison, owned a taxi company with his brother, Doc Harrison, as driver of his other taxi. Apparently, Pete and Doc, noted for always being cordial and pleasant, had exclusive license and authority to operate from the Southern Railroad Depot at South Main Street-Industrial Boulevard.

Nearby on the west side of Athens Street was the Clearview Restaurant operated in the 1930s by the Neals (Bessie, Jack, R. D., George, and Ida) who owned the building and operated another taxi company there. In the 1950s, the restaurant was operated by Raymond Maxey, father of W. H. Maxey[60].

The Avion, at Broad and Sycamore Streets, Gainesville's finest eating establishment for the post-war years developed by the McKibbon family. The site is presently occupied by a carwash at E. E. Butler Parkway, Jesse Jewell Parkway, and Broad Street.

COURTESY OF JACK MCKIBBON, JR.

CHAPTER 3 ENDNOTES

1. J. D. Matthews residence (1932).
2. H. H. Dean residence, c. 1910, replaced in 1962 by the First Baptist Church.
3. Henry Washington residence (1938).
4. Dr. Cleve Whelchel residence (1937).
5. Built for Congressman B. Frank Whelchel, Prater' s last project (1947).
6. For photo of the property on East Spring Street (p. 40) and tornado information, see *A City Laid Waste*, 1936, W. M. Brice, author. James and Harold DeLong succeeded to ownership of the Buick dealership, later being acquired by Jim Hardman. "Dub" and Dan Jacobs succeeded to ownership of the Oldsmobile-Cadillac dealership, later selling to Moss Robinson in the 1990s.
7. The American Legion Post No. 7 fielded youth baseball teams practicing at Chicopee and Gainesville Mill fields comprised mostly of sons of WWI veterans, coached and managed by Ed Sarratt.
8. Since the 1970s: Wachovia acquired Gainesville National Bank. Regions Bank acquired First National Bank. SunTrust acquired Home Federal Savings and Loan. Citizens Bank was acquired by Bank South, then NationsBank, and then Bank of America. Gainesville Bank and Trust was organized. Lanier National Bank and Georgia First Bank were organized, then acquired by CenturySouth.
9. The history of the Great Tornado of April 6, 1936 owes much to W. M. Brice and his *A City Laid Waste*. Without his vision and publication, much history of that event would be lost. A second edition was printed in the 1990s and sold by his heirs at Pardue's Newsstand. Mr. and Mrs. Brice Pardue graciously urged references by the Hall County Historical Society to that book, which the Society recommends.
10. "Archives of Hall County." http://ngeorgia.com/county/hall.html, September 19, 2000.
11. See *A City Laid Waste*, W. M. Brice, copyright 1936 (127 pages).
12. See *A City Laid Waste*, supra, p. 70 reference "civic center" planning and redevelopment. In the 1970s the unique and beautiful Government Center was lost by the locally planned and federally funded construction of the undistinguished Georgia Mountains Center, cluttered on the lawns of the County Courthouse and City Hall blocks, the closing of East Broad and South Bradford Streets, and the removal of three blocks of retail business buildings on South Bradford, South Main, East Spring Streets (facing the Square).
13. "Ivy," named after the English Ivy growing in the park opposite the homes.
14. Located at 7 North Green Street next door to the 1906 First Presbyterian Church formerly Merck & Elliott Buick dealership building (in the block now occupied by SunTrust Bank) between East Washington Street and Brenau Boulevard, H. Earl Terrell, manager.
15. Thereafter, a grateful Gainesville reportedly contributed for many years more per capita to the Red Cross than any other similar city. The memory of the beneficial services of the Red Cross in the aftermath of the 1936 tornado is still strong in Gainesville and Hall County in annual giving drives and when disasters occur.
16. See articles regarding church services and pages 117 to 126 regarding surviving businesses in *A City Laid Waste* by W. M. Brice (c. 1936).
17. Photographs over the years reveal numerous styles of landscaping of the Square, for example: trees, shrubs; no trees, no shrubs; light posts, no light posts; circle of standing utility posts and transmission wires; wires underground (1950s); but again in 1960s, wires on poles on the Square and adjoining streets along the Square area. That is, landscaping and utility posts, on again, off again.
18. Herbert Bell, whose family operated Bell's Mill on Little River three miles north on Cleveland Highway from the early 1930s through WWII.
19. Jesse Jewell received many honors of industrial and civic acclaim for his leadership in business and creation of a southern poultry industry that resulted in great prosperity for countless small farmers and individual growers, feed dealers, and hatcheries which stimulated the entire Georgia and southern economy. Jewell organized the National Broiler Council in Washington, D.C., and became its first president. He was elected the first reorganization president of the Georgia Chamber of Commerce (1955), which had become dormant during WWII. This was the first time a Gainesville citizen had been honored by election to that position and it was not until the year 2000 that another Gainesville native, Philip Wilheit, owner and operator of Tom Wilheit Paper Company, citizen extraordinaire, was named president of the Georgia Chamber. During the same period, Charles Thurmond, a boyhood friend of Jewell and general counsel of J. D. Jewell in the 1940s and '50s, and president in the 1960s, was elected (1956) president of Associated Industries of Georgia (A.I.G.), the oldest business association in Georgia (originally, Georgia Manufacturers Association in 1906). In January 2000, *Georgia Trend Magazine* named Jesse D. Jewell among the one hundred most influential Georgians of the twentieth century.
20. Former owners of Martin Chevrolet, South Main Street near Broad Street.
21. In the 1960s, Bruce & Wilson (Homer Wilson, Max Ward, and James Evans) formed Select Laboratories, Inc., which, in a few years, became the largest manufacturer of poultry medication. Subsequently it was sold to Merial Select, Inc., now managed by Stan Appleton.

[22] Constructed in the 1920s with a gymnasium added in 1936. Both were severely damaged by the 1936 tornado and the gym was reconstructed in 1937. The school building was abandoned in the 1960s and Gainesville High School moved several blocks down West Washington Street off Oak Street. The former school structure was destroyed, but the 1937 Gymnasium remains as an office building owned by realty developer, David Mercer.

[23] Due to tremendous growth, another Hall County High School. Flowery Branch High School located on Hog Mountain Road and Chestatee High School in North Hall are scheduled to open in the fall of 2002.

[24] Later, in the 1980s, Smithgall, Fockele and Robert Fowler associated to acquire several local weeklies in Cumming, Buford, Norcross, Winder, and Lawrenceville and organized the very successful *Gwinnett Daily News* which they sold in the 1980s to the *New York Times* which desired to expand it as a competitive metropolitan Atlanta newspaper. During the 1970-90s, Smithgall organized other radio stations and cable TV services in other cities and assembled some four thousand acres of North Georgia wilderness forestlands at Duke's Creek near Helen, Georgia and R. B. Russell Highway. It became Smithgall Woods State Park due to the vision and generosity of the Smithgall family. The January 2000 issue of *Georgia Trend* named Charles Smithgall one of the one hundred most influential Georgians of the twentieth century.

[25] Dixie Hunt (25 South Main Street), Princeton (2 North Main Street) and Wheeler (North Main Street).

[26] Palmour Hardware which, by 1919, had added a full line of auto supplies for the locally growing trade (47 South Main Street); Western Auto (South Main Street); Tanners; Goforth Brothers (33 South Bradford Street); also, J. D. Matthews Toys, Cycles, Appliances (35 South Main Street); Kleckley's Appliances (South Main Street, adjoining Dixie Hunt Hotel); Ed Jewell's Hardware (South Bradford Street); Pruitt-Barrett Hardware (20 South Bradford Street at the corner of East Spring-North Bradford Streets prior to the 1936 tornado, during which it was destroyed and never rebuilt). After WWII, Tom Paris, Sr., and James D. Dunlap established Paris-Dunlap Hardware Company (Wholesale) on South Bradford Street.

[27] Perfect Service, also known as Woco Pep, Wofford Oil Co., and Pure Oil (North Green Street at Brenau Avenue); Howard Fuller Standard Oil, later "Fat" Smith (South Green and East Spring Streets); Waters-Sinclair; Curtis Prickett, also known as Gulf Oil (Grove and East Spring Streets); Ed "Neighbor" Hughs' Motor Inn, also known as Standard Oil (on West Spring Street behind Dixie Hunt Hotel); Jimmy Wood Standard Oil (East Broad Street at South Main Street); and J. D. Williams Texaco (Grove and West Broad Streets.)

[28] Harrison's Goodyear Tire Store (Grove Street); DeLong's Firestone Tire Store (Main Street); Dayton Tire Store (Main Street); J. D. Williams Tire Store (Grove and West Broad Streets); and others.

[29] Moved from Athens Street and located with *The Daily Times* (West Spring and Grove Streets), and then on South Main Street.

[30] Mundy's on West Broad Street opposite West Avenue, now Queen City Parkway. Pete and Doc Harrison; Neals; both Athens Street.

[31] Whatleys, formerly known as Queen City (East Spring Street) and Dixie (25 South Main Street); Piedmont (45 South Bradford Street at East Washington Street); Imperial (1 West Washington Street at Washington and North Bradford Streets); and Stringer Brothers Confectioners, later owned by "Steamboat" Ledford Drug Co. (10 East Washington Street, opposite the Jackson Building).

[32] Frierson-McEver (on the corner of South Main and East Spring Streets, but moved to East Washington Street in the 1940s); Jake Sacks (14 South Bradford Street); Whitfields (East Spring Street); Hulsey's, formerly Hulsey-Roper, which sold men's clothes (8 South Bradford Street); Pauls (men's clothes); Saul's, which sold ladies' ready-to-wear and shoes (East Spring Street, and later North Main Street at West Washington Street); L. B. Adams, which sold men's clothes (South Bradford Street); Mrs. Ollie McCormell sold women's clothes; Mrs. J. N. Harrison Millinery, Furs and Hats (East Washington Street, next to W. R. Hughes Jewelry); Ronald's (East Washington Street across from the Jackson Building); Modrey's (East Washington Street across from the Jackson Building); The Hub (South Bradford Street); J. M. Parks & Son (South Bradford Street in the building that became *The Leader*). Ned Parks on the east side of the Square sold dry goods, shoes and clothing, including overalls at $1.90 a pair; Little New Yorker; Little Shop (East Washington Street); Millner's sold ladies' ready-to-wear (South Main Street); Fair Store, dry goods and ready-to-wear garments.

[33] Newman's (Newman, Frierson and McEver Department Store), which existed from the 1920s to the 1940s at the corner of South Main and East Spring, promoted a style trend by advertising "hair bobbing by a man barber - 35 cents;" Estes, owned by George P. Estes Co. (17 West Washington Street); and Gallant-Belk (East Spring and South Bradford Streets). After WWII JCPenney moved in Newman's space at corner of West Spring-South Main Streets.

[34] Claims have been made that the first bank in Northeast Georgia was the "Bank of Banks Brothers" located on the corner of Washington and Bradford Streets and organized by D. E. Banks and J. H. Banks, sons of Dr. Richard Banks; sold in the 1880s to C. C. and M. M. Sanders who renamed it State Bank until it failed at the beginning of the Great Depression. With the progress brought about by railroads and textile manufacturing, the First National Bank, which later became Regions Bank (9 South Main Street, then North Green Street at East Washington Street, and then across the street to South Green Street at the corners of Green and Washington Streets), was formed on May 22, 1889 under the leadership of Charles Banks, son of Dr. Richard Banks and father of Rafe Banks, Sr., and, on April 5, 1905, the Gainesville National Bank (with two locations, the Square and then to North Green Street in 1967 where it became First Atlanta and then Wachovia) opened with Samuel C. Dunlap as the bank's president. In June 1913 John H. Hosch and other Gainesvillians started the Citizens Bank. Banks in Clermont, Cleveland, Gillsville, and Maysville were formed in the 1920s, but all failed around 1928-29.

35 Byron Mitchell, later Butch Reynolds (originally located at 6 South Bradford Street, then on South Main Street adjoining Royal Theatre); Toy Minor (North Bradford Street and Brenau Boulevard).

36 Rogers, became Big Star and Colonial (North Bradford Street); A&P, managed by Jack Elrod (North Bradford Street); Piggly Wiggly, owned by Jack McKibbon, Sr. (S. Bradford Street at Broad Street); The Minor family owned Bee Hive Market (North Bradford Street at Brenau Boulevard); Red Grocery, owned by the Shiretzki family (24 South Main Street near Royal Theatre); and Porter's.

37 Purple Top, so named by owner William Hogsed (father of Bill Hogsed, Georgia Tech, and Robert Hogsed, U.S. Naval Academy) for the color of the felt covers of the tables (West Spring Street); Lee Crow's, later known as Pete Tankersley's (South Main Street next door to Palmour Hardware and close to Royal Theatre).

38 *Gainesville News* (established in 1888), owned by Albert Hardy, Sr., and, later, Charles Hardy (38 South Main Street); Eagle Publishing Company, owned by Austin Dean which produced the *Gainesville Eagle Weekly* (established in 1860, 35 North Bradford Street). In 1947, Eagle Publishing was acquired by Charles Smithgall, who then began Southland Publishing and *The Gainesville Daily Times.*

39 WGGA was first located at Athens Highway, then South Main Street, and then West Spring Street with *The Times*. The creation of the Northeast Georgia Broadcasting Company was announced in November of 1947 and plans were made public for a new AM and FM station to be managed by John W. Jacobs, Jr. WDUN opened in early April of 1949.

40 The State (East Washington Street), Royal (South Main Street), and Ritz (North Bradford Street) were all owned by the Paul Plaginos family. Late in the summer of 1946 the region's first "colored theatre" opened, The Roxy (Athens Street). The Roxy was located in the remodeled former Kidd Building on Athens Street and managed for the Georgia Theater chain by Harry E. Martin. Martin and Chief Projectionist Richard Atkins were the only white Roxy employees. "Doc" Lowe, Jr., Imogene Peeks, Cicero Daniels, Lucinda Davis, and Charles Williams rounded out the staff taking care of ticket and refreshment sales, maintenance, and upkeep of the theater. Meanwhile a drive-in theater on Atlanta Highway between Gainesville and Chicopee was opened in 1948 by John Thompson, and another outdoor theater was opened on Thompson Bridge Road at Nancy Creek Road, another sign of the local culture getting in step with the national trends in modern entertainment media.

41 N. C. White and Milton Hardy's were in adjoining locations on South Main Street across from the Royal Theatre. Hardy was son of Albert Hardy, Sr., owner of *Gainesville News*. Ramsey's, later Leonard Cinciolo (above Imperial Drug and later at Prior and Park Streets).

42 Newton and Ward, formerly Hansford-Newton Co. (West Washington Street at Maple Street, then Ward's), later moved to South Main Street; Stowe, Bell & Co. (45 South Main Street), then D. C. Stowe (East Spring Street.)

43 Smith Brothers; Pirkle's Café; Dixie Hunt Coffee Shop; Wheeler Hotel Coffee Shop; Princeton Coffee Shop; Wisteria Café; Mayflower Café; Cinciola's; and Cookie Jar, which mainly served Brenau College (East Washington Street at Boulevard). In the 1930s the Cookie Jar was managed by Eber Collins. After WWII, it was managed by "Spec" Moore.

44 Pilgrim-Estes (2 East Washington Street, later South Main Street at West Washington Street, and then North Bradford Street); Martin-Johnson, later Martin (North Bradford Street); Jimmy Reeves (North Green Street); Mather (South Green Street); B. H. Moore (North Bradford Street at Brenau Boulevard); Rhodes-Wood (South Main Street); and William Hood (South Main Street.)

45 Mintz, W. R. Hughes, and C. R. Hammond (later Courtenay's) were all located on East Washington Street at the Square. The Gem was located on South Bradford Street.

46 McClellans (West Washington and South Main Streets); Rose's (West Washington Street); Woolworth's (North Main Street at West Washington Street); and Frank's (South Bradford Street).

47 First Baptist (South Green Street at East Washington Street); First Presbyterian (North Green Street at Brenau Boulevard); First Methodist (North Green Street at Academy and Brenau Boulevard); St. Paul Methodist (West Washington Street at Grove Street.)

48 DeLong Buick-GMC (South Main Street), Jacobs Olds-Cadillac (Main and West Spring Streets). Jacobs and Delong later occupied adjoining buildings at East Spring Street. C. V. Nalley Dodge, later Sawyer & Womack Dodge (East Spring Street, then North Green Street at Brenau Boulevard); D. T. Pethel Pontiac and used cars (Main Street); Martin Chevrolet (South Main Street); Jimmy Haynes Chrysler-Plymouth, (East Broad Street); and O. B. Leverette's Gainesville Ford Company (South Main Street).

49 Hosch Brothers, which sold dry goods and school supplies from the 1880s to the 1970s (West Washington-Maple Streets). In the 1970s the building occupied by Hosch Brothers was sold to the law firm of Stevens & Shuler. Carter Grocery Company (Maple-Church Streets, now Jesse Jewell Parkway); H. A. Terrell & Son, formerly Gainesville Grocery Company (41 Maple Street between West Spring and West Broad Streets at Gainesville Midland Railroad, and 54 West Spring Street.)

50 Brogdon's, East Spring Street (facing Square); Smith & Pierce (East Washington Street, opposite the Jackson Building); Princeton Hotel, Barber Shop (West Washington Street adjoining the Princeton Hotel); and the Dixie Hunt Barber Shop, (part of the Dixie Hunt Hotel, South Main Street).

51 Barron's Shoe Shop was in business from the 1920s to the 1960s (North Bradford Street, then North Main Street). Upon the death of its original owner, Barron's was purchased by Tom Carter, a black businessman who owned Carter's Shoe Shop on Athens Street (now E. E. Butler Boulevard between Atlanta and Summit Streets). Carter moved to North Main Street in the 1960s. Later, Carter's son, Ben, took over

the business and opened Ben's Shoe Shop on College Avenue; Niven's Shoe Shop, which was in business from 1945-1960 (in the alley behind the Jackson Building).

[52] Robert's Book Store (East Washington Street); Ragland's (East Washington Street); Crescent Ice Cream (West Spring Street); Wright's Ice Cream (South Main Street); Nickleback Shoes (Jim Cash)(North Bradford Street); Southern Shoes (East Spring Street); Motor Finance (H. M. Burns)(Jackson Building); C. H. Martin Coal Company (Parker at Grove Street)(on Gainesville Midland tracks); George W. Moore & Sons (on Southern Railroad tracks at Industrial Boulevard near Main Street).

[53] Dr. C. J. Welborn, Dr. W. A. Palmour, and Dr. R. L. Rogers all in the Jackson Building as were Dr. Hartwell Joiner and Dr. H. S. Titshaw. Dr. J. C. Morrison, an optometrist (between Piedmont Drug and Hulsey's on South Bradford Street); Dr. J. K. Burns, Jr. (4 South Sycamore). One block off the Square for over thirty years after 1925, a house on North Green Street at Brenau Boulevard was the office of Dr. Jesse Meeks, Dr. R. L. Garner, and Dr. Bradley Davis (a pediatric specialist), Dr. Pratt Cheek, Dr. Mark, Dr. Clarence E. Butler, and Dr. Eugene Ward (an eye, ear, nose and throat specialist). Drs. Ward and Butler later moved to Academy Street and E. E. Butler Parkway. Also, in the early 1900s, Dr. W. N. Downey was at the North Green Street-Brenau house before forming W. N. Downey Hospital with Dr. Cleveland D. Whelchel and Dr. John Burns on Sycamore Street in the late 1920s. Dr. John B. Rudolph and Dr. H. Latimer Rudolph officed at 23 East Washington Street. Dentist offices in the Jackson Building included Dr. W. H. Miller, Dr. J. L. Thomas, Dr. J. J. Powell, Dr. C. R. Brice, Dr. John Scott, Dr. K. C. Maddox, and Dr. Clabus Lloyd. Dr. E. M. Whelchel was a dentist on Athens Street. The Gainesville Dental Parlor over Newman, Frierson and McEver had "full sets of suction teeth from five to ten dollars, gold crowns $3.50 and up."

[54] During WWII, the Hall County Commission created a hospital on the hill overlooking the Atlanta Highway, headed by Dr. R. L. Rogers, Sr. WWII also brought additional medical practitioners to Gainesville in the form of Gainesville native, Dr. Pierpoint F. Brown, Jr., who attracted Dr. P. K. Dixon. Both Dixon and Brown were from the Emory University Medical School and had extensive surgical experience in the Veterans Administration hospital in Atlanta. To the internal medicine specialty came doctors Henry Jennings, Jr., and Dr. Samuel O. Poole, graduates of Emory University and participants in the original Emory Clinic, joined by Dr. Warren Stribling, Jr. Gainesville native Rafe Banks returned after attending Emory University and Harvard University Medical School, and completing training in New York City and Boston to start his urology practice. Drs. Brown, Dixon, Jennings, Stribling and Poole built substantial specialty firms amid the development of the Hall County Hospital, subsequently named Northeast Georgia Medical Center and Lanier Park Hospital.

[55] Lawyers above the Gainesville National Bank (30½ South Bradford Street) included Pinckney Whelchel, Edgar B. Dunlap (later Dunlap & Dunlap, later Whelchel & Dunlap), Ernest Smith, and Ernest Palmour, Jr. Lawyers in the Jackson Building included B. P. Gaillard, who became a judge in the early 1930s; Charles S. Reid, later chief justice of the Georgia Supreme Court; Ed Quillian, who operated in the 1920s and '30s; Fred Kelley; Lilly, Charters & Wheeler (later Charters & Wheeler, later Wheeler & Kenyon, later Wheeler, Robinson and Thurmond, later Wheeler, Robinson and Norton in 1958 when Thurmond became president of J. D. Jewell, Inc.); Kenyon & Kenyon; R. Wilson Smith, Jr., Sloan & Sloan (W. W. Sloan and W. B. Sloan); Jeff Wayne; W. Boyd Sloan became Superior Court judge. When Sloan resigned, Joe K. Telford and W. Boyd Sloan formed Sloan and Telford, and later Telford, Wayne and Smith, when Sloan became U.S. district judge. Later Sidney O. Smith, Jr., became Superior Court judge, eventually succeeding Sloan as U.S. district judge. Law Firms above Estes Department Store (Masonic Hall on top floor above Estes) included Joe Blackshear, later Superior Court judge; W. N. Oliver and Perry Oliver in the Jackson Building; William J. Phillips at South Bradford Street.

[56] Sidney O. Smith Insurance Agency (Jackson Building, later North Bradford Street); Loudermilk Insurance Agency (North Bradford Street, above Citizens Bank); Kimbrough Insurance Agency (Estes Department Store Building); Bill Dewitt Insurance Agency (Jackson Building); W. L. Norton Agency, Inc. (Jackson Building, later across from the Jackson Building, later 393 Green Street, and then 434 Green Street); W. C. Ham and Henry Washington, later Sidney O. Smith Agency. Also W. A. Roper Real Estate was located in the Jackson Building.

[57] Small & Estes, in business during the 1930s and '40s (North Bradford Street); Cake Box, which was owned by Vern Sayre, was located on East Washington Street before moving to Thompson Bridge Road in 1950s.

[58] Bay Way (West Broad and Grove Streets); Gainesville Steam, owned by the Porter family (62 South Main Street at Broad Street); George Stephens, a black-owned dry cleaner and tailor (35 West Spring Street, then Maple Street behind McLellan's & First National Bank adjoining Ward's Funeral Home). In the 1940s Stephens moved to his residence on College Avenue near Prior Street where he owned several properties.

[59] All the buildings on the east and west sides of Athens Street near Summit Street were removed about 1977 by an Urban Renewal Program and the widening of Athens Street into E. E. Butler Parkway.

[60] W. H. Maxey was chef at the Elk's Club (Riverside Drive) and Avion Restaurant (East Broad at Sycamore Street). He was chef at Holiday Inn and Holiday Hall (West Broad) for fifteen years, until 1996. In the 1970s he became the managing chef at The Landings at Thompson Bridge Road, and Athens and Buford, Georgia, and Anderson and Greenville, South Carolina, and other locations. When The Landings was sold in the 1980s, he rented the vacant Gym of '36 (Grove, West Washington, and Maple Streets) and instituted The Dry Dock, which catered to Gainesville businesses, citizens, and visitors, busy with both black and white customers until it was destroyed by fire in 1987.

CHAPTER IV

WAY OF LIFE — THE MID-TWENTIETH CENTURY

In 1949, J. D. Cash of Flowery Branch, president of the Hall County Farm Bureau, reported local agricultural developments. Milk, beef, hogs, poultry products, corn and small grains joined cotton as export crops in Hall County. Farming was diversifying, becoming more scientific, calling for larger investments in equipment, and requiring greater and greater management and marketing skills. Small farms seemed in jeopardy.

Library services made their way into the countryside in 1950 as the bookmobile became an important feature of Hall in February that year. The bookmobile ran from Gainesville Mill to New Holland, and on to Sardis, Candler, Belton School, Corinth, Murrayville, Brookton, Bethel, Cross Plains, Chestnut School, Blackshear, Oakwood[1], Timber Ridge, Mt. Zion, Harmony Church, Flowery Branch, Zion Hill, Clermont, Gillsville, River Bend, Whitehall, and Jefferson Academy over a two week schedule, then started over again. Adults and students alike eagerly awaited the chance for more to read.

The stability of the economics of merchants and ownership of buildings on the Square (and at least one block in all directions) was tremendously stable during the 1920s, '30s, and '40s. During those years, seldom did a merchant go out of business; when there was a vacancy, the space immediately rented and a successor owner or a new business continued occupancy. Following WWII, businesses began to replace some of the residences along South Main and South Bradford. When zoning ordinances and a Planning Commission were established in the late 1940s, all of the areas of West Washington Street, East Spring, East Washington, and most everything north of East Washington were zoned R-1 (single family residence), including North Green Street and further north. Gradual exceptions were made beginning in the downtown area where First Baptist Church at Green and Washington Streets, First Presbyterian Church at Green Street and Brenau Avenue, First Methodist Church at Green and Academy Streets had located in 1906-07. Prominent residential houses were replaced. The First National Bank moved from

The Fair Street High School Band in a parade down East Washington Street in 1954. Note the Dixie 5&10, Courtenay's Jeweler, Ruth's Beauty Shop (next to W. R. Hughes Jewelry), Ledford's Pharmacy, Bell's Cleaners, Ronald's, Cake Box, Georgia Gas Company, Western Union, and Georgia Power. Note the front of the Jackson Building and the Modern Beauty Shop sign, and the edge of the First Baptist Church on Green Street.

COURTESY OF PATRICIA HUDSON.

the west side of the Square on Main Street and replaced the Pierpoint F. Brown house at the corner of North Green and East Washington Streets with a new bank building and parking area. After the fire of 1959 at the First Baptist Church at Green Street, the First National Bank (now Regions Bank) purchased the site, including the former Southern Bell site, and the adjoining Standard Oil Service Station site at Green and Spring Streets, thus owning the entire block to Sycamore Street. It erected a larger multi-story bank building at North Green facing the Post Office and Federal Building[2].

Following World War II and the accelerated automobile age, congestion increased and limited parking spaces around and near the Square presented problems. Thus businesses sought other locations.

The rest of Hall County fared better. Postwar prosperity and an industry friendly labor situation made Hall County a promising site for industrial expansion in the 1950s and '60s. In 1954 Brunner Manufacturing opened a $400,000 plant to manufacture air conditioning and refrigeration equipment. In 1956 Warren-Featherbone located a baby-clothes manufacturing plant in Gainesville. Capital expenditures on new plants and equipment grew by 129 percent in Hall County between 1954 and 1963 and manufacturing employment rose 53 percent between 1947 and 1963 in Hall. Median income grew from $1,770 in 1950 to $4,027 in 1960 and $7,778 by 1970.

National politics occupied center stage by late 1960 in the Kennedy-Nixon contest. East Hall High School students staged a mock campaign and election which locals said would "likely be the first two-party election in Hall County since Reconstruction." On October 12, Senator Lyndon B. Johnson, JFK's running mate visited Gainesville. He was the first national executive level candidate to visit locally since Wilson was here in 1914. Johnson spoke for about four minutes off the back of a train at the depot in much the same way Wilson had.

School business was much on local minds in the 1960s[3].

Integration threatened not only racial separation, but also the public schools themselves as Georgians debated giving them up rather than giving in to government

Top: President Lyndon Johnson and Lady Bird Johnson with Mayor Henry Ward at an appearance in Gainesville, 1964. After his visit, Johnson sent Ward a letter expressing his gratitude (middle).
COURTESY OF HENRY WARD.

Bottom: The first Fair Street High School football team, the Tigers, in 1951. First row (from left to right): George Goss (8), James Westbrooks (22), Leroy Wright (7), Hayward Clyde (3), Otis Sanders (10), Paul Wilkens (24), and Raymond Hudson (4). Second row: Mascot Robert Morrow, Asberry Turner (18), Jack Pitman (9), Jimmy Thompson (5), Edward Hunter (21), Cleo Saddler (11), Stanford Summerour (23), Alvin Johnson (17), Charles Ivory (26), Tommie Holland (20), and Mascot June Johnson. Third row: Trainer Virgel Blake, Robin Hudson (25), Doyle Butts (2), Amos Goudlock (14), T. J. Hawkins (15), Lenord Cantrell (19), Scipio Jackson (1), Robert Cantrell (12), Winfred Cobb (16), Bobby Pitman (6), Maynard Brown (13), and Coach E. L. Cabbell.
COURTESY OF PATRICIA HUDSON AND ASBERRY TURNER.

Opposite, top: The Gainesville Midland remained a local institution well beyond mid-century (now SSX).
COURTESY OF WALTER BYRD.

Opposite, middle: The "roots" of NASCAR? The Hall County region has a mixed reputation for its part in the birth of auto racing. Legends of talents honed in the liquor-running business persist. Shown in this photo is an "organized racer," with the weapon of choice, a Ford of course, c. 1950.
COURTESY OF IRIS FRY.

Opposite, bottom: The Perry Business School was an important local source of post/ secondary education in the late 1940s and through the '50s. The school was located at the site of the former W. N. Downey Hospital on Sycamore Street.
COURTESY OF DIXIE RAMSEY & THE RAMSEY COLLECTION.

directives about race mixing. Sylvan Meyer, editor of *The Daily Times* was an effective writer of editorials on this and other "civil rights" issues in the period between 1948 and 1965. "We are," Meyer offered, "one of the few communities in Georgia with peaceful, working interracial communications, and no one wants this relatively placid condition disturbed. When we are deciding in our own community the fate of our own children, free us from the stampede and let us go our own way without hindrance."

In May 1964, Lyndon Johnson, now president of the U.S., returned to Gainesville to deliver a prominent national speech initiating his "War on Poverty" for the Appalachian area, to be waged concurrently with the Viet Nam War. The President's speech included his advocation of the civil rights agenda. A *Times* reporter observed "there was a noticeable lack of applause at his remarks concerning civil rights." However, the crowd on Broad Street between the Courthouse and City Hall, estimated at

THE WHITE HOUSE
WASHINGTON

May 12, 1964

Dear Mayor Ward:

Gainesville will forever remain a warm memory for me as a result of the wonderful welcome Lynda and I received there last week.

It was a pleasure to be with you, and I am deeply grateful for your providing such a richly satisfying experience.

My warmest personal regards.

Sincerely,

[signature]

The Honorable Henry Ward
Mayor of Gainesville
City Hall,
Gainesville, Georgia

thirty thousand, was enthusiastic about the visit. Johnson reminded locals of the spirit which came after the 1936 tornado and he called on Hall County folks to "rebuild and move

Above: Chattahoochee Park (Dunlap Dam-Lake Warner) as photographed in the early 1900s by W. J. Ramsey.

COURTESY OF DIXIE RAMSEY & THE RAMSEY COLLECTION.

Below: One of the many county roads lost to the flooding in the mid-fifties. As some feared, the lake was both a blessing and a curse and getting through town became more complicated.

COURTESY OF MRS. LEE GILMER.

forward." Keying on his "Great Society" theme, the President asked "for you and for your heart and your hand to guide a greater society and invite all to come in."

In 1965 the County School System announced its desegregation plan, a freedom-of-choice scheme involving grades 1, 7, 9, and 12 in the initial year and grades 2, 8, 10, and 11 in the 1967-68 year. In the summer of '65 Hall County conducted a racially integrated summer school at E. E. Butler High School. Hall County students had "their first taste of integration." The Gainesville city

desegregation plan was approved in July, a combination of geographic attendance zone and freedom-of-choice arrangement. E. E. Butler High School, built in 1961 as a black segregated school, was closed in 1967 and its closing was a loss to the core community and a difficult step in the process of school integration for those whose heritage went back to Butler and Fair Street Schools.

Race relations in Gainesville seemed always to be good, certainly far better than most communities in the South. Before the Supreme Court Decision and Civil Rights legislation of the 1960s, Gainesville had not only black policemen, but black members appointed to the City School Board.

The Gainesville School Board during the late 1950s first named as members Dr. E. E. Butler, J. Wesley Merritt, D. S. ("Doc") Lowe and John Morrow. In January 1985 John Morrow, sixty-five, whose father had swept the streets of Gainesville to help make ends meet, after several years as city commissioner and member of the City School Board, became the first black mayor of Gainesville. Morrow's legacy has been honored by dedication of a mini-park on E. E. Butler Parkway and a prominent parkway bearing his name.

In 1995, Ms. Myrtle Figueras, long time Gainesville High School teacher, succeeded John Morrow as the first black female city commissioner and, in 2001, became Gainesville's first black female mayor.

LAKE SIDNEY LANIER

Completed in January 1950, Lake Allatoona in Bartow County was designated strictly as a flood control watershed designed to protect the homeowners and businesses in the Etowah Valley. In the summer of 1950 construction of the Buford Dam was announced following several years of promotion, planning, and debate.

Lake Lanier was formed by the waters of the Chattahoochee and the Chestatee Rivers as a multi-purpose lake to provide drinking water, power generation and recreation and to aid navigation on the Chattahoochee further south.

Lake Lanier borders five counties in Georgia—Forsyth, Dawson, Lumpkin, Hall,

and Gwinnett. Before World War II, the rivers through western and northern Georgia seemed to accommodate the population's water needs. But as times changed and population increased in the Atlanta and North Georgia area, this was no longer the case. A growing population became more concerned about the effects of flooding, water supply, power production, and transportation. It seemed obvious that the Chattahoochee and Chestatee Rivers were valuable natural resources that should be more fully utilized for the necessities of the increasing population.

The prospect of flooding thirty-eight thousand acres of rolling farmland was a concern for many. There was limited local enthusiasm for the project which was expected to take five years to complete. Charles Hardy, owner and editor of the *Gainesville News*, found little to be cheerful about regarding the project. He and many others in Hall County felt that the dam and lake would benefit Atlanta and others to the south, but that in Hall County there would be problems and inconveniences. Bottom lands would be flooded, more than a dozen bridges submerged, eliminating transportation access to Gainesville and Hall County, a new water and sewage-disposal plant would be necessary. The flooding of 500 to 600 of the best farmlands would drive thousands out of the County, the covering of old roads and bridges would divert and concentrate traffic into the commercial center in Gainesville, without adequate means and resources for alternative north and south transportation routes. Surely, the dam and what would become the resort area of Lake Lanier[4] would change things, some quite adversely for Gainesville.

Others similarly questioned the lake but their concerns were not universal in the community. Many of the land owners were pleased to sell and others welcomed the prospects of change. Senator Richard Russell heard from all sides, but in a letter to one anti-dam correspondent from Hall County he replied that he found no "organized and determined opposition" to the project in Gainesville.

Wallace Hugh Warren, in his University of Georgia thesis on the socio-economic history of this area in the twentieth century, writes:

If any period marks the pinnacle of the transition in the Georgia foothills from tradition to modernity, from cotton to chickens, from subsistence farming to large-scaled agriculture, from agriculture to industry, the years of Buford Dam's construction…probably served best. Lake Lanier became trickle-down economics in actuality. It bore physical testimony to [the] dictum that a rising tide raises all boats. It may have submerged the farms of the people who lived in the river's bottoms, but it also rose the motley flotilla of sailboats, ski boats, bass boats, houseboats, pontoon boats, and paddle boats that came to cruise the lake's waters every Sunday.

Lake Lanier, truly a gem of north Georgia, is strategically located between State Road 400 and I-85 northeast of Atlanta, and is perhaps the largest economic force of the area. Since completion it has been the most visited and popular Corps of Engineers recreation lake in the United States. Yet, the water supply is under siege from the growth of the population of the several adjoining counties, and the many areas downstream to Columbus and Florida. Environmental concerns abound. Realization is upon many that water is the single most important aspect of population and commercial expansion. And it is a sobering reality that the finite source of clean water of the Chattahoochee River Valley is insufficient now and the future for the unchecked current growth of north Georgia and Atlanta.

The 1938 Hall County Courthouse courtroom, c. 2000.

COURTESY OF WILLIAM L. NORTON, JR.

*Above: The 1970 Hall County Courthouse
Annex, c. 2000.*

COURTESY OF WILLIAM L. NORTON, JR.

*Below: A 1985 illustration of several houses
from the Green Street Historic District by
artist John Kollock, including the Charters-
Smith house, Smith-Estes house, Newman-
Quinlan House, First Baptist Church, and
Pruitt-Wheeler house.*

CHANGES IN THE SQUARE

Late in 1963 it was announced that Hall County would be the site of a new University System of Georgia two-year college with an anticipated enrollment of three to four hundred students. The site selected for the Gainesville institution was pastoral acreage at Oakwood and Blackshear Place. At the same time the Lanier Technical Institute (now College) was located on adjoining acreage. By 2000, Gainesville Junior College, now Gainesville College, posted an enrollment of more than three thousand students on its campus adjacent to I-985.

Hugh Mills, Gainesville College president since its beginnings in 1965, announced his retirement in the fall of 1982. Mills, a South Georgian of impressive family leadership heritage, who came to love and be loved by the citizens of Northeast Georgia for his important leadership, left a substantial legacy of opportunity. His enlightened guidance inspired the development of new generations of leadership in the region. Without Gainesville College, many might not have a chance for a college education. Hugh Mills and the Technical College management immediately worked together to minimize duplication of curriculum by cross-acceptance of academic courses for graduation credits at both institutions. Their aggressive cooperation has been a model of mutual conservation of resources. J. Foster Watkins, the college's second president, and today, Martha Nesbitt, have expanded the goals established by Mills and the faculty and staff of Gainesville College, and have broadened the mission into what Mills frequently called "Emerging Northeast Georgia."

As the mid eighties ushered in a wave of new economic activities, some of the community's oldest and most influential entities faded. Gainesville Mill announced closing in 1985 following more than eighty years as a major economic force in the region. Its establishment in Gainesville at the turn of the century had marked the beginning of an important era of mill influence in all phases of local life when such facilities as Gainesville Mill, New Holland Mill, Chicopee, and Owen Osborne supplied much of the lifeblood in the local economy and provided a strong spirit of community among mill workers and villages. Three hundred jobs were lost in the 1985 closing of Milliken's Gainesville Mill. Similarly, Chadborn Mills, successor to the Owen Osborne and Best mills, closed in the 1960s. Much of the blame was laid to the competition of cheaper imports, a charge leveled throughout much of the textile regions.

It was in those same booming building years of the mid and late 1980s that the new at times displaced the old to the disappointment of many. There was a considerable outcry of disappointment and despair when in July 1987 the Strickland Funeral Home building on West Broad Street, identified as the "oldest structure in Gainesville," was astoundingly destroyed for a new bank site. On the positive side of the ledger the creation of the Chicopee Woods Commission signaled the magnificent gift of twenty-five hundred acres of Chicopee Wilderness watershed lands from Johnson & Johnson, Inc. The subsequent golf course, Elachee Nature Center, the Equestrian Center, and wilderness trails add much to the quality of life in Gainesville and Hall County.

FLIGHT FROM THE SQUARE

Even though growth was beginning to overtake Gainesville, by 1960 the Square was declining in activity. Stores moved out to other locations on West Broad, Atlanta Highway, Thompson Bridge Road, and the new Colonial Lakeshore Mall, developed by Pearl Nix between Dawsonville Highway and Shallowford Road, and a newer Sherwood Shopping Center, developed by H. W. "Washy" Wallis on the newly located Enota Drive just beyond the new Hall County Hospital (now

Northeast Georgia Medical Center). Gainesville's merchants on and around the Square promoted "Downtown, The Business Section of a City," in a full page advertisement in the November 24, 1963 *Gainesville Daily Times*, an obvious slap at the rising threat of shopping centers and malls to the downtown merchants of Gainesville. Thirty local establishments were listed around "downtown" and readers were urged to: "Shop at the following downtown Gainesville merchants for complete satisfaction."

Not until the late 1950s did commercialism hit the prestigious, most beautiful and significant residential neighborhood, North Green Street. First came the Gainesville Coca-Cola Bottling Plant from North Green Street at Brenau Avenue and First Federal Savings and Loan, from North Bradford Street just off the Square, to relocate on North Green Street at Academy Street across from the historic 1906 First Methodist Church. The balance of North Green Street and most of North Gainesville remained single family residential and R-1 zone until the U.S. Post Office in 1965 announced it was moving from the corner of East Washington Street and North Green Street to North Green Street, stretching to Brenau Avenue and Green Street Place, and replacing several residences. The relocation to North Green Street was opposed by Square merchants and professions, countless citizens, the Chamber of Commerce, and the Planning and Zoning Commission. The Planning Commission, chaired by Dr. W. D. (Dick) Stribling, joined by historical preservationists, opposed the destruction of the several traditional historic residences and impacting an R-1 area. The City Council offered no opposition and announced: "A city can't do anything about applying zoning restrictions on the location of federal government facilities." Despite that erroneous argument and predominant citizen opposition, the City Council immediately rezoned North Green Street to "Central Business" to Green Street Place, and relocation was effected by the Postal Service. An exodus of Square businesses replacing several residences on North Green Street promptly followed to be near the Post Office, including *The Times*, and the Gainesville National Bank.

EXPANSION OF THE CENTRAL BUSINESS DISTRICT

The flight to North Green Street and Colonial Lakeshore Mall and Sherwood Shopping Center and the like found Gainesville and Hall County, in the 1970s and '80s, taking on the look and feel that was to be the community at the end of the century. As the Post Office and other businesses relocated on historic North Green Street, a 1967 decision to rebuild a large section of the south side of the City of Gainesville resulted in the launching in 1973 of the Model Cities program, a program of the "Great Society" of President Johnson. A survey carried out by the University of Georgia enumerated the most pressing problems as housing, education, the physical environment, employment, economic development, crime, delinquency, and health and social services. The area south of Spring

Above: The East Hall High School Marching Band on the 1938 Courthouse Campus facing South Bradford Street. It was closed in the 1970s upon the enclosure of the 1938 Courthouse and City Hall by other buildings. The Gallant-Belk store and others in the block were removed for the construction of the Georgia Mountains Center, c. 1968.
COURTESY OF PAT PATTERSON.

Below: Johnson High School Pep Band in what looks like the cusp of the modish-post-hippie days of the late '60s and early '70s. Recognize any friends?
COURTESY OF THE HALL COUNTY LIBRARY.

The 1911 Gainesville U.S. Post Office until 1967 was housed in what is now the 1936 Federal Building/U.S. Courthouse at East Washington, East Spring and North Green Streets.

Street received the largest share of attention in the effort to address these problems.

By 1975 the Square was only a sad reminder of its glory days. In 1975, the City employed an independent study by Hamner-Siler Associates. The report recognized the flight of merchandising and recommended expansion of the Central Business area by construction of a major circumferential road encircling an expanded Central Business Area (i.e.: West Academy, E. E. Butler Parkway and Jesse Jewell Parkway). The study urged adoption of a City policy to encourage expansion of the critical mass of retail merchants around the Square and Central Business District, and to specify that no additional government facilities should be included within the area. Following a bond issue of $3 million for the road construction, the City (with Georgia and federal DOT assistance) constructed part of the planned circumferential thoroughfares.

But instead of attracting more retail merchant facilities as recommended by the Hamner-Siler study, it eliminated three streets and numerous business locations and substituted the Georgia Mountains Center-City/County Administration complex. Consequently, the greatest change to the historic Square area since 1821, and certainly 1872, was the reduction of retailing facilities by elimination of several city blocks of period mercantile buildings on the southside of the Square and closing of South Bradford, South

Main and East Broad Streets. The substantial urban destruction and loss of the distinguished campus of the historic 1938 "Civic Center[5]" made way for what many describe as the sprawling, Georgia Mountains Center and City/County Administration Building.

The decision of City and County governments in the 1970s to reduce numerous period retail merchants in the South Bradford-South Main-Church Streets blocks plus the Spring Street stores facing the Square produced lasting economic changes. With the loss of two to three blocks of retail merchants, and no movies or other entertainment, customers and sales decreased. By 1980 the Square was all but deserted during weekends. More new businesses located on nearby highways. Property values plummeted and with it the City's traditional tax base. Several well intended but failed efforts were conducted during the 1980s and '90s to revitalize the central business area. All seemed lost.

REACTION TO COMMERCIAL EXPANSION

The location of the Post Office and commercial moves to North Green Street in the 1960s and loss of historic, architecturally significant houses led to the formation and incorporation of the Hall County Historical

Society in 1968 "to foster historical education, conduct historical tours, to maintain historical documents and information, to produce writings on historical subjects, to preserve our historical sites and structures and to preserve our quality of life."

Historical preservation proponents avowed that Gainesville was sacrificing irreplaceable assets of its heritage and the attractiveness of the architecture and environment of the Victorian village that gave Gainesville its charm and appeal. The establishment of the Green Street Historic District (including Green Street Circle) and Brenau College Historic District by the Hall County Historical Society followed in 1975-76.

The Hall County Historical Society has long recognized that the historic status of the Green Street properties on the National Register does not protect the properties from individual alterations and additions which may change the architectural appearance of the structure and possibly erode values of neighborhood properties. Neither does the status protect the property from change in zoning from R-1. Thus, the Society began discussions with the City planning department to establish a historic-professional zone to allow zoning changes from residential to commercial but limited to occupancy by defined professions. The ordinance enacted in the late 1960s defined allowed professions and in time the properties changed from totally single family residential to predominately professional occupancy. Yet the existence of the Historic District and "Professional Zone" did not protected the neighborhood from destruction of former residences and construction of commercial buildings for general offices north of Green Street Place. In early 1980, the City disastrously allowed BellSouth to construct a large office building at the corner of Green Street and R-1 residential Ridgewood Avenue which replaced four historic residences in the historic district. In 1999 the Hall County Historical Society founded the Gainesville-Hall Trust for Historic Preservation as an adjunct to concentrate on historical preservation of heritage. Other cities have found a partial solution to continued erosion of historic and architectural significant neighborhoods by the enactment of a local Historic Preservation Ordinance. By 1999 over one hundred cities in Georgia had adopted local Historic Preservation Ordinances pursuant to the Georgia Historic Preservation Act which are designed to protect the architectural character and environment of historic and traditional neighborhoods. In a demonstration of historical preservation cooperation and leadership, the City Council of Gainesville moved in the fall of 2000 and 2001 toward enactment of such a historic ordinance.

To provide greater coordination of community arts and cultural activities, the Arts Council was

Above: Charles Smithgall, Jr., in Viet Nam. This episode in American history changed the lives of many Hall Countians and how we all looked at our foreign policy and our part in what seemed to be remote corners of the globe.
COURTESY OF LESSIE SMITHGALL.

Below: The 1938 Gainesville Federal Courtroom, c. 2000.
COURTESY OF WILLIAM L. NORTON, JR

Civic organizations like the Rotary Club swept America in the twenties. Gainesville's club was established in 1922, a sure sign that the boosterism thrust of the "roaring twenties" had come even to the hills of Northeast Georgia. Ed Dodd, creator of "Mark Trail" and a member of the local club, created the following images as part of a series of member sketches in the mid-thirties, including:

Top, left: Educator Haywood J. Pearce of Brenau College.

Top, right: Leslie F. Quinlan of hosiery manufacturer Owen Osborne.

Bottom, left: Riverside Military Academy owner Sandy Beaver.

Bottom, right: Conrad J. Romberg of City Ice Company.

HAYWOOD WAS BORN ON THE 26TH OF AUGUST IN COLUMBUS, GEORGIA. IN 1904 HE MARRIED MISS LUCILLE TOWNSEND. THERE ARE TWO SONS AND TWO DAUGHTERS.

HE IS A METHODIST AND A MASON; A CHARTER MEMBER OF GAINESVILLE ROTARY, ORGANIZED IN 1922, AND A PAST PRESIDENT OF THE LOCAL CLUB.

HAYWOOD IS A "SHO' 'NOUGH" FISHERMAN.

"HAYWOOD"

THERE IS A MAN IN OUR TOWN, AND IS HE WISE? O BROTHER! HE RUNS A COLLEGE WITH ONE HAND AND FISHES WITH THE OTHER.

HAYWOOD J. PEARCE
COLLEGE FOR WOMEN

LESLIE WAS BORN ON JULY 31ST IN PHILADELPHIA. IN 1918 HE MARRIED MISS EDITH RUTTER. THEY HAVE TWO DAUGHTERS AND ONE SON.

HE IS AN EPISCOPALIAN AND ONE OF GAINESVILLE'S LEADING GOLFERS.

LESLIE'S FAVORITE SPORT IS FOOTBALL.

"LES"

HE MAKES HOSE FOR A LIVING HE PLAYS GOLF FOR HIS HEALTH. AS LONG AS HE LIVES IN GAINESVILLE HE'LL NEVER BE PUT ON THE SHELF.

LESLIE F. QUINLAN
HOSIERY

SANDY WAS BORN IN AUGUSTA GA. ON OCT. 5. IN 1912 HE MARRIED MISS ANNICE LOWRY. THEY HAVE FOUR CHILDREN, A SON AND THREE DAUGHTERS.

HE IS A PRESBYTERIAN, A MASON AND A SHRINER.

HIS HOBBY IS WORK AND HIS GREATEST INTEREST IS RIVERSIDE MILITARY ACADEMY.

SANDY'S SCHOOL IS UNIQUE IN THAT HALF THE SCHOOL TERM IS SPENT IN FLORIDA, HALF IN GAINESVILLE.

"SANDY"

SANDY RUNS A BOY'S SCHOOL, HE CARRIES HIS LADS TO FLORIDA, HE IS A MAN OF MANY AFFAIRS, HE'S BEEN SEEN IN THE CAPITOL'S CORRIDOR.

SANDY BEAVER.
EDUCATION - BOY'S SCHOOL

CONRAD WAS BORN IN HOLLAND, TEXAS, ON THE 25TH OF SEPTEMBER. IN 1932 HE MARRIED MISS ELIZABETH ASHFORD. THEY HAVE ONE DAUGHTER AND TWO SONS.

HE IS A METHODIST AND A MASON. HE LOVES TO WATCH FOOTBALL AND TO CATCH FISH.

CONRAD'S HOBBY IS CARPENTRY AND MECHANICS.

HE BECAME A ROTARIAN IN 1930

"CONRAD"

CONRAD IS A PRETTY GOOD GUY, THOUGH RATHER LIKE HIS BROTHER. IN SUMMER HE'LL FREEZE YOU WITH ICE, IN WINTER WITH HIS HEAT YOU WILL SMOTHER.

CONRAD J. ROMBERG.
ICE. MANUFACTURING

incorporated in 1972. In 2000 the Arts Council had a full-time staff and a jewel box of a home base/cultural center located in the restored historic Gainesville Midland Railroad Depot. Exhibits, concerts on the green, and support for a wide variety of arts activities in the schools and among cultural interest groups and organizations around the County make the Arts Council one of the community's most dynamic players, made

possible by the consistent significant leadership and generosity of silent benefactors. The Council expands the cultural opportunities initiated by the Gainesville Art Association in the 1930s and the creation of the Quinlan Art Center in 1963.

Miss Bessie Bickers, a lifelong Gainesvillian, a career Candler Street School teacher, and a First Methodist Church Sunday School teacher, was a lifelong promoter of human respect and care for

RED WAS BORN
ON JANUARY 24TH
IN ATLANTA,
HE MARRIED
MISS REBIE
TANNER IN
1921. THEY
HAVE ONE SON
AND ONE
DAUGHTER.

HE IS A MEMBER
OF THE
PRESBYTERIAN
CHURCH.

RED'S FAVORITE
SPORT IS GOLF,
AND IT'S HIS
HOBBY, TOO.

HE BECAME A
ROTARIAN IN 1925.

"RED"

NO HAIR ON HIS HEAD, BIG SHOES ON HIS FEET,
RED AMBLES GENTLY ALONG THE STREET.
HE SELLS MEN'S CLOTHES AND LADIES' READY-TO-WEAR.
WHEN HE'S CALLED TO WORK, HE'S ALWAYS THERE.

CHARLES R. FRIERSON
MEN'S CLOTHING

HENRY WAS BORN
IN GAINESVILLE, GA.
ON JANUARY 28TH.

HE IS A BAPTIST
AND A MASON.
HE BECAME A
ROTARIAN IN
1923.

HENRY'S
HOBBY IS
READING. HIS
FAVORITE SPORT
IS MAKING
GAINESVILLE
THE
QUEEN CITY.

"HENRY".

I LOVE ITS GENTLE WARBLE,
I LOVE ITS RAPID FLOW,
I LOVE TO WIND MY TONGUE UP
AND I LOVE TO HEAR IT GO.

HENRY H. ESTES
.OUTDOOR ADVERTISING.

Other Rotarians who were illustrated by Ed Dodd included:

Top, left: Haberdasher Charles R. Frierson of Frierson-McEver.

Top, right: Henry H. Estes, owner of Estes Department Store.

Bottom, left: Famous athlete and local businessman Tom Paris.

Bottom, right: Albert S. Hardy, owner and editor of the Gainesville News.

ALL IMAGES COURTESY OF DAN HUGHS.

TOMMY WAS
BORN IN
GAINESVILLE,
GEORGIA ON
MARCH 2ND,
IN 1931 HE
MARRIED
MISS MARY
FOOTE SIMMONS.
THEY HAVE
ONE DAUGHTER.

HE IS A
MEMBER OF
THE METHODIST
CHURCH. HE
JOINED THE
ROTARY CLUB
IN 1936.

TOMMY'S HOBBY
IS GOLF, AND
WHAT GOLF! HIS
FAVORITE SPORT
IS FOOTBALL.

"TOMMY"

"PENALIZING PARIS" THEY CALL HIM IN FUN,
BUT WHEN YOU WANT A GAME CALLED STRAIGHT
JUST GIVE HIM A WHISTLE AND RELAX IN YOUR SEAT
FOR HE'S THE BEST REFEREE IN THE STATE.

.TOM PARIS.
.HARDWARE.

ALBERT WAS
BORN ON
MARCH 30TH
IN JASPER COUNTY
GEORGIA. HE
MARRIED
ROTARYANNE
MABEL IN
1898. THEY
HAVE THREE
SONS.

HE IS A
BAPTIST AND
A PAST PRESIDENT
OF GAINESVILLE
ROTARY.

ALBERT'S FAVORITE
SPORTS ARE
HUNTING AND
FISHING. HIS HOBBY
IS COLLECTING STORIES
OF THESE SPORTS.

HE IS A LEADING LIGHT
IN THE GEORGIA PRESS
INSTITUTE.

"ALBERT"

A WEEKLY PAPER THAT IS FULL OF NEWS
IS PUBLISHED BY ALBERT HARDY.
BUT THE THING THAT IS NEAREST HIS HEART
IS THE SUCCESS OF THE DEMOCRATIC PARTY.

.ALBERT S. HARDY.
.NEWSPAPER.

animals and pets. She originated and founded in 1913 one of the first humane societies in the United States and first non-profit organizations in North Georgia, the Hall County Humane Society. Because it was unacceptable at that time for a woman to sign a charter, her name does not appear there, although the community admirably recognizes her lifelong devotion and leadership to the Hall County Humane Society.

The Humane Society is now managed by a caring board and exceptional professional staff at modern facilities on Ridge Road substantially enlarged in 2001. Miss Bickers would be gratified with the annual Humane Society Bessie Bickers Day and pet parade at the historic Hosch House in Green Street and Brenau College Historic Districts and the annual pet acquaintance walk in historic Longstreet Hills subdivision.

Famous artist Ed Dodd celebrates Mark Trail's thirty-ninth birthday. Dodd was a conservationist when there was not a name for it. He introduced millions to the outdoors and tried to teach them some manners in the process.

COURTESY OF ED DUNLAP, JR.

One of the community's residents and adopted sons of the late 1920s, Ed Dodd, long retired from an active role in his famous "Back Home Again" and "Mark Trail" comic strip creations (the latter now carried on by artist, Jack Elrod, a Gainesville native), wrote an occasional article for *The Times* under the heading "Rambling Trails." Dodd, commenced his career in Gainesville as a Boy Scout executive and budding cartoonist in a shared office in the Jackson Building in 1928, had seen Gainesville and Hall County consistently up close for over a half century. His recollections in the eighties of earlier, simpler times were a welcomed break from the steady drum beats of progress, change and growth that seemed to be sounding throughout Hall County. Dodd's death in 1991 took him out of these streams of change, but the spirit he so well cultivated over his many years as an advocate for nature and the out-of-doors survived him in the very significant number of conservation and preservation groups that worked diligently to ensure that, even with all the change going on, the legacy would endure. The Elachee Nature Center, The Lake Watch Group, The Lake Lanier Association, Hall Clean Council, The Friends of the Park, Hall County Historical Society, Gainesville-Hall Trust for Historic Preservation, The Longstreet Society, Georgia Mountains History Museum at Brenau

(formerly the Georgia Mountains Museum), the Arts Council, Friends of Georgia State Parks and Historic Sites, individual nature conservationists, and the effective generosity of civic benefactors continue to ensure that Hall County will retain important examples of the land and heritage as it was found almost two hundred years earlier.

Dodd would have been pleased with the leadership and generosity of Charles and Lessie Smithgall in establishing in 1992 the approximately four-thousand-acre wilderness area called Smithgall Woods State Park at Duke's Creek in White County, near Richard B. Russell Highway and Helen; and in the gift in 2000 of some 160 acres at their Gainesville residence as a horticultural park to be perpetually managed by the Atlanta Botanical Gardens.

And Dodd would have been delighted with the potential for parks and greenspace expansion and preservation in Hall County and North Georgia by the acquisition of Chicopee Woods by the City of Gainesville and the Chicopee Woods Commission, and the acquisition of some one thousand acres of wilderness along the Chattahoochee River in North Hall County near I-985 and Lula by the Department of Natural Resources. Likewise, Dodd would have been supportive of the activities currently advocated by the Hall County Historical Society, the Gainesville-Hall Trust for Historic Preservation, the Friends of the Parks of Gainesville, the Friends of the Georgia State Parks and Historic Sites, and the leadership for greenspace and parks preservation currently being sponsored by Governor Roy Barnes.

Another aspect of the cultural heritage has been provided by Don Cooley who brought to Hall County in the 1980s, the cabin of his great-grandfather, Cherokee Chief White Path. Cooley had found, disassembled, moved and reassembled the cabin of Chief White Path at Skyview Place at the rear of the Bamboo Gardens restaurant of Dawsonville Highway. The Georgia Mountains Historical and Cultural Trust worked with Cooley to have the cabin moved again to some other location as a public museum of the Cherokee frontier history in northeast Georgia. Reinhart College in Waleska has a new magnificent museum on sixteen acres on the campus dedicated to Native American history.

Today White Path's cabin relocated on the campus of Brenau University is part of a growing complex of cultural landmarks which may include a promising Georgia Mountains History Museum at Brenau. Lectures and tours of the cabin and museum provide a popular activity for area schools and visitors.

Dodd would also have been thrilled with the recent encouraging leadership of the current Gainesville City Council and staff by the initiation of a study, including property owners and citizens comprising an active "advisory committee," to promulgate a Master Plan for "renaissance," revitalization and historic preservation of the designated approximately 360 acres of the so-called "Midtown" area of Gainesville south of Jesse Jewell Parkway to the Norfolk Southern Railroad tracks and west of Queen City Parkway and east of E. E. Butler Parkway.

ETHNIC & CULTURAL ADDITIONS

It was toward the close of the eighties that perhaps the most significant cultural change in the local community's twentieth century history began to be noticed. In the October 21, 1988 issue of the *Atlanta Journal* an article explained that "Jobs lure Hispanics to Gainesville." It noted that from only "a few hundred" the ranks of Hispanics in Hall had

swelled in five years from an estimated 3,000 to 3,500 and that local "poultry plant managers welcome the newcomers."

Hall County and Gainesville public schools felt the wave of increasing Hispanic immigration to the community. In 1994 Hall County school figures showed a rise from 243 Hispanic students in 1989 to 790 in 1993, a 225 percent increase in four short years.

"Hall Faces Diverse Future," said the headlines of January 1, 1999. From 1990 to 1997 the local Hispanic population had grown by 103% and was still on the rise. Advanced estimates of the national census of 2000 advise that those newcomers exceed 4,000. Everywhere poultry, construction, and services work were being done, they were more frequently being done by newcomers from south of the border, dark-haired and eyed, hard workers who brought legendary dependability to whatever job they secured. By century's end they seemed here to stay and some wonder how anyone ever got any jobs done before their arrival. And with the addition of the Hispanic, Asian, and other cultures has evolved the need to foster mutual understanding of traditional historical local heritage with new imported customs and the challenge to solve the language barriers, produce bilingual jobs, and establish dual-language skills among the "new" and "native, i.e. old-line citizens." As with the farmers, gold miners, railroads, textile mill workers, manufacturing, poultry industry, resort tourists, lake residents and commuters, this new influx of ethnic and cultural diversity is being welcomed by these natives to the larger community.

More recent signs of an ever evolving local culture.

Top, left: The Smithgall Arts Center, formerly and the Arts Council Depot and the Gainesville Midland Railroad Depot, has become a downtown focal point for cultural events like this outdoor concert.
COURTESY OF THE GAINESVILLE ARTS COUNCIL.

Top, right: Ruth Waters, history teacher, lived, breathed, and passed along history— Georgia history, local history and family history. She was always active in the Hall County Historical Society. In the 1980s Waters was designated as "Hall County historian" by the Hall County Historical Society. Every community, every generation needs a Ruth Waters.
COURTESY OF THE HALL COUNTY LIBRARY.

REVITALIZATION RENAISSANCE

Gainesville's Green Street Historic District, a treasured beauty under pressures of traffic and commercialism, long has been a focal point of historic preservation concerns for local citizens and the Hall County Historical Society. All North Georgians express pride in this "most distinguished North Georgia area." Other traditional and historic residential neighborhoods adjoining are likewise in jeopardy of erosion and destruction of character and environment. America is undergoing a revival of admiration and love for community heritage and historical preservation. The movement in Gainesville for broad historic preservation throughout the City and County has been growing in citizen support for several years. In 1998 the Hall County Historical Society organized the Gainesville-Hall Trust for Historic Preservation to focus on promoting and helping fund and manage several anticipated local restoration projects. Restoration of General Longstreet's Piedmont Hotel became the Trust's first project of a series of preservation and restoration efforts which include the 1906 First Methodist Church, New Holland United Methodist Church, Healan Mill, the Southern Railroad Depot, Gainesville Mill Village, New Holland Village, Chicopee Village, New Town, and the homes of Ivy Terrace. It is hoped that this history book will help stimulate interest and support in these on-going policies and objectives for protection of

the heritage and quality of life traditions in Hall County. Fortunately the Main Street Program, a national effort of the National Trust for Historic Preservation and the Georgia Trust for Historic Preservation to restore downtowns to original architectural and environmental character and revive economic viability, was brought to Gainesville in 1995, endorsed and supported by an awakened, enlightened City government.

More and new boutique merchants are sought to locate on the Square to replace non-merchant occupants and restore the necessary critical mass of retail services. The Square is again becoming a vital and attractive place to visit and shop. Historical restoration and preservation has become acceptable and desirable to many property owners. In 2000 the Square was designated as a historic district on the National Register of Historic Places. Some structures are being restored to the original architectural style. Perhaps other owners will follow and a Master Plan of historical preservation can be effected, as some have proposed consistently since World War II, to make the downtown Square area an unique and appealing shopping and historical visitation destination.

Owners of properties and merchants on the Square are expressing intention to work together with the City to maintain Gainesville

essentially as the Victorian Village which has been its traditional heritage and charm. Similar, but less organized, preservation efforts are moving in Flowery Branch, Clermont, Lula, Gillsville, Oakwood, Murrayville, Chicopee Village, Gainesville Mill Village, and New Holland Village.

Citizen interest and spirit in the Square and other traditional commercial and residential downtown areas is strong. People are beginning to come back to the Square. Much is left for the future. The County, the City, Main Street Gainesville, and other parties are cooperating to

agree on a Master Plan to improve the Square center and Roosevelt Square, which are seldom the visiting, strolling or lounging places of citizens or visitors. Perhaps the current Main Street, Gainesville (1998-2001) revitalization plan will make the Square center again a significant plaza. The current design suggests a "Veterans Wall of Honor" or "Pantheon of Heroes" featuring the names of all the Hall County Veterans of all the wars: Spanish-American, World War I, World War II, Korean, Viet Nam, and Desert Storm, and a small monument to each war, to join the historic, beloved Civil War Veterans Memorial. The design proposals for the "Veterans Wall of Honor" and small war monuments have been endorsed by Post 7 and Post 308 and the Oakwood Post of the American Legion and the

Top, left: The next addition to Hall County's governmental complex is underway in this spring 2000 view toward the new Courthouse additions.
COURTESY OF RICHARD STONE.

Top, right: Rabbit Town's "Rabbit."
COURTESY OF RICHARD STONE.

Bottom, left: Murrayville sustains its traditions with annual gatherings. Shown here are Ronnie and Judy Green at a Murrayville Gathering in the late 1990s.
COURTESY OF ROBERT SPRIGGS.

Bottom, right: The east side of the Square, c. 2000.
COURTESY OF WILLIAM L. NORTON, JR.

Veterans of Foreign Wars Post, Beulah Rucker Museum, and other organizations. The expressed desire is to enhance City and County pride in the cherished historic "Ole Joe" memorial to Civil War veterans and also to honor veterans of other wars. They aspire that the Square, the center of Hall County, will become an attraction as a historical educational outdoor classroom for students, citizens and visitors to come to rest, make and hear speeches, celebrate, or just have fun and enjoy the gathering place and distinctive boutique shopping center.

In conclusion, about the only thing that has not changed since the founding of Gainesville-Hall County is the sky above. Visitor John Muir observed the place in 1867 when little had changed; he found a river with trees right to the bank and a small town pleasantly shaded with an abundance of trees and farms.

But after the Gold rush, railroads and electricity, the maturity of the textile and poultry industries and the development of Lake Lanier, change has come. The present population arrived long after Eden, and they did not come to farm. Population growth, expansion of neighborhoods and change seems inevitable, and the fact is that most Hall Countians would not be here if not for change. The challenge for the new millennium is to accommodate inevitable change and diversity of cultures within a policy of education and continued preservation of present historical heritage and cherished traditional quality of life to the benefit and satisfaction of all citizens.

Doug Ivester, former president of Coca-Cola and native of New Holland and Gainesville, carries the torch for the 1996 Olympics, in the Gainesville leg of the torch run which was widely witnessed by locals, even those who didn't see the rowing events on Lanier.
COURTESY OF HALL COUNTY PUBLIC INFORMATION.

THE 1996 ATLANTA OLYMPICS

Excitement of the first order hit the community in late December of 1993 when it was announced that Lake Lanier had been selected as the venue for rowing, canoeing and kayaking for the July 1996 Olympics.

The Lanier bid for a role in the games was the result of tremendous leadership efforts on the part of dozens of organizations and legions of local volunteers. Activities surrounding the lake events brought thousands into direct contact with the spectacle. On July 15 the passage of the Olympic flame through the community had an estimated 18,000 gathered about Gainesville along the route of the flame bearers. Spectators who never saw the later lake rowing events or any of the other later events of the Games, even on TV, swelled with pride as the colorful parade passed in and out of light showers. Local papers carried special Olympic editions before and during the events. The official parking facilities at Gainesville College made Oakwood "ground zero" for the initial impact of thousands of visitors who parked there and were shuttled by buses to the Lake for the rowing events off Clark's Bridge Road.

Suddenly it was over, the crowds were gone, the banners hauled down, but the Olympic spirit has lingered in the history of Hall, and the Olympic venue area at Clark's Bridge has continued as the world's premier boating training and competition facility.

CHAPTER IV ENDNOTES

[1] First called "O'Dells Crossing."

[2] In the 1960s the Gainesville National Bank (now Wachovia) moved from the corner of South Bradford and East Spring Streets to the three-story building that formerly was the Estes Department Store at the corner of North Main and West Washington Streets, and then to North Green Street in 1968. In the1970s Citizens Bank (now Bank of America) moved from the Square to East Washington Street.

[3] Others presidents to visit were General Andrew Jackson, who camped with his troops near Young's Cemetery at Hog Mountain Road and U.S. Highway 23; Franklin D. Roosevelt who visited Gainesville twice, on April 9, 1936, and March 23, 1938; and Jimmy Carter, who visited Gainesville prior to the election of 1976.

[4] In a 1954 *Gainesville News* column written by Hardy, came the suggestion to name the water formed behind the Buford Dam "Lake Sidney Lanier" after nineteenth century poet Sidney Clopton Lanier. A Georgia native, Lanier wrote the poem *Song of the Chattahoochee.*

[5] Subsequently, in 1996-2000, the location of the needed addition to the Hall County Courthouse caused quite a stir. The 1996 plans were to adjoin the 1980s Annex to, and further desecrate, the historic 1938 Courthouse and straddle and close off part of Green Street. Some local critics of that approach bemoaned closing South Green Street and adding another wall to "fortress Gainesville." Already by the 1990s fewer and fewer residents and visitors knew that the parking decks and Georgia Mountains Center-Administrative Complex surrounded a beautiful little greenspace park containing a view of the historic 1938 marble City Hall and 1938 marble Courthouse and memorials to a number of events important to local history. So few people ever entered that hidden space that a dry fountain and a sometimes extinguished "eternal flame" and the historic Roosevelt Park area had little notice or attention. The public storm of late 1996 persuaded the County Commission to cancel the plan to connect the new courthouse structure with the Courthouse Annex and close Green Street. Subsequently (2000), the County Commission determined to locate the new Courthouse of questioned adequate capacity across Green Street adjoining the parking deck amid highly criticized continued plans to close South Green Street.

Clermont Hotel, Clermont, Georgia.

Charters-Smith House. *The house is*
located at 625 Green Street in the Historic
District, Gainesville, Georgia.
COURTESY OF GEORGE EVANS. WATERCOLOR, 2000.
PRINT SIZE 15 X 20 INCHES.

SHARING THE HERITAGE

historic profiles of businesses and

organizations that have contributed to

the development and economic base of

Gainesville and Hall County

SPECIAL
THANKS TO

City Plumbing and Electric
Supply Company

Hall County
Board of Commissioners

ZF INDUSTRIES, INC.

Above: ZF Industries, Inc. of Gainesville, GA, in 1999.

Below: The Industrial Park South in May 6, 1988. ZF Industries is in the foreground on the right.

When ZF Group began its operations in North America, ZF Industries, Inc. of Gainesville was the second facility the company opened, in 1987. Today, Gainesville is one of twelve United States production facilities of ZF Group North American Organization (ZF NAO), the North American subsidiary of ZF Group, one of the world's largest independent industrial suppliers and a world leader in drivetrain technology.

At 300 workers and growing, ZFI Gainesville is one of Hall County's largest employers. In the tradition of ZF Group, the facility has been an active member of Hall County civic and corporate communities since beginning operations.

The 162,000-square-foot facility produces more than 80,000 five- and six-speed manual transmissions per year for light trucks such as the Ford F-250 and F-350 and the GIVIC Sierra. Beginning in August 2000, the facility will also produce transmissions for the Chevrolet Silverado.

The facility also produces 11,000 transmissions yearly for off-road vehicles such as John Deer front-end loaders and Omniquip backhoe loaders. The Gainesville plant also manufactures parking brakes for Ford pick up trucks and a number of recreational vehicles.

ZFI Gainesville celebrated its millionth transmission in 1997, but the second million is expected to come much faster. That same year, the company added a new high-volume line for its advanced transmissions, and fifty percent growth in production expected by 2002.

But productivity is just one part of the equation that has made ZF Group a world leader in the design and production of gearing products. Another cornerstone of the ZF philosophy is quality. That commitment begins with a level of employee involvement and attention to detail that has earned high recognition.

ZFI Gainesville has ninety-eight percent employee involvement in education and development courses, ranging from specialized in-house training to MBA programs. A record of quality and productivity that is second to none rewards such commitment to its employees. By May of 2000, ZFI Gainesville had achieved a remarkable PPM record with Ford of zero defective parts in twenty-nine months and still counting. "That's pretty much unprecedented in the industry," said plant manager Elizabeth Umberson. ZFI Gainesville has also earned the John Deere Key Supplier and numerous other awards from its customers.

Rolf Lutz, vice president of Commercial Transmissions, attributes the plant's outstanding record to a number of factors, beginning with ZF's program of "very intensive" worker training. ZF uses no temporary workers, and strives to promote quality in all phases of its operations. "We try to design mistake proofing into our assembly line and involve our employees early in the process," Lutz said.

The company's comprehensive quality assurance system means more than defect-free parts. Recognizing that quality is the most important factor in stacking up against competitors and is the foundation of a good reputation. ZF also is committed to meeting the requirements of its customers and of national and international authorities such as the American Bureau of Shipping, European Environment Protection

Systems Audit, the International ISO 9000 Standard and the QS 9000 U.S. requirements.

As ZF Gainesville looks to its own future, it has also become strongly involved in community life of the Hall County area and in preparing workers to take their place in the twenty-first century workforce.

ZF participation includes involvement in the United Way, the Industry Round Table and many other programs of the Greater Hall County Chamber of Commerce. The plant is a Partner in Education, supporting activities at the C. W. Davis Middle School in Flowery Branch, and is also involved in educational programs at Lanier Technical Institute.

The company has also been a partner in the Chamber's QUEST (Quality Education Strategy Team) since its 1994 inception. QUEST promotes a highly qualified workforce by linking students and teachers with industry and business.

Since 1995, twenty-one area students have gone on to full-time employment after participating in the QUEST youth apprenticeship program at ZF Gainesville, completing a 2,000-hour apprenticeship beginning in the junior year of high school. Twelve to fourteen students are enrolled in the youth apprenticeship program at all times, and many of them also begin studies in college or technical school after completing the program.

The company's commitment to its host community is not only to the people, but also to the environment. ZF Gainesville is one of just a handful of Georgia plants to earn ISO 140001 certification. The certificate, awarded only after a thorough audit, is recognition of engineering and manufacturing processes that minimize waste generation. ZF Gainesville is classified as the lowest class of waste generator.

The Gainesville plant, founded in 1987, is relatively young. But it is heir to a long tradition of excellence that began in the second decade of the twentieth century.

The company's history is linked to the legendary name of Ferdinand Graf von Zeppelin, who began manufacturing his famous Zeppelin airships in the early part of this century. In 1915, he founded another company called Zahnradfabrik Friedrichshafen to manufacturing transmissions for his gearing for the airships.

After reconstruction of destroyed plants following World War II, ZF in 1959 set off on the path that has now established the company as a leading global manufacturer of drivetrain technology. In that year, ZF do Brasil S.A. was founded in Sao Paulo, Brazil.

Today the global ZF Group employs more than 35,000 people worldwide, with facilities that span the globe. Headquartered in Friedrichshafen, Germany, ZF operates more than fifty production facilities in seventeen countries, among them Germany, Belgium, the United States, Spain, France, China, Japan, South Africa, Argentina, and Mexico. The company marked nearly $6 billion in 1998 sales.

ZF produces transmissions, steering gears, axles, chassis components and complete systems for installation in passenger cars,

Above: A Zeppelin launch at Lake Constance in Friedrichshafen, Germany in the early twentieth century. Ferdinand Graf von Zeppelin, father of the Zeppelin aircraft, founded Zahnradfabrik Friedrichshafen, which later became the ZF Group, parent company of ZF Industries, Inc. of Gainesville.

Below: Five Speed transmission.

Top, left: Off Highway Line—backhoe or tractor transmissions.

Top, right: On Highway Line—five-speeds for pick up trucks.

commercial vehicles and off-road equipment. ZF also produces drive technology for boats, railways and helicopters.

One company unit, ZF Marine Group, is also the world's largest producer of marine gearing systems. The new high-speed ferry "Corsaire 13000," for example, relies on a ZF gearbox. Built by the French shipyard Alstom Leroux Naval, the 134-meter vessel has a capacity of 1,100 passengers and 250 vehicles.

Established as an entity in 1997, ZF NAO, including the Gainesville facility, is together one of the fastest growing units of ZF Group. Headquartered in Florence, Kentucky, just south of Cincinnati, ZF NAO operates twelve production facilities in seven states, a technical center in the Detroit area and three sales and service centers.

A key site is ZF Batavia, located in Ohio. The new company is a joint venture with Ford Motor Company, and combines ZF's transmission technology with Ford's know-how of high-volume manufacturing. The company's main product is the CVT (continuously variable transmission), which will begin production in late 2001.

With strong roots in the past, ZF Group looks ever to the future, knowing that only through innovation can it stay ahead of the competition. ZF Group's corporate research and development center in Germany is the base for more than 500 of the company's 2,400 development engineers. In Plymouth/Detroit Michigan, fifty highly trained engineers attend to customer needs at the company's technical center.

That commitment to technological leadership is the key to ZF's strong market position, and pays constant dividends. Today, a third of ZF Group sales come from products brought to the marketplace within the past five years. Last year, ZF unveiled the world's first six-speed automatic transmission.

As ZF Gainesville enters the twenty-first century, the company will continue to operate with the objective of winning new customers and programs on the foundation of manufacturing excellence. Being a good corporate partner in Hall County means that ZF will continue to play an active role in the community, particularly in the area of education. ZF has actively supported the advancement of manufacturing education and technology in local colleges and universities, and is the area's largest employer of youth apprentices. ZF's commitment to its employees centers around the belief that our people are the most valuable asset, and the single biggest reason for the plant's successful growth.

Established by an act Congress in 1916 as a federally-charter agricultural lending institution, North Georgia Farm Credit was in the forefront of Northeast Georgia's growth and economic success for nearly a century.

With the merger of North Georgia Farm Credit and South Central Farm Credit in July 1999, the newly-incorporated AgGeorgia Farm Credit boasts a diversified agricultural portfolio and capital in excess of $125 million to serve the state's number one industry.

The credit institution, with more than 5,000 stockholders, promotes the success of cooperative members by providing superior financial services and products in a safe, sound and reliable manner. In 1999, AgGeorgia Farm Credit had dedicated loans of approximately $600 million statewide, with over 900 loans totaling $71 million in Hall County alone.

In the early days of Farm Credit, the North Georgia office provided lending services for row crop and corn growers. As growth of the poultry industry accelerated throughout the region, the company dedicated its resources to serve an area that has become the world's largest broiler producer.

In Hall County, AgGeorgia Farm Credit provides everything from short-term operating money to long-term mortgages, facility and home construction loans. The company also offers life insurance, appraisal services, crop insurance, and equipment leasing services. Member-borrowers who purchase stock/participation certificates in the cooperative own farm credit. AgGeorgia Farm Credit has distributed patronages of more than $157 million, including $80 million in cash, to its members since 1988. These patronages have worked to reduce the effective cost of borrowing for farmers.

In Gainesville, the Northern Division office of AgGeorgia serves 38 counties, with eight administrative employees in the central office and nine employees serving Hall County. The Hall County branch primarily works with poultry farmers in the construction of poultry houses, equipment, and purchase of land. The significance of the area's poultry industry can't be overstated. With more than 31 million birds, the economic impact of agriculture in Hall County is estimated at $583 million annually.

The local office also promotes the endeavors of the part-time grower.

As committed partners in each community it serves, AgGeorgia Farm Credit sponsors and promotes the activities of Future Farmers of America and 4-H and is actively involved in fundraising for the Children's Miracle Network and the March of Dimes. The company sponsors annual Agricultural Expos and Cattle Shows as part of its continued community involvement.

The dedicated staff of professionals at AgGeorgia Farm Credit has built lasting relationships with generations of farmers in Northeast Georgia with an acute understanding of their needs. As it continually adapts to those needs in the future, AgGeorgia is positioned as a stable and reliable source for agricultural lending.

AgGeorgia Farm Credit

Below: The Gainesville North Division office of AgGeorgia Farm Credit serves 38 counties.

Bottom: AgGeorgia Farm Credit provides a full range of financial services for the farming community.

MILTON MARTIN TOYOTA

Thirty years hasn't changed Milton Martin's own style of success and consistency in being Georgia's oldest Toyota dealer.

Whoever claimed "nothing stays the same" obviously never visited one of Hall County's mainstays—Milton Martin Toyota.

On an early Monday morning, another bustling business week begins there-a week not so different from the first one thirty years before. A small boy sits curled up on a sofa before a television set in Milton Martin Toyota's customer waiting area. Occasionally, he lets out a burst of laughter while he watches Mr. Rogers. Behind him, just on the other side of the glass and paneled walls, one of the ladies in the office proudly unveils the chocolate-pecan fudge she made the night before

for co-workers to share. A few steps away in the service area, customers shake off the cold with coffee and warm conversation.

Milton Martin may have become one of Georgia's largest Toyota dealers in the automotive sales industry, but a personal hometown atmosphere still lingers here. It's an atmosphere reminiscent of the days of old general stores and such. Yes, it may be 2000. But after three decades in business some things at Milton Martin Toyota just haven't changed. Things like a friendly handshake and a pat on the back. Things like loyalty and trust and satisfaction guaranteed.

Maybe that's why Milton Martin Toyota has something to celebrate. If you thought it was because of thirty years in the automobile

business, you stand slightly corrected. Milton Martin, the industrious man behind the success of this story, will tell it's the people business he's in. Sure, he sells automobiles. But he prefers to think of it as meeting one of people's basic human needs—that of providing quality transportation they can depend on. In his words, the goal is "to meet a human need and not for a motive of greed."

He's never failed to do that, he says. And he has the letters from satisfied customers to prove it. It's the reason his business has prospered over the years, growing from three employees in 1961 when Martin began selling used cars in Gainesville to more than eighty-five employees today.

Enterprising and enthusiastic, dynamic and driven, Martin is a man whom ideas continually bubble from what seems like some eternal, underlying spring. Whether it's from an ambitious desire to succeed or just a zest for life, the effect of his contagious enthusiasm is the same. It motivates all who are around him. "Never a dull moment," his employees exclaim. And that's the way they like it.

Martin brought his own style of success to Gainesville in January 1950. A graduate of Sardis High School, he had attended Young Harris College, and later, Southern Business University in Atlanta. He served in the Navy as a dispersing clerk from 1948 to 1950, and upon arriving in Gainesville, took a job as a bookkeeper for C. V. Nalley, Sr., a local automobile dealer who would pass along to Martin a passion for the business. For ten years, the young Martin worked for what later became Nalley Chevrolet and for Nalley Discount Company, a business that financed automobiles.

In 1961 the time had arrived for Martin to make a name for himself in the business. In January that year, a new sign, "Milton Martin Autos," went up where today the Gainesville parking deck stands. The modest used-car operation had two employees: Milton and his brother Merritt. From the time they were boys, the brothers had followed a "work together" philosophy. The basic founding philosophy "satisfaction guaranteed" is "what's built this business," Martin says today.

Throughout the years, he's practiced what he's preached. And so has everyone who has ever worked for him and stayed on the payroll.

Another building block for Martin was added in 1969 when new 1970 model Toyota cars and trucks arrived on the lot. The dealership moved to Browns Bridge Road where it had room to grow and, for the first time, many North Georgians saw the first of what became an influx of Japanese automobiles into the area and the country.

"I felt like if I had a franchise, I'd have a source of used cars," Martin explains of his reason for adding the new car line. "Since all of the domestic franchises were represented in Gainesville, I couldn't get a known name. I saw these Toyotas and I thought, "Well, that's a doggone good-looking car." After I got all of my input, I found out it was a successful-selling automobile over in Japan." News came from the West Coast that people were buying the car there as well.

Above: Milton Martin Toyota is Georgia's oldest Toyota dealer.

Below: The Parts & Service Department.

Because of Martin's reputation for selling quality used cars, the Toyotas began to sell instantly. Martin remembers the first Toyota he sold was a 1970 four-door Corona. "Nobody knew what a Toyota was, so I told the first customer who bought one that if he would keep it serviced, I would guarantee it for life. That's how good a car I thought it was. And that's how good a car it turned out to be."

In November 1973, Martin said a fuel crisis fed the demand for gasoline-efficient automobiles. People became more concerned about driving gas-guzzlers and began to look to cars that go a long way on a little fuel. Martin's new Toyotas could get thirty to thirty-five miles per gallon easily. "The fuel-efficiency (of the Toyota) was what got the job done," he said. "It gave the American consumer an option. We were at the right place at the right time.... Preparation always meets opportunity...that's what I always say."

Martin also says he believes the durability, and fuel efficiency of the early imports has made domestic cars, which he also continues to sell, a much better product.

"The consumer has always been the benefactor of worldwide competition," Martin said.

On the subject of worldwide competition, in 1987, Milton Martin received the Presidential Award for "Achievement of the Toyota Touch Goal of Unmatched Excellence in Customer Satisfaction Through Superior Dealership Performance." For Martin it symbolized the loyalty and trust he has worked so diligently to achieve from the thousands of customers he serves.

There are now seven freestanding buildings on the Milton Martin Toyota property, including the parts and service departments, the business office and the new car showroom. Sitting directly behind that building is the reconditioning shop for new and used cars. The building just to the right of the used car pavilion is leased to Enterprise Rent-A-Car. Just up the hill is Milton Martin Tours and Rentals. The Milton Martin Collision Center sits between Milton Martin Tour and the reconditioning shop.

Milton Martin's belief in carrying on a tradition of excellence through his family is an ongoing factor in the company's long-term success. Martin's five sons and one daughter have all worked at the dealership at one time or another. Mike Martin, following in his father's footsteps, is the current company president and general manager. Ricky Martin is vice president and sales manager. A third generation has now joined the ranks, with Milton's grandson Tommy Martin as the company's assistant sales manager and Brandon Martin as sales consultant.

Ask him if it's true that nothing's stayed the same over the past thirty years at Milton Martin Toyota and he'll tell you that hasn't been his experience. It's true there have been a lot of changes and growth, but "Everyone is still basically trusting the seller to offer a good product, good service, and to be treated fairly."

Top: The largest American flag in Hall County.

Below: The Milton Martin Toyota Collision Center.

The Norton Institutes on Bankruptcy Law, founded in Gainesville in 1986 by retired United States Bankruptcy Judge William L. Norton, Jr., conducts national seminar events that foster and promote legal education on bankruptcy law and practice. The Institutes are an expansion of the educational presence of *Norton Bankruptcy Law and Practice* (thirteen volumes) and other Norton law publications.

Engaged by Callaghan & Co., Chicago, in 1978, Judge Norton, a tax planning and litigation attorney in Gainesville and Atlanta (1950-71), completed in 1982 the first six volumes of the *Norton Bankruptcy Law and Practice*, an encyclopedic treatise on the new Bankruptcy Reform Act. Previously U.S. Bankruptcy Judge Norton (Northern District of Georgia, 1971-1986) authored *Norton Real Property Arrangements on Chapter XII, Federal Bankruptcy Act* (1977) and *Norton Evidence in Trials under the Bankruptcy Act* (1978) for The Harrison Company in Atlanta.

Also in 1982, with a small bankruptcy law publisher in Washington, D.C., the non-profit Institutes on Bankruptcy Law, Inc. was organized to sponsor seminars on bankruptcy law, primarily at resort venues. The faculty of each seminar is drawn exclusively from the several highly respected contributing editors of the Norton Publications recruited by Judge Norton and Bill Norton III. The Institutes allow the Nortons and contributing editors to meet together more than once per year to plan, expand, and improve the Treatise and other publications.

Since 1982 Norton Institutes has managed the planning and conducting of seminar responsibilities regularly in San Francisco, Jackson Hole, Wyoming; Quebec City, Quebec; Palm Beach, Florida; Washington, D.C.; New York City; Park City, Utah; Phoenix; Boston; San Diego; and Las Vegas. Registrants at the seminars typically number 150 to 200 from over thirty states. Each advanced level, intense Institute is four hours, mornings only, for four days, thereby allowing registrants and families to enjoy the facilities of each distinguished popular resort site.

In 1983 the Nortons began publication of a monthly newsletter, *Norton Bankruptcy Law Advisor*, which contains articles solicited from several hundred "correspondents" widely enlisted from registrants at the seminars, judges, law clerks, professors, and other attorneys and judges around the world.

In 1991-1994, after several mergers of publishers, the Nortons revised *Norton Bankruptcy Law and Practice* (nine volumes) into a second edition of thirteen volumes, *Norton Bankruptcy Law and Practice, Second Edition* (West Group). The thirteen-volume hard copy, CD-ROM, and online editions of *Norton Bankruptcy Law and Practice, Second Edition*, constitute the widest distributed and used bankruptcy publications.

Other Norton-West Group publications include *Norton Bankruptcy Law Adviser, Norton Annual Survey of Bankruptcy Law, Norton Bankruptcy Code, Pamphlet Edition, Norton Bankruptcy Rules, Pamphlet Edition, Norton Quick Reference Code and Rules, Norton on Creditors' Rights,* and *Norton Handbook for Bankruptcy Trustees, Debtor in Possession and Committees.*

For more information about Norton Institutes on Bankruptcy Law and its publications, please call (770)-535-7722 or fax (770) 536-7072. The Norton Institutes can also be reached through e-mail at nortoninst@aol.com and its website, www.nortoninstitutes.org.

Above: William L. Norton III and Sallie Norton.

Top, left: The Honorable William L. Norton, Jr.

Left: The office staff of the Norton Institutes on Bankruptcy Law. Front row (from left to right): Martha Norton Hodge and Adelaide Norton. Back row (from left to right): Joyce Frankum Seabolt, Susan M. Corby, and Lee F. Wood.

HALL COUNTY HISTORICAL SOCIETY & GAINESVILLE-HALL TRUST FOR HISTORIC PRESERVATION

Above: The Society is encouraging the formation of chapters, such as the Flowery Branch Chapter of the Hall County Historical Society. Potential chapters include Candler, Chestnut Mountain, Chicopee Mill Village, Clermont, Gainesville Mill Village, Gillsville, Lula, Murrayville, New Holland Mill Village, and Oakwood.

Below: The destruction of several distinguished residences on North Green Street beginning in early 1960s with the location of First Federal Savings Bank, the Post Office, Gainesville National Bank and others, precipitated the organization of the Society with one of its objectives to preserve the beauty and heritage of the neighborhood. Commercialization attracted more traffic to the residential environment of North Green Street and the adjoining neighborhoods.

Since 1968, the Hall County Historical Society has been actively involved in promoting and preserving historical interests. Its purposes and objectives are: to foster historical education of our heritage; to conduct historical tours; to attract and maintain historical documents and information; to produce writings on historical subjects; to preserve historical sites and structures; and to preserve traditional environmental character and quality of life.

Former presidents and officers have included Ted Oglesby, William L. Norton, Jr., Marie Carter, Sybil McRay, Dr. Rafe Banks, Andrew Fuller, Lydia Banks McCrary Henley, Marsha Hopkins, William M. House, Eula Mae Grigg Pearce, L. W. Richardson, Mrs. Danny Scroggs, Henry O. Ward, Ruth Waters, and June Smith Woodruff. Former directors include Roger Brown, Dallas Chrisner, Marian Ledford Chrisner, Mary Cleveland, Rosemary Johnson Dodd, Charles Edmondson, Charles Frierson, Jr., Heyward Hosch, Jr., Lester Hosch, Mrs. A. R. Kenyon, Happy Garner Kilpatrick, Annadell Moore, Dr. Martin Smith, Loyd Strickland, Joe K. Telford, Lura Whitehead, and Claude Williams, Sr.

In 1975 the Society established the Green Street Historic District and Brenau College Historic District on the National Register of

Historic Places and supported a zoning change from residential to "Professional Offices." The original "Historic and Professional Office Zone" of 1977 defined some professions and government to exclude retail business and professions which were considered traffic magnets in order to minimize traffic and commercialization along Green Street.

The Society has opposed attempts to widen North Green Street, which would destroy Gainesville's most beautiful and historical environment. To protect this area, since 1975 the Society has opposed further "sprawl" and supported the national concept of "new urbanism" and efforts to improve traffic conditions on Green Street and adjoining residential neighborhoods which are all receiving excess traffic.

Recognizing that opponents to widening Green Street should support viable alternatives, the Society has:

- Endorsed the completion of the long planned (since 1957) inner city northern loop project from "the rock" at Pearl Nix Parkway across Dixon Drive to Enota Drive and thence to Downey Boulevard and Myrtle Street (M.L. King Boulevard);
- Endorsed the completion of the long-planned (since 1945) inner city southern loop from Queen City Parkway to Limestone Parkway; or the improvement of Industrial Boulevard from the Atlanta Highway to E.E. Butler Parkway and Limestone Parkway;
- Consistently recommended the City and County to jointly initiate a bypass thoroughfare north of Lake Lanier from Dawsonville Highway at Sardis to

Thompson Bridge Road south of Murrayville, to Clarks Bridge Road and I-985 near Lula.

The Society supports the enactment and enforcement of the Gainesville Historic Preservation Ordinance in compliance with the Georgia Historic Preservation Act.

Please join the Hall County Historical Society and the Gainesville-Hall Trust for Historical Preservation by becoming an active participant in your community to aid in preserving and creating a better quality of life for yourself, family and posterity. Committees include the Task Force for Transportation, the Beautification and Trees Committee, the Task Force for Removal of the Gainesville Downtown Post Office from Green Street and the Green Street Christmas Lighting Festival. Its offices are at 380 Green Street Historic District Gainesville, Georgia 30503. Visit us on the Web at www.hallcountyhistoricalsociety.org or call 770-503-1319 or fax 770-536-7072.

Top: In 1999 the Society organized the Gainesville-Hall Trust for Historic Preservation, Inc. as an IRS-approved charitable corporation to concentrate on funding preservation and restoration projects. The first project is the historic Longstreet Piedmont Hotel, which was operated by General James Longstreet from 1874-1903. Other fostered projects include the 1906 First Methodist Church, North Green Street Historic District; United Methodist Church, New Holland; Brenau-Hall County Museum; the Beulah Rucker Museum; Healan Mill; Chicopee Village; New Holland Village; and Gainesville Mill Village.

Below: The Healan Mill near Lula is being converted into a greenspace and recreation park with walking trails.

LANIER PARK HOSPITAL

Lanier Park Hospital was born out of the vision of long-time Gainesville physician P. K. Dixon, who saw a need for additional quality services in the growing region.

Building the hospital "seemed necessary to improve the quality of healthcare for the Gainesville community." Dixon said in an interview twenty years after Lanier Park's 1977 opening.

Ground was broken in 1976 for the $7 million, sixteen-acre Lanier Park Hospital, which opened in 1977 as an acute care facility offering general medical and surgical services including nuclear medicine, intensive care, respiratory therapy, physical therapy and a wide array of imaging services.

Then as now, the hospital was committed to the care and improvement of human life, striving to deliver high-quality, cost effective healthcare. Recognizing the unique value of each individual, the mission of Lanier Park employees is to treat all they serve with compassion and kindness, as they work to restore and improve the health of the community.

Lanier Park admitted its first patient, for gall bladder surgery, June 12, 1977. Dixon completed the case, and then presided over a steak dinner to celebrate the milestone.

Over a quarter of a century later, the 113-bed hospital is one of the state's most comprehensive healthcare facilities. Fully accredited

by the Joint Commission on the Accreditation of Healthcare Organizations, the hospital has more than 200 high trained physicians, a medical support staff of more than 400 employees, and goodwill developed through twenty-three years of service to the people of northeast Georgia. The hospital offers a wide variety of inpatient and outpatient services, community wellness programs, and free monthly screenings.

Annual reinvestment exceeds $1.5 million per year in technology, equipment, and furnishings to meet the hospital's commitment to state-of-the-art facilities and services.

Lanier Park's facilities and services have grown over the past twenty-three years to meet community needs. In 1985 a $2.6 million addition/renovation project added 12,000 square feet of hospital space and renovated 5,000 square feet of existing space. In 1992 a $4.6 million, 48,000-square-foot medical office building was completed. The two-story Atrium also serves as the hospital's main entrance. In 1997 the Women's Health Center opened, offering diagnostic procedures and treatment specifically for women.

In 2000, the MRI department was upgraded with a $1.8 million construction and services renovation and a new OB unit was added.

In addition, Lanier Park offers:

- A fully staffed emergency department, open twenty-four hours a day, seven days a week
- Outpatient surgery services that give the comfort of same day recovery at home, and include minimally invasive and laparoscopic surgery techniques. They include specialties in gynecology, urology, orthopedics, thoracic, maxillofacial, and vascular and laser surgery
- Women's Health Center offering such services as mammograms, stereotactic breast biopsy, ultrasound, bone density scans, and stat lab. Monthly seminars, pre- and post-surgery education, a lending library, and support groups give both the knowledge and emotional support that patients need
- Cardiac rehabilitation services offering a full array of services for cardiac patients. Targeting patients who have had a heart attack, heart surgery, or who have been diagnosed with stable angina, the service brings specialists together with the patient's personal physician for precise diagnosis and a rehabilitation program tailored to the individual
- The Transitional Care Unit, offering comprehensive rehabilitation services to residents, seven days a week, includes physical therapy, occupational therapy and speech therapy. The unit also offers twenty-four-hour skilled nursing coverage by experienced RNs and LPNs
- Corporate health programs in partnership with area businesses, including drug screening, medical care for work-related injuries and other occupational medical needs

- An active schedule of community education and wellness programs conducted on-site and in schools, businesses and other locations throughout northeast Georgia. Programs such as nutritional counseling offer community-wide help to control and sometimes even prevent nutritionally related diseases such as strokes, some cancers, diabetes, osteoporosis, and coronary heart disease
- A state-of-the-art obstetrics unit that opened on July 24, 2000
- Lanier Park's reach is extended by a series of primary care centers that offer non-emergency treatment and diagnosis by a physician. Locations include Flowery Branch, Browns Bridge, and Thompson Bridge

Gerald N. "Jerry" Fulks, Lanier Park's CEO since 1992, was named chairman of the Board of Trustees for the Georgia Hospital Association in 2000. He is active in the United Way and other civic activities.

Under Fulks' leadership Lanier Park has received Certificate of Need approval to expand the facility. Construction is expected to being in late 2001 and will add approximately 30,000 square feet to the outpatient services area. An expanded Emergency Department, a new outpatient entrance, and a dedicated cardiovascular center are the key components of the plan.

Says Fulks, "The community support of Lanier Park Hospital has allowed us to grow to meet the ever increasing needs of our citizens. As we move forward we will continue to focus on providing care in state-of-the-art facilities, while treating each patient with warmth and compassion."

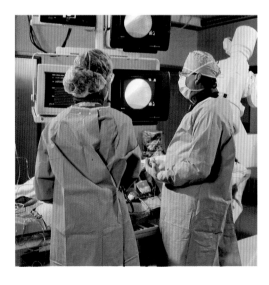

RIVERSIDE MILITARY ACADEMY

Through nearly a century, Riverside Military Academy has pursued one goal: to educate, train and inspire young men for success in college and in life.

Haywood J. Pearce and A. W. Van Hoose founded the academy in 1907. Pearce was president of nearby Brenau College. The founders chose a site in the rolling Blue Ridge Mountain foothills for their 252-acre campus. Situated near Gainesville, Georgia, beside Lake Lanier, the school is an hour from Atlanta and Hartsfield International Airport.

As president for half a century, from 1913 to 1969, longtime board of regents member Sandy Beaver saw Riverside grow from a small school to one of the nation's largest and most respected military academies.

Today, Riverside's enrollment includes more than 450 young men grades eighth through twelfth from 31 states and 13 foreign countries. The academy's faculty consists of 47 full-time teachers, most of them with advanced degrees.

Under the leadership of Superintendent Colonel Michael Hughes, a career military officer and a nationally respected educator, Riverside Military Academy has embarked on a course aimed at a future that already includes some of the best teaching facilities anywhere.

With small class sizes, one-on-one attention and weekly grade reports, Riverside offers a strong advantage over the typical school.

Riverside's educators seek young men of high moral character and the willingness to set and achieve worthy goals. At Riverside, they are provided a challenging but supportive learning environment designed to develop both mind and body. In the words of the Riverside's mission statement, the school strives "to provide a supportive and challenging educational environment that fosters scholarly competence and intellectual curiosity, enhances spiritual and physical fitness, develops leadership skill and the strength of character necessary for success in college and life."

While maintaining a ninety-four-year heritage, Riverside is devoted to helping boys build successful futures in a rapidly changing world. The school's Student Success program helps young men develop skills to achieve long-term goals throughout their lives.

Top priority is given to college preparation, the next big step for cadets. Experienced college counselors work with each young man to choose appropriate school and career directions, and guide them to successful completion of Riverside's thorough college-prep curriculum.

New instructional facilities include four up-to-date computer science laboratories equipped with Pentium computers and a wide array of software and Internet access. The language lab includes twenty individual sound-protected cubicles for one-on-one communication with an instructor.

Riverside's comprehensive interscholastic and intramural programs include football, soccer, baseball, basketball, wrestling, swimming, diving, water polo, track, golf, cross country, tennis, riflery, and crew.

However, some of the school's most enriching activities occur outside classroom walls. A visitor is likely to see cadets learning life-saving techniques or conducting biology experiments on the lake, attending Chapel or serving guard duty, practicing their music or marching before a meal on the quadrangle.

Cadets adhere to a disciplined schedule, with two hours of supervised study time each Sunday through Thursday evening, but are allowed time for relaxation, independent study, letter-writing and socializing.

Special events are a constant feature of the Riverside cadet's calendar, and include activities such as lectures, drama, entertainment programs, and dances, among many others. The frequent off-campus activities include ski trips, white-water rafting, amusement parks and many other activities aimed at both learning and enjoyment. Longstanding annual events include Parents' Weekend, the formal Military Ball, and Holiday Banquet.

For the past five years, Riverside has achieved one hundred percent college acceptance to top schools across America. Riverside graduates currently attend Vanderbilt University, Georgia Tech, the University of Georgia, The Citadel, Tulane, The University of North Carolina, and the United States Military Academy, among others.

Riverside's growing facilities include full science laboratories, computer and language labs, a twenty-unit computerized algebra lab and a forty-thousand-volume library.

Cadets are housed two to a room in a newly finished quadrangle complex wired and built to fit the needs of the twenty-first century. Each room is equipped with a computer and software that includes cadet e-mail. The building also includes faculty apartments, a modern, fully equipped thirty-bed infirmary, nurse's station and quarters, and a dining hall with three fireplaces, built to accommodate the entire cadet corps and faculty.

The 250,000-square-foot building was the first phase of an ambitious, multi-year, multi-million dollar expansion project designed to enhance Riverside Military Academy's national reputation. The second phase, now complete, was the renovation of Lanier Hall to house all student services, including The Grill, a longtime favorite of RMA cadets.

A third project, completed in 2000, is the complete reconstruction of Elkin Hall, the school's primary academic building, which contains most of Riverside's classrooms and specialized learning environments.

"We want to give cadets the learning environment of the new millennium," explained Frank Wiegand, chairman of the Riverside Military Academy Board of Trustees. "The architects and engineers have designed buildings with technology options for today and tomorrow. By accommodating the dreams and predictions of future classrooms, the new academic hall will ensure Riverside is at the forefront of the twenty-first century."

Upcoming projects include a fine arts building with auditorium and practice rooms for band and chorus, a new gymnasium and a new library.

db TELECOM TECHNOLOGIES, INC.
DBA TELETECH

Dr. Sam F. Dayton in front of TeleTech Center in Gainesville, Georgia.

If you use a mobile telephone or beeper, communicate over a wireless radio, or use a wireless device to access Internet service, the odds are good in the Southeastern United States that you are communicating, in part, over a telecommunications system built by Hall County-based db Telecom Technologies.

Registered under the Georgia trade name of "TeleTech," the company was founded in 1994 by Gainesville native and CEO Sam F. Dayton and his business partner, James L. Bruce, Jr., of Cornelia. The two had seen the growing business opportunities in wireless communications and wanted to be a part of what they saw as "the wave of the future in electronic communications." They were also provided with an incentive to form their own business when AT&T and other major telephone companies began outsourcing the building, testing, maintaining, and providing technology upgrades for telecommunication systems.

As has been the case with many native Hall Countians who have returned to the county, Dayton, a graduate of Gainesville High School, spent considerable time away from

Georgia in his early professional years. In addition to university degrees through the doctorate, he obtained valuable experience in electronic communications intelligence with the U.S. Army Security Agency in Southeast Asia, and in working with other telecommunications companies. His other relevant experience included time as a research geophysicist, as a public agency head where he put together one of the first multi-jurisdictional computer service bureaus for governments in our nation, and as a college department head.

David L. Nix of Gainesville was the first employee to join Dayton as a full-time employee of the company. At the end of the first year, senior staff had been added which had an aggregate of over fifty years experience in the electronic communications industry. The customer base had also been broadened and then included BellSouth, AT&T, Sprint, and GTE. In the following years, additional customers including Alltel, Nextel, Powertel, Southern Linc, Triton, and Knology would be added.

Having established its corporate headquarters in Gainesville in 1994, the company opened a second regional office in Durham, North Carolina in 1995. Building on the early success of TeleTech, Dayton and Bruce, along with David Rush Mauney, Dayton's brother-in-law, founded GlobalTech Industries, Inc. in late 1995. The new company had its corporate headquarters in Gainesville and its first manufacturing plant in Cornelia. Dayton, Bruce, and Mauney had found that there was an opportunity to apply modern manufacturing technology to produce upscale decorator candles. Five years later, their candles can be found in better gift shops in malls across the United States.

In March 1996 Dayton incorporated an Internet service provider company in Atlanta. His partners in this venture were Bruce, and two of the original employees of MindSpring, Cary Howell and Ed Landa. This company provides high-speed connectivity, managed server services, and collocation of computer and communications equipment. Its customers include mid-size companies, institutions, and the military.

TeleTech had grown from nine employees in 1995 to over fifty by 1999; the Atlanta Internet company had grown to over sixty employees and was destined to be bought by a larger NASDAQ-listed company in the year 2000. GlobalTech Industries had grown to over three hundred employees.

During the period 1995-2000 TeleTech had broadened its communications services by adding the assessment and studies of existing systems; development of system plans; implementation of satellite services; antenna installations of all types; development of facility housing and shelters; wiring of all types including fiber optics, coaxial cable, and copper; grounding of any type of communications system; civil construction and construction management related to communications systems; antenna sweeping and testing; coordination with local zoning and code officials; and assistance in financial planning for communications systems. The company served the role of general contractor in the development of both analog and digital personal communications services systems.

In the year 1999 the company formed a sales and services division, which concentrated on miniaturized wireless devices for homes, schools, and businesses and wireless access to the Internet. Future plans call for a serious look at Linux operating systems and their relationships to wireless communications. In addition, the company is currently considering two major foreign projects which will blend wired and wireless systems with links to the Internet that will be designed to serve businesses at the local and national levels in two countries.

In commenting on the companies which he has created or caused to be created, Dayton commented, "I am pleased that my business partners and I could play a small role in the creation of jobs for our country which are based on the New Economy, technology jobs which offer more current income and long-range growth potential for so many Americans. Also of great importance to me is the fact that we did this without any assistance from any level of government and with no tax breaks of any nature. That is the way it was when capitalism started in our country and now is a worthy goal for modern capitalists as well."

Sam F. Dayton was born in Hall County, Georgia and is married to the former Beth Mauney of Cleveland, Georgia. Dayton has four children, Mike, a graduate of Johns Hopkins University, who is a vice president of a Georgia-based technology company; Leslie, a graduate of the Medical College of Georgia who is a senior employee of a technology company in central North Carolina; and Mary and Katherine, who are students at Lakeview Academy in Gainesville, Georgia.

The Dayton Family. Front row (from left to right): Katherine Dayton and Matt Olsen. Middle row: Mary Frances Dayton, Beth Dayton, Angie Dayton, and Clara Olsen. Back row: Sam Dayton, Leslie Dayton, and Mike Dayton.

NINTH DISTRICT OPPORTUNITY, INC.

Ninth District Opportunity's first central office at 123 Main Street. This office was occupied from 1967-1983.

Through the decades of change since its founding in 1967, the Ninth District Opportunity Community Action Agency has held steadfast to its purpose: serving the poor and underprivileged in Northeast Georgia.

From weatherproofing initiatives for substandard housing to Head Start programs for early childhood education, the private, non-profit entity has consistently demonstrated its dedication to helping low-income people help themselves.

The beginnings of Ninth District are rooted in our country's war against poverty. Prompted by then President Lyndon Johnson, the U.S. Congress adopted the Economic Opportunity Act in 1964. Congressman Phil Landrum of Jasper, Georgia played an instrumental role in seeing the bill's passage through the House of Representatives. The act established ten regions throughout the U.S. including the Region IV Office of Economic Opportunity in Atlanta. The State of Georgia in turn, delegated the responsibility for carrying out the mandates of the act to Area Planning and Development Commissions. Frank Moore, who later served in the Carter administration, served as the OEO administrator for the area's first Community Action Programs.

In 1967 the initial Ninth District Opportunity offices, so named after the Congressional District that Landrum served and in which Gainesville is located, were established to address the needs of the economically disadvantaged. The office was led by second OEO Administrator James (Jim) Redmond. Initially serving sixteen Northeast Georgia counties, the NDO CAA headquarters on Main Street consisted of fifteen staff members, which were directed by a volunteer board of directors.

The Community Action Agency has grown to include 600 employees and 300 delegate agency staff members in a 20-county service area, including 38 in the Gainesville central administrative offices. Through thirteen community service offices and 35 childcare centers, the Agency provides a myriad of services for the economically disadvantaged including, among others, emergency food and shelter, employment counseling, energy assistance, weatherization-housing rehabilitation, Head Start/Pre-Kindergarten, food distribution, transportation, youth services, and parenting skills training.

Ninth District Opportunity uses federal income guidelines as a primary criterion for serving individuals. In Hall County, the agency serves about 1,000 clients each year.

The multi-county agency had an annual budget in 1999 of $26 million including more than $1.5 million in expenditures for programs administered in Hall County. While much of its funding comes from federal block grants distributed through various state agencies, Ninth District Opportunity also relies heavily upon advocacy and volunteerism in the communities it serves. One of the major factors of Ninth District Opportunity's success is volunteer participation in its community-based programs. The CAA works hand in hand with elected officials, business and industry, and local and state agencies such as the Department of Human Resources, Department of Community Affairs and the Georgia Environmental Facilities Authority in partnerships that benefit those most in need.

In 1989 the Agency established Housing Opportunity, Inc. to address the area's housing needs. This affiliate non-profit provides affordable housing to Hall County citizens

through two multi-family complexes located in Gainesville and Flowery Branch.

Housing Opportunity, Inc. plans to continue acquiring housing properties across the North Georgia region for resale or rental. Though NDO coordinators throughout North Georgia may aid clients in obtaining available local housing, future plans also include developing a comprehensive counseling program in order to prepare families to become homeowners.

Ninth District Opportunity's Head Start/Pre-Kindergarten and early Head Start programs, which serve 380 children in Hall County and nearly 4,000 within the district, offer comprehensive child development for three and four year-olds. Children in the programs, which are recognized as among the top childcare initiatives in the state, participate in planned activities that contribute to their intellectual and social growth. The programs are unique in their ability to blend both federal and state resources to provide the quality of child development services the families need. Their success is attributed to skilled and caring staff members, cooperation from local school systems and county governments and the many residents who serve as volunteers. With the movement in Georgia and the nation toward renewed emphasis on childcare, Ninth District's programs will continue to play a relevant and crucial role in the communities it serves.

Ninth District Opportunity has weathered its share of change over the years as federal legislation has evolved to redefine the Community Action Agency's roles in the community. Its central offices moved from Main Street to Pine Street to its present location on Spring Street. But leadership has stayed relatively stable, with only two executive directors in the past three decades. Janice Riley, who initially became involved with the Agency through the Cherokee County Head Start Program, succeeded Redmond, in 1981. That same year Ninth District Opportunity assumed service duties in Hall County which were previously provided by Allied Community Services.

As one of twenty community action agencies in Georgia and more than 1,000 nationwide, Ninth District Opportunity reaches into the communities it serves to make a difference in the lives of the poor.

Above: The second NDO central office at 810 Pine Street in Gainesville. This office served the community from 1983-1997.

Below: The current NDO offices at 308 Spring Street in Gainesville.

THE HOME PLACE

At The Home Place, a professional building consultant assists customers in choosing what home plan is best for them and guides them through many options.

Since 1972, The Home Place has been building homes to help Hall County residents build families.

Its number one concern is making the home-building experience a good one for its customers. The Home Place builds for families who have their own land, with home plans ranging from the $50,000's to $150,000+. To serve its customers more effectively, The Home Place has developed a network of sales offices in Georgia, South Carolina, North Carolina, Tennessee, Alabama, Kentucky, Florida, and Mississippi, consisting of production crews and corporate teams. Currently, it has over 375 full-time

staff members and some 4,000 construction workers. In fact, it is one of the nation's largest "on your lot" homebuilders.

At each of the sales offices, customers will see over 60 custom home plans and designs for all types of housing needs. A professional building consultant assists customers in choosing what home plan is best for them and guides them through the many options.

Building consultants are experienced professionals who are able to discuss the different sources of financing and advise each customer on the best source for them. Once an application is made, customers may begin decorating their home.

Each showroom features a color selection area with a variety of selections including roof, bath fixture colors, siding and shutter colors, cabinet and countertop colors and many more. This enables customers to completely decorate their new home at one location and eliminate the burden of going to several different places to make choices.

The Home Place is proud of the caliber of its building superintendents and construction workers. Through its 27 years of experience, The Home Place has developed a system of site meetings and pre-construction meetings prior to beginning construction to assure that customers are confident in what they can expect and what they are getting in their new home. Customers work directly with their building superintendent. Every stage of construction is checked by a building superintendent to assure that quality standards are being met. Approximately two weeks prior to occupancy, a thorough inspection is made to identify all items of minor nature which should be corrected. Service crews will then complete these items so that the customer's new home will be completed when they move in.

All homes incorporate cost-effective, energy-saving features. Thus, customers have the assurance that their home will have a high resale value, year after year.

After the customers occupy their home, one of The Home Place's most important jobs begins—standing behind its warranty on the customer's new home. The Home Place has a reputation for honoring their warranty and feels that this reputation is its greatest asset.

Brick by brick, Simpson Brick has helped build the future in Northeast Georgia for more than twenty years.

The beginnings of Gainesville's first local brick distributor are rooted in one man's devotion to family and a desire to stay in the community. It was 1977, and Charley D. Simpson Sr., of Fitzgerald had spent ten years as a Hall County area representative for Macon-based Cherokee Brick and Tile. Settled in Gainesville and faced with a job transfer to Tampa, Simpson chose instead to branch out on his own, and found quick support from the local building industry. For the first year, Simpson ran the business out of his home with his wife, Dixie keeping the books. He sold around half a million bricks that year.

Today, Simpson Brick employs forty-five people, a fleet of nineteen trucks, and has three locations, providing more than forty million bricks annually for the building industry. That's 80,000 tons of masonry products the company moves each year.

Charley's son Jake, who took over from his brother Dave in 1998, now heads Simpson Brick. Brothers Jake, Dave, and the late Tony Simpson worked to maintain the business standards of hard work, honesty

and respect for the customer that their father instilled in them.

When Charley Simpson retired in 1995, Simpson Brick was an established distributor that had carved out a respectable market share in the region. Since then, the growth has continued. The economic prosperity of the state and the ensuing building boom of the late 1990s has led to an enormous expansion of the company in the latter part of the decade.

Simpson Brick has grown by an average of thirty percent annually over the past nine years, opening a showroom in Athens and a central distribution facility in Commerce. Positioned to compete with metro Atlanta distributors, Simpson Brick serves a fourteen-county area of Northeast Georgia along the Interstate 85 corridor.

Over the years Simpson Brick has shipped the bricks that built Hall County's Johnson High School, Spout Springs Elementary and nearly every other public school building erected in Hall County over the past two decades. More recent projects include the expansion of Gainesville's Riverside Military Academy, SunTrust Bank, the Ace Hardware Distribution Center at Hall County's Airport Industrial Park, and the Gilbert Health Center at the University of Georgia in Athens. The company also supplies bricks for a large portion of the area's residential developments.

A commitment to the community, faith in a quality product and a trusting relationship with its customers—those are the cornerstones of Simpson Brick's success.

SIMPSON BRICK

Above: Simpson Brick founder Charley Simpson and wife, Dixie.

Below: Simpson Brick's Gainesville office serves a fourteen-county area in Northeast Georgia providing more than forty million bricks annually for the building industry.

HALL COUNTY LIBRARY SYSTEM

The Hall County Library offers over 190,000 books, videos, cassettes, magazines, and newspapers in its collection. A full complement of computer resources is available in all five-branch facilities. Access to electronic information includes Internet links to magazine databases, business resources, and genealogy materials. The library has one of the largest local history collections in North Georgia with visitors coming from across the United States to conduct research into their family histories. The library system is developing a Spanish language collection to serve the needs of its rapidly growing Hispanic population. Those with Internet access can visit the library at www.hall.public.lib.ga.us.

Attempts to establish a public library in the county date back to the late 1890s. These attempts were generally unsuccessful until sometime before 1933 when a group of women from the Grace Episcopal Church started a small community library in the church basement. This library remained in use until the devastating tornado of 1936 destroyed the library and church.

Following the tornado, interested citizens declared May 21, 1937 as Library Day. Gifts of money and books were accepted for a new facility. In March 1938, Ethel Roark of Clermont became the first librarian of the new

Hall County Library. Located in the basement of the Hall County Courthouse, its opening day collection consisted of many of the books that had been salvaged from the destroyed church library.

The 1940s were a period of growth for the library. Branch libraries were established in Clermont and Lula. The Lula Branch was located in the town hall. Depository libraries were placed in a beauty shop in the city of Flowery Branch and in a combination grocery store/post office in the community of Murrayville. Another branch was established in the late 1940s in a classroom in the Northwestern School, a private school in Gainesville for black students.

In the 1950s the library added a bookmobile that was stocked with more then 1,000 books. Library circulation for the system increased to over 20,000 items checked out in the first year the bookmobile operated, 14,505 of which were borrowed from the bookmobile.

Hall voters approved the construction of the existing main library located in downtown Gainesville in 1967. It was dedicated in 1970 as the Chestatee Regional Library from which library service was provided to Hall, Dawson and Lumpkin Counties.

Hall County left the Chestatee Regional Library System in 1997 and established the Hall County Library System as a single county Georgia library system.

Top: Mrs. Almera Austin is shown on the Hall County Library's new bookmobile with a group of children, 1950.

Below: Hall County Library headquarters in Gainesville today.

Brenau University's roots of tradition run deep as Gainesville's preeminent institution of higher learning.

Founded in 1878 as Georgia Baptist Female Seminary, the institution became Brenau College in 1900 when Dr. H.J. Pearce purchased the campus. "Brenau" derived from German and Latin means "refined gold," a fitting moniker for this campus established in a region once rich in gold.

Brenau was privately owned until 1911, when a board of trustees assumed stewardship of the college, as is the case today. In 1928, Brenau created a female, residential, college preparatory school, grades nine through twelve. And, in the early 1970s, Brenau began offering evening and weekend classes to both men and women. In March, 1992, the board of trustees voted unanimously to convert the college to a university. Dr. John S. Burd, its eighth president, who has held the position since 1985, leads the institution.

Brenau University is a comprehensive university that includes the Women's College, the Evening and Weekend College and the Academy. These three divisions, distinct yet complimentary, offer diverse educational opportunities founded in the liberal arts which lead to intellectual and professional development, foster personal growth, encourage community responsibility and global understanding.

By the end of the twentieth century, Brenau's total enrollment reached 2,472 students, including 664 in the Women's College, eighty in the Academy, and 1,728 in the Evening and Weekend College.

Brenau offers more than thirty majors for students in the Women's College, from performing arts to applied sciences, from broadcasting to education, and from healthcare to marketing. Graduate and undergraduate degrees are offered through the EWC at six locations in Georgia.

In more than a century of existence, Brenau has forged a sterling reputation for its devotion to the fine arts in the Northeast Georgia community. The university presents music recitals, dramas, dance performances, and art exhibitions by campus, local, regional, national, and international artists. Brenau is home to art organizations such as the Gainesville Ballet Company, Gainesville Pro Musica, and Wonderquest, the local children's theatre.

At the dawn of a new century, Brenau has renewed its promise to meet the cultural needs of its students and the region. Brenau is building a new Performing Arts Center on Academy Street, to include a 400-seat auditorium and 100-seat recital hall along with music faculty studios, classrooms and practice rooms. The new $13 million facility will bring much-needed relief to venerable Pearce Auditorium, in use since its opening in 1897.

Like gold, a Brenau education is an investment of lasting value. Tomorrow's doctors, lawyers, business and community leaders, researchers, scientists and performers are the students at Brenau today.

BRENAU UNIVERSITY

Top: Today's Brenau students benefit from modern facilities and resources.

Below: Brenau University has a rich legacy dating back more than a century.

LUNSFORD GRADING AND HAULING

Above: Glenn Lunsford, grandfather of Lunsford Grading and Hauling founder Gregg Lunsford, worked extensively in Hall County's agricultural industry in the 1950s and 1960s.

Below: Lunsford Grading and Hauling working on a local project.

Lunsford Grading and Hauling, a Hall County contractor that performs clearing, grading, pipe work, demolition, and hauling, is a company rooted in family history.

Glenn Lunsford life's work was in the grading and hauling profession, clearing fields and moving land for the hundreds of chicken houses that sprouted up in Hall County as a result of the burgeoning poultry industry in the 1950s and 1960s. Lunsford, who worked mainly in agricultural grading, passed his knowledge of the profession on to his grandson Gregg.

"As a kid growing up and hearing all of his stories, that's all I ever wanted to do," said Lunsford Grading and Hauling founder Gregg Lunsford. Gregg was twenty-one when he started the business out of his South Hall County home in 1987. Back then he had only one loader and a dump truck, performing mostly residential work by himself. Lunsford saw some lean years in the beginning, especially in the slower winter months. "It took two or three years to get my foot in the door," Gregg said.

Slowly but surely business began to pick up and, by 1994, the workload became more than one person could keep up with, and Gregg hired his first employee. Today, Lunsford Grading and Hauling employs five people, operating two loaders, a dozer, backhoe, scraper, and two tandem dump trucks. Gregg stores the equipment at the same shop that his grandfather used more than thirty years earlier.

With the building boom of the 1990s in full swing, Lunsford Grading and Hauling has worked on numerous residential and commercial projects, from Hall and Gwinnett County subdivisions to small industrial sites.

As one of the few medium-sized grading and hauling operations in the area Lunsford Grading and Hauling maintains close relations with the builders and contractors it serves.

Lunsford looks for a modest rate of growth in the company while maintaining the quality and dependability of its work.

Since 1987 Lunsford Grading and Hauling has held true to the principals of good business: "We try to do a good job at a fair price and treat people the way we would want to be treated."

Regions Bank of Gainesville, the oldest and largest bank in northeast Georgia, has been a key* mover in Gainesville's history since the bank was founded as the First National Bank of Gainesville in 1889. In that year Gainesville business partners Samuel C. Dunlap, J. W. Smith, Ratliff Palmour and Z. T. Castleberry put together thirty-five stockholders and raised the $50,000 they needed to qualify for a federal charter.

More than a century later, Gainesville is the Regions Bank headquarters for the Eastern Region that includes South Carolina, Georgia, and Florida. The bank's Hall County assets are $700 million. Hall County brings a full forty percent of its banking business to Regions Bank—far more than any other bank. It is considered one of the top performing banks within the Regions Financial Corporation, which has total combined assets of $43 billion dollars. Regions Bank has shown an increase in net income every year since it was founded in 1971.

The bank provides work for over 340 people in Hall County, and also returns to the community over $250,000 in charitable contributions annually through the bank and the Roy C. Moore Foundation.

It was good timing for the stockholders when the bank opened its doors 111 years ago. Hall County was about to undergo an era of rapid growth. The nearby cotton fields, improving roads and a ready supply of labor

REGIONS BANK OF GAINESVILLE

First National Bank of Gainesville, the city's oldest bank, founded in 1889, was the predecessor to today's Regions Bank of Hall County.

were bringing textile mills to the area, which grew by fifty percent between 1900 and 1930, when the census counted more than 30,000 people in Hall County.

In the 1930s First National Bank became a leader in financing local entrepreneurs, and became a leader in finding ways to finance the growth of the poultry processing business. That partnership brought Gainesville a global role as a world center of poultry agriculture.

As Gainesville and the Hall County economy grew, so did First National, but even so the bank did not leave the downtown square for sixty-two years. In 1951, however, First National Bank outgrew its longtime home and moved to Green Street, where customers had more parking and could use Gainesville's very first drive-in window.

"That kind of innovation and community involvement will continue to be a hallmark of the bank," said Regions Bank of Gainesville President Rich White. White was named president of First National Bank in 1990 and has continued in the position after 1996, when Regions Financial Corp. of Birmingham, Alabama purchased the bank.

"Our goal is continued growth in Hall County, and a major goal is to differentiate ourselves from other banks by providing superior products and the highest level of community service," White said.

RWH TRUCKING, INC.
SOUTHEASTERN SERVICES

Above: Southeastern Services has gained a number of accounts with some of the country's largest food companies through its high standards of service, which include a ninety-seven percent on-time delivery record.

Below: Robert Howard, founder of Southeastern Services.

Southeastern Services, Inc., founded in 1989, has grown from modest beginnings into one of the largest trucking and freight brokerage firms in Northeast Georgia, with state-of-the-art equipment and dedicated, long-term employees ensuring its success.

Robert Howard, a veteran of the trucking business since 1980, founded Southeastern Services as a one-man freight brokerage operation out of a small leased office on Mundy Mill Road in April 1989, following in the footsteps of his father Grady, who trucked poultry products for the Hall County agricultural industry in the 1950s and 1960s.

Today, with approximately 175 employees, Southeastern Services has grown out of an initial $10,000 small business loan and into a $23 million company, with sixty percent of its business in dedicated trucking and forty percent in freight brokerage, or logistics. Southeastern Services covers the lower forty-eight states, transporting dry goods, perishables, produce, paper products, and marble more than fourteen million miles annually.

Southeastern Services relies on the latest in computer tracking software and satellite navigation systems to ensure that its clients receive freight on schedule. Over the years Southeastern Services has gained a number of accounts with some of the country's largest food companies through its high standards of

service, which include a ninety-seven percent on-time delivery record.

Southeastern Services, the largest locally-owned refrigerated trucking company in Northeast Georgia, has enjoyed a long-standing business relationship with Hall County's poultry industry, as well as Wrigley Gum, Nestle Ice Cream, Mrs. Smith's Pies, Hershey's Candies, International Paper, Conagra, Mohawk Carpets, and Georgia Marble. The company, with about eighty percent of its trucking operations dedicated to refrigerated products, hauls produce for Wal-Mart and cold storage pro-ducts for Sysco Foods.

With 110 tractor rigs and 155 trailers, the company employs 140 drivers who move products across the country in a safe, dependable and timely manner. By providing top notch equipment and competitive pay rates and benefits, Southeastern Services enjoys a low driver turnover rate, with many of the drivers employed by the company since dedicated trucking operations began in earnest in 1994, when gross annual revenues reached $6 million.

By 2000 gross annual revenues had expanded to $23 million, and plans at the South Hall facility called for fifteen percent growth per year over the next five years or more.

While Southeastern Services relies on high-tech computer technology and the latest in trucking equipment to meet customer demand, it's the people that have made the difference. "The success of this company has been related to the dedicated, quality employees that have really made it happen," Howard said.

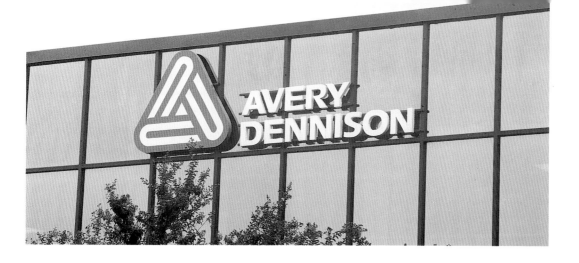

Established in 1975, Avery Dennison's manufacturing facility in Flowery Branch has grown along with Hall County. One of 200 Avery Dennison manufacturing facilities worldwide, Avery Dennison's Hall County operation has more than doubled in size in that time, to more than 300 employees today.

As a global leader in pressure-sensitive technology and innovative self-adhesive solutions for consumer products and label materials, the company's 1999 sales increased 8.9 percent to a record $3.8 billion worldwide. Pasadena-based Avery Dennison ranked number 429 on the 1999 Fortune 500 list of the largest U.S. companies.

Employing more than 17,000 people worldwide, Avery Dennison develops, manufactures and markets consumer and industrial products at 200 manufacturing facilities and sales offices in 39 countries. With active product sales in eighty-nine countries, Avery products are used in virtually every industry.

The company is best known for its Avery-brand office automation and consumer products, Fasson-brand self-adhesive materials, peel-and-stick postage stamps, battery labels, reflective highway safety products, automated retail tag and labeling systems, and specialty tapes and chemicals. Avery Dennison products such as the Avery Marks-A-Lot and Hi-Liter brands are recognized worldwide.

The Avery Dennison facility in Hall County is part of the company's largest division, the Office Products Group. Receiving shipments of components from suppliers worldwide, the facility ships a wide range of products throughout the United States.

That long product list includes file folders, pressure-sensitive labels, and color-coding dots. Greeting cards, brochures, gift cards, and labels are among a growing list of products for

personal computer printers produced in the Hall County facility—examples of ongoing product development, an Avery Dennison hallmark, and a reflection of the company's strategic focus on high-technology solutions for consumers. Innovative product brands produced in Hall County include Avery ink jet labels, laser labels, and specialty items.

Avery Dennison and its employees also participate in Hall County civic life through on-site American Red Cross blood drives, the United Way, American Cancer Society Walk-a-thons and other community efforts. A member of the Hall County Chamber of Commerce, Avery Dennison's Flowery Branch facility is also a Partner in Education with nearby Enota Elementary School.

Both the company's business success and community involvement grow out of a set of fundamental values: integrity, service, teamwork, innovation, excellence and community.

Founded in 1935 Avery began selling to worldwide markets in 1945, and soon emerged as a global industry leader, guided by a vision of changing the way people work by providing creative solutions, unique services and innovative products for the office, school and home.

ALPINE PSYCHOEDUCATIONAL PROGRAM

Alpine Psychoeducational Program, a state-funded educational resource for children with severe emotional disorders and autism, has served the students of Hall County and the students of the counties in the surrounding region since 1973.

In 1970 the Rutland Program in Athens became the prototype for a statewide network for serving emotionally disturbed children in public schools. Concern among parents, teachers, clinicians and legislators about a lack of services for these children led to the creation of the Georgia Psychoeducational Network. This network was built around four basic convictions for reducing severe emotional behavioral problems among young children. Specifically,

the network would offer comprehensive child services in their communities, and not in residential programs; it would keep the children's families involved in supportive ways; it would keep children in regular school with active teacher involvement while special help is provided; and it would use specialists from various child professions in a collective effort to help children.

In 1972 the Georgia Board of Education and the Georgia Board of Health approved a network design based on the pioneering Rutland Program. That same year, the Georgia General Assembly approved funding for the Georgia Psychoeducational Network, which was formally established July 1, 1972.

In Hall County, the Alpine Psychoeducational Program started with a staff of six members in 1973 to serve the region's severely emotionally disturbed children. Initially, the Program was supported with local funds and supervised by Pioneer CESA, now known as Pioneer RESA, a cooperative education service that shares resources among school systems.

Dr. Mary Wood, developer of the Developmental Therapy Model that was the philosophical basis of Alpine, played an instrumental role in the origins of the Alpine Program. Over three decades, Dr. Frances Gotesky, Dr. Linda Berknopf, Dick Downey, and Dr. Wayne Moffett have served as the Program's director.

Currently serving fourteen school systems in Northeast Georgia, Alpine Psychoeducational Program is one of twenty-four state-funded service providers for emotionally disturbed and autistic children. Employing forty-nine staff members and operating with a budget of more than $2 million the Program has classroom facilities in Hall, Habersham, Union, and Towns Counties, and classes in Lavonia that serve Stephens, Hart, and Franklin Counties.

The Alpine Psychoeducational Program provides therapeutic and academic instruction to encourage and nurture both student achievement and social and emotional growth for children. The comprehensive special education program offers a cost-effective alternative for residential treatment, and a curriculum to support students becoming productive, contributing members of society.

Mar-Jac Poultry is committed to producing a product that is wholesome, valuable and of the highest quality. We are also committed to producing that product with a sincere love for people—those we work with and those we serve. These principles guide our business daily.

In the early days of Hall County's poultry industry, each component of the production chain operated independently of each other. Egg companies produced and sold hatching eggs; hatcheries bought eggs and sold baby chicks; grow-out companies bought chicks and feed and sold broilers to processing plants. One Hall County processing plant of the mid-1950s was Mar-Jac, founded by brothers Marvin and Jack McKibbon in 1956.

In a move to integrate their poultry operations, the Mar-Jac processing facility was purchased in 1962 by a group of broiler grow-out companies: Bruce-Wilson, founded by Alton Bruce and Homer Wilson; A. C. Smith and Mark Heard of Forsyth County; Twin Oaks Hatchery, owned by Max Ward and John Cromartie; and Emerson Stowe, sales manager for Mar-Jac. The Mar-Jac name was retained for market recognition. By the mid-'60s, Mar-Jac was owned by Bruce-Wilson, A. C. Smith, and Twin Oaks. In 1969 this group built HFC Feed Mill to further consolidate their feed manufacturing in Hall County. This feed mill is still in operation as of year 2001, but is scheduled for replacement in 2002. In 1984 SAAR Foundation, a Virginia investment firm, purchased the entire poultry operations of Mar-Jac and its related companies.

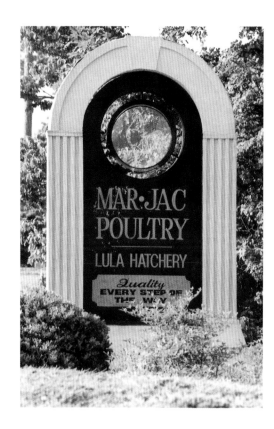

MAR-JAC POULTRY, INC.

Mar-Jac Poultry is committed to producing a product that is wholesome, valuable and of the highest quality. Automation combined with hands-on inspection provide the highest quality poultry available anywhere (above). The end result is a nutritious food that is absolutely delicious (below)!

Mar-Jac's processing plant is located on the same site where it was founded. A continuous series of equipment innovations and plant modifications has enabled an increase in production from 600,000 birds per week in the 1980s to 1.6 million birds per week in the year 2001.

Today, Mar-Jac Poultry, Inc. is a recognized leader in poultry production and processing techniques. Mar-Jac is thankful that God has provided the fifteen hundred employees and associates that make Mar-Jac Poultry, Inc. one of the best poultry companies in the world.

NORTHEAST GEORGIA MEDICAL CENTER

Above: The new emergency room entrance at Northeast Georgia Medical Center.

Below: A neonatology unit opened in the 1990s to help treat infants born at risk.

For nearly fifty years, Northeast Georgia Medical Center has provided quality healthcare services for Hall County and the surrounding area. With a continued commitment to providing the very latest in medical advances combined with a personal touch, the institution that began as the Hall County Hospital is counted on by thousands of patients every year.

Opening in September of 1951 with a ninety-bed capacity, expansion of the facility on Gainesville's Spring Street moved rapidly through the next two decades, with two additions in 1958 and 1967 increasing the capacity to 147 beds, then 252 beds. From its beginning, the hospital has been supported by a strong auxiliary of dedicated volunteers. Over 500 active volunteers give generously of their time to help support the Medical Center's mission.

Today, the hub of Northeast Georgia Medical Center and Health System is Gainesville's 315-bed facility, which caters to a vast range of healthcare needs in the community. The Medical Center is a regional referral hospital supported by over 200 physicians trained in a variety of medical specialties.

Northeast Georgia Health System helps provide the community with convenient access to primary healthcare through Neighborhood Healthcare Centers located throughout Northeast Georgia. NGHS also provides mental health, alcohol and drug abuse services for the community through Laurelwood. The New Horizons facilities help meet patients' needs for long term care. Other services, such as wellness and Hospice care are also part of the full range of services provided for the community.

Northeast Georgia Medical Center is a not-for-profit community hospital, which means that all revenue in excess of expenses is reinvested into healthcare services for the community. Led by volunteer boards, made up of community leaders, the hospital system serves over twenty counties.

For decades, the hospital has been a leader of progress. In 1960 the steady growth of the hospital generated an increased need for nurses, prompting the founding of the Hall County School of Nursing. Later, that program was transitioned to Brenau College and changed from a nursing degree program to bachelors' program.

Hall County Hospital was one of the first small hospitals in the state to have an Intensive Coronary Care, which opened in December 1967. In 1976 a $10 million expansion to the hospital was completed. It was in this year that Hall County Hospital's name was changed to Northeast Georgia Medical Center to more accurately represent the hospital's provision of healthcare to citizens throughout Northeast Georgia.

In 1980 the Northeast Georgia Medical Center Auxiliary began the annual Love Light Tree celebration, a holiday fundraising event that has generated more than $650,000 for needed healthcare services since the tradition began.

The Medical Center's Outpatient Services Building opened in 1985, providing space for a new radiation oncology treatment department for cancer patients, outpatient cardiology services, a new clinical laboratory, dialysis, outpatient surgery services and Fit for Life, a community wellness center.

The 1990s has seen the opening of the new neonatology unit for infants born at risk, renovations of the Medical Center's Pediatric Unit, a new Surgery Pavilion, a new sleep disorders center, and a renovated and expanded emergency department to meet the healthcare needs of a rapidly growing community.

As we greet the twenty-first century, Northeast Georgia Medical Center continues its pursuit of medical advancements to meet the healthcare needs of the community and is making plans to provide open-heart surgery by Summer 2002.

The first two decades of the 1800s saw an influx of people crossing the borders from the east into Georgia. By 1821 Gainesville was officially a city and the county seat of Hall County. It has enjoyed a diverse history rich in heritage and triumph over tragedy. Gainesville has gone through many eras of growth including being known for its healing mineral waters and, after World War II, being known as the Poultry Capital of the World. In 1903 and 1936 devastating storms claimed many lives and left much destruction in their wakes. In the span of almost 180 years, Gainesville has grown from virgin forest to become an economic, medical, cultural, and recreational center of Northeast Georgia, its achievements recognized in early 2000 by being named one of Georgia's ten "Cities of Excellence."

Gainesville is the largest of the six cities of Hall County and operates under a council-manager form of government. Every two years the council elects from their membership a mayor and mayor pro-tem. These two offices represent Gainesville's five voting precincts. Under the guidance of these offices, the City of Gainesville provides a full range of services and activities, while aggressively recruiting new industry to the area.

Recent awards for City departments include: a nationally accredited Police Department; a nationally accredited Parks and Recreation Agency; and award-winning Finance, Public Utilities, and Main Street programs.

In downtown Gainesville improvements are ongoing at the Georgia Mountains Center to make it even more attractive to the people of the community and to draw people from miles around. The multi-purpose facility is estimated to have had a net community economic impact of about $8 million in 1999.

One of the City's newest projects is the construction of the Allen Creek Soccer Complex that will feature nine soccer fields and state-of-the-art amenities.

Water demands for Gainesville are supplied by Lake Lanier serving an estimated 33,000 accounts. Partnering with Hall and Forsyth Counties to conduct a Watershed Assessment Study, Gainesville remains committed to protecting the environment and enhancing the quality of life for all who live in the watershed.

The Public Works Department is one of the few remaining in the U.S. to provide back door garbage pick-up twice a week. One of its most significant projects is the Downtown Streetscape program, now in Phase II. This program will revitalize downtown with brick sidewalks, ornamental lighting and more. In the spring of 1999 the National Trust recognized the Gainesville Main Street Program for Historic Preservation for its work in saving historic buildings that make up the character and heritage of the community.

Gainesville is a city on the move committed to a strong future and a quality of life to rival none. More information about this award-winning city can be seen on TV-18, a government access channel jointly owned and operated by the City of Gainesville and Hall County.

CITY OF GAINESVILLE

The Gainesville City Council. Front row (left to right): Mayor Pro Tem Sissy Lawson and Myrtle Figueras. Back row (left to right): Jim West, Mayor Bob Hamrick, and George Wangemann.

HALL COUNTY BOARD OF COMMISSIONERS

As the twentieth century gives way to the twenty-first, the Hall County government is working to ensure the quality of Hall County life remains high as the county continues its unprecedented growth.

A poultry industry which generates more than $720 million annually and a $258 million annual tourism industry centered around 38,000-acre Lake Sidney Lanier remain the cornerstones of a strong $1.5-billion annual economy. But today's industrial mix is increasingly diversified. Hall is now home to 35 Fortune 500 companies and about 300 manufacturing facilities, attracted by a low cost of living, a quality workforce and other advantages.

The Hall County government is led by a five-member Board of Commissioners serving staggered four-year terms to ensure consistency. Voters elect four by district. The county at large elects the chairperson. Brenda Branch represents District 1, Roger Cole District 2, Stephen Black District 3, Frances Meadows District 4, and Gary Gibbs is the chair.

They oversee a county workforce of over twelve hundred employees, including a full-time county manager. Services and facilities include emergency medical services; fire protection; planning and zoning; building permits and code enforcement; business licenses; water and sewer services; law enforcement; animal control; parks and leisure services; health department; senior center activities; Hall County transit; Hall County Library System; recycling centers and resource recovery program; landfill; and Chicopee Woods Agricultural Center.

Looking to the future, Hall County is also making major investments in infrastructure to attract large, clean industries to the community. Most of these projects are being accomplished through voter-approved Special Purpose Local Option Sales Taxes (SPLOST), one factor which has allowed the government to reduce the tax burden on owners of property in Hall County.

After a 1994 SPLOST measure generated more than $75 million in revenue and interest, voters in 1999 approved a continuation of the tax to fund an additional $144 million for community needs, including five fire stations, water and sewer projects, road improvements and three community centers.

Other projects underway to enhance the quality of life in Hall County include measures designed to ensure the supply of clean drinking water into the future and a major youth soccer facility built in cooperation with the City of Gainesville.

Limited revenue sources and unfunded mandates from state and local governments are continuous challenges, but have not dimmed the Hall County government's progress in promoting a strong, diversified economy and a constantly improving quality of life for Hall County citizens.

SunTrust Bank, Northeast Georgia traces its origins back to 1957 when its predecessor, Home Federal Savings and Loan Association, began operation. Founded by a group of local businessmen, including James A. Dunlap, James E. Mathis, Sr., Carl Romberg, Leslie Quinlan, Winston Garth, Carl Lawson, William Crow, Hubert Deaton and William Gignilliat. Home Federal was created to provide the opportunity of home ownership and savings growth to the residents of Hall County.

In 1985 Home Federal became a publicly traded stock institution. To expand the bank's product base and to better serve its customers, Home Federal converted to a state-chartered commercial bank in 1991 and changed its name to Home Trust Bank.

In 1993 Home Trust Bank was purchased by Trust Company Bank of Georgia, a subsidiary of SunTrust Banks, Inc., and became SunTrust Bank of North Georgia. A 1995 merger with SunTrust Bank, Northeast Georgia, which began business in 1866, and a name change to that of its parent company made SunTrust a household name for banking in the southern and mid-Atlantic states.

In addition to Hall County, SunTrust Northeast Georgia serves Forsyth, Fannin, Morgan, Oconee and Clarke Counties with a total of eighteen full service branches. Robert D. Bishop of Athens is the CEO, Martha Simmons is president of the Gainesville Division, and Lana Nix is executive vice president in charge of Retail Banking.

SunTrust's involvement in its community is deep and wide with SunTrust employees volunteering in churches, schools, Chamber of Commerce, nonprofit boards of directors, and community groups, to mention a few. SunTrust believes in its role as a mainstay of community leadership in Gainesville-Hall County.

During the bank's almost forty-five years of service to this community, this solid financial institution has consistently provided banking services to enable this region to grow and develop.

SunTrust Banks, Inc., with assets of $103.5 billion, is among the nation's largest financial holding companies. Its principal subsidiary, SunTrust Bank, offers a full line of financial services for consumers and businesses. SunTrust serves more than 3.7 million customer households through a regional organizational structure that encompasses more than 1,100 branches and 1,900 ATMs in six states—Alabama, Florida, Georgia, Maryland, Tennessee, and Virginia—plus the

District of Columbia. SunTrust also offers twenty-four-hour delivery channels including Internet and telephone banking. In addition to traditional deposit, credit and trust and investment services offered by SunTrust Bank, other SunTrust subsidiaries provide mortgage banking, commercial and auto leasing, credit-related insurance, asset management, discount brokerage and capital market services. As of December 31, 2000, SunTrust had total trust assets of $138.4 billion, including more than $91.6 billion in discretionary trust assets, and a mortgage-servicing portfolio in excess of $42.3 billion.

SunTrust benefits from a distinct combination of strengths: an enviable franchise in very attractive markets, a good business mix, a strong balance sheet, a the necessary capital, technology and human resources, and a proven execution capability.

CITY OF
OAKWOOD

Nestled between Interstate 985 and Lake Lanier, Oakwood has its beginnings in 1873 with the completion of a railroad track between Charlotte and Atlanta. Originally called Odell's Crossing the name was later changed to Oakwood because it was the regular stop for wood burning locomotives to pick up their fuel, oak wood. It became a thriving small railroad stop with a depot and passengers and goods being loaded and unloaded. This attracted industry, among those early industries were a brick making facility and a bottle-making plant.

When the settlement was incorporated in 1903 its population stood at about 250; by 1980 the population was 750; and today Oakwood has a population estimated at about 2,000.

In the earlier parts of this century, Oakwood was home to one of the finest institutes of higher learning in North Georgia, the Oakwood Academy. People came from all over North Georgia to attend the school. The town grew in response and boarding houses, stores, and a hotel were established to meet the demands. Today that fine tradition of education is carried forward with the Gainesville College established in the 1960s and again attracting students from all over North Georgia.

With the building of Highway 365 (the predecessor to I-985), the construction of Lake Lanier, and the establishment of the college, the town began to grow rapidly in the '70s, '80s, and '90s. City officials responded by directing the growth toward industrial expansion as well as residential expansion.

With that challenge in mind, Oakwood's mayor and five council members, all elected at large, took a step in 1998 destined to shape the city's future. The city purchased 250 acres for the city's first industrial park, Oakwood South Industrial Park. Now under development by the Pattillo Construction Company, Oakwood South offers thirteen sites from 7.2 acres to 32.7 acres. By 2000, one 83,000-square-foot facility was already under construction, and a second had been sold.

In cooperation with the government of Hall County, the city was also in the process of buying right-of-way for an east-west connector to open a new industrial corridor in south Hall County.

Those forward-looking decisions follow something of a city tradition planning for the future. After all, Oakwood had the first school bus in the state in 1921, when driver Ernest Tanner logged a daily forty-four miles.

More recent milestones came in 1966, when Oakwood turned on residential natural gas service for the first time. In 1984 came another big step—the city's first sewer line, which paved the way for much of the industrial and commercial development now occurring in Oakwood.

As the city has grown, so has the demand for city services. With fourteen city employees, Oakwood city government provides police protection, street maintenance, weekly garbage and recycling pick-up, street lights and a municipal court, as well as services for building permits, business licenses and zoning.

The city's annual budget had reached $1.5 million by 1999, but not through higher taxes. After coming down steadily for several years, the millage rate stood at 2.48 in 2000, an average of $70 to $110 per home.

Below: Residential gas service turned on for the first time in 1966.

Bottom: The City of Oakwood railroad depot.

LANIER
TECHNICAL
INSTITUTE

At the flagship campus, 1,150 students prepare for careers ranging from surgical technology to law enforcement, with more than eight in ten availing themselves of Georgia's lottery-funded HOPE grant for education. Quick Start, the state initiative that provides job skill training for new industries to the area, has served over 200 businesses and 10,000 workers in the school's thirty-plus year existence.

Dr. Joe E. Hill, president of Lanier Technical Institute since 1984, carries on the traditions of progressive technical education initiatives begun by Lloyd and his successors, John McCormick (1968-1975) and Dr. Ken Breeden (1975-1984).

Hill oversees a staff of 137 full-time employees at both campuses, many bringing the professional skills and knowledge of the private sector into the classroom.

A proven leader among the state's thirty-three technical institutes, Lanier Tech has grown with the industrial and commercial base it serves to provide the Northeast Georgia area with the skilled, proficient and knowledgeable employees needed to guide the region into the next century.

When former Lockheed manager Dr. John Lloyd helped start the Gainesville-Hall County Area Vocational Trade School in 1965, the only class space the school had to offer was in churches, high schools, and a converted gas company service center. As architects readied the plans for the Oakwood School which eventually became known as Lanier Technical Institute, seventy students signed up for classes in blueprint reading, drafting, electricity, and technical math.

By the time the first class of fifty-one graduated from the school in June 1967, a 47,000 square-foot campus in South Hall County was open, bringing job skill training opportunities to Northeast Georgia that continue expanding to this day.

From its modest course offerings of the early days to the vast career-building options of the present, Lanier Tech has grown with the technical needs of the region. Today, Lanier Technical Institute offers twenty-seven diploma programs, thirty-five technical certificate programs, and, through a partnership with Gainesville College, twenty associate degree programs. Class and facility space has more than doubled since the first foundation was poured, with the campus now encompassing more than 85,000 square feet over twenty-nine acres. Plans are on the drawing board for another 40,000-square-foot, $3 million addition.

The growth of Lanier Tech hasn't been limited to its Oakwood location. In January 1998, the school opened its satellite campus in Forsyth County, a thirty-five-acre, 57,000-square-foot facility that saw initial enrollment of 179 and grew within a year to 850 students.

Below: Lanier Technical Institute offers high-tech career training in more than 30 fields of study.

TURBO
LOGISTICS

Below: Turbo Logistics' first tiny office near the Gainesville Depot with (left to right) Steve Syfan, Scott Sapp, and Gloria Syfan.

Bottom: Turbo Logistics' present location in North Hall County. Pictured are (left to right) CEO Jim Syfan, President Greg Syfan, Vice President of Dedicated Division Mort Goldsmith (kneeling), and Executive Vice President Steve Syfan.

Founded in 1982 by Jim Syfan, his wife Gloria, and sons Steve and Greg in a tiny office near the Gainesville Depot, Hall County based Turbo Logistics has grown into one of the largest and most sophisticated transportation and logistics firms in the nation.

Jim Syfan had worked as an executive in Atlanta for Firestone Rubber Company and dabbled in real estate, insurance, and printing, before moving to North Georgia in 1970, where he purchased a Dahlonega Restaurant. Syfan was hired in 1970 as a dispatcher for Furman Greer's Arrow Truck Lines Company, and worked through the mid-1970s for Interstate Transport Company before deciding to start out on his own.

Turbo Logistics was then and is today a company that matches commercial freight with trucking companies, the "logistics" of commercial transportation. Two decades after its founding, Syfan laughed when describing the cramped working conditions at the first Turbo office, situated near train tracks in downtown Gainesville "My wife had to literally climb on top of the desk to get behind it," he recalled. "When trains came by, we had to put customers on hold."

By 1984 Syfan was able to quit a second job in Atlanta as a trucking consultant and buy three acres of land in North Hall County, where he built the first Turbo Logistics building. Over the years the facility would grow to encompass twenty acres, employing more than 100 people with annual revenues of $75 million.

"We developed our business culture and philosophies during the first few years," Syfan said. "We take excellent care of our employees, and if we don't put our customers first, someone else will. We also made it our business to be active participants in what the community was doing" through charitable fund raising and volunteerism.

Turbo Logistics has developed into six divisions: the original Turbo Transport, dedicated trucking, refrigerated division, dry van division, government contracts division, and enhanced computer solutions, its software division.

Through its logistics operations, the company contracts with approximately 9,000 trucking concerns across the country. The dedicated trucking division, with about 70 tractors and 134 trailers, transports freight for a wide range of clients, from poultry to postal shipments to non-armed nuclear weapons for the U.S. Department of Defense.

The company's high-tech transportation system is overseen by a staff of more than fifty logistics professionals with experience that covers millions of miles. Turbo Logistics meets customer demand with a highly advanced computerized operation system supplemented by software developed by its computer solutions division. With service as the base, technology as the tool and teamwork as the driving force, Turbo Logistics uses all of its resources—every day, every load—to meet and exceed the needs of the customer.

As the only locally owned financial institution headquartered in Gainesville, Gainesville Bank & Trust takes pride in being the "hometown" bank that offers its customers personal one-to-one service.

Recognizing the need for a true community bank in Hall County, real estate developer Don Carter assembled eight local businessmen as a core-organizing group in 1986. Initial stock sales in July 1987 raised a record $7 million in capital in just seven weeks; an accomplishment not matched by another Georgia bank in that short a span.

On February 1, 1988, Gainesville Bank & Trust opened its doors for business at its former location at 441 Sycamore Street. Atlanta veteran banker, Richard Hunt, had been recruited as president and CEO, a position he continues to hold today. By 1990, GB&T had moved into its current main office located at 500 Jesse Jewell Parkway and opened its first branch office in Oakwood in August of that year.

In 1996, the board of directors endorsed an aggressive strategic growth plan, which included the ambitious goal to double the size of the bank over a three-year period and pave the way for expansion in the services the bank offered to the community. In January 1998, shareholders approved the formation of the holding company, GB&T Bancshares, Inc. that positioned the organization for optimum growth and profitability through diversification into additional business activities and through alliances with financial institutions throughout North Georgia. On January 5, 1999, the company's stock began trading on the Nasdaq national market under the trading symbol GBTB (Nasdaq:GBTB).

As of December 31, 1999, the original $7 million in starting capital had grown to more than $250 million in total assets, and GB&T Bancshares, Inc. was recently listed as one of Georgia's top 200 public companies ranked by annual revenue. While many banks have an average growth rate of eight to ten percent, GB&T grew at a rate of over 100 percent between 1996 and 1999, as the board realized its three-year goal.

In May 2000, GB&T Bancshares was recognized as one of Georgia's 100 top performing companies and was the only top company headquartered in Gainesville,

Gainesville Bank & Trust has seven branch offices located throughout Hall County, including the newest Friendship Road office, completed in December 2000. Employing approximately ninety people, GB&T is committed to personal service, not often provided by larger regional financial institutions. The company believes strongly that its phenomenal growth can be directly attributed to building its customer base through the quality personal service it provides.

Today, Gainesville Bank & Trust continues to position itself as Hall County's premiere hometown bank with decisions made locally by people with interest in the community.

GAINESVILLE BANK & TRUST

Above: President & CEO Richard Hunt (standing) and Board Chairman Abit Massey.

Below: Gainesville Bank & Trust main office located at 500 Jesse Jewell Parkway.

CENTURYSOUTH BANK OF NORTHEAST GEORGIA

CenturySouth Bank of Northeast Georgia combines personal focus with world-class capabilities to provide banking solutions as unique as every customer.

As the result of a February 2000 merger between Lanier National Bank and Georgia First Bank, the new CenturySouth Bank of Northeast Georgia has nearly $300 million in assets. Officials with Lanier National saw the merger as an opportunity to join a community-based holding company that could provide more products and services to customers and enable the bank to make larger loans.

Lanier National was founded on August 1, 1989, and operated out of a storefront at the Goody's shopping center on Washington Street its first year. Led by President Joe Chipman, who had spent thirteen years with The Citizens Bank, the founding board of directors included Chairman C. E. Daniel, Tom Jarrard, Gene Mooney, Austin Edmondson, Ed Teaver, John Browning, Jerry Jackson, Buddy Wallis, and Carl Rogers. Lanier National Bank capitalized with $5.25 million, with 600 original shareholders and eight employees. By the time the bank opened its Washington Street building in 1990, assets had grown to $22 million. At the time of its merger, Lanier National Bank had $125 million in assets and forty-five employees, with four full service locations in Hall County.

Georgia First Bank was chartered locally in 1985, with a branch on the downtown square in Gainesville, and had $165 million in assets at the time of the merger. In 1995 it was acquired by the CenturySouth holding company, a publicly traded company listed on the NASDAQ stock exchange with assets of $1.6 billion.

CenturySouth Bank bases its success on three essential elements: delivering excellent service to its customers, providing a great place for its employees to work, and ensuring a superior return to its shareholders. CenturySouth Bank's corporate beliefs are deeply rooted in a foundation of excellence, hard work and fairness. CenturySouth has a strong and sincere interest in its customers and strives to serve them in a resourceful, professional and friendly manner. The company is committed to developing a corps of well-trained relationship bankers, and believes in using available technology to enhance performance and service. CenturySouth believes in empowered community banks, where local directors and management in each community are challenged to develop according to the unique characteristics and demands of their respective communities.

Though the names have changed over the years, Wachovia Bank in Gainesville provides the same level of strength, stability, and service to its customers and shareholders as when its predecessor first opened its doors in Hall County at the turn of the twentieth century.

Founded as Gainesville National Bank in 1905, one of Hall County's oldest financial institutions was formed by a board of directors that included prominent Atlanta lawyers J. J. Spalding and R. D. Spalding, and Gainesville natives Samuel C. Dunlap, E. E. Kimbrough, Sr., A. J. Mundy, M. M. Hamm, and B. M. Stallworth.

The bank was founded in anticipation of the newly opened Pacelot Mills' (Milliken) payroll and business requirements, with an initial stock issue of 500 shares of $100 each. In 1921, Gainesville National merged with the Farmers and Merchants Bank.

Over the years, Gainesville National ushered in a number of banking "firsts" in the Hall County area, particularly in the era overseen by bank President O. J. Lilly in the 1950s and '60s. Drive-in windows (1957), branch banking (1962), Bank-Americard, now Visa (1968), and computerized banking (1969) were all services first introduced to local customers by Gainesville National.

The 1970s was a period of tremendous growth and expansion for Gainesville National, with assets growing from $31.9 million to $108.6 million.

In 1983, First Atlanta acquired Gainesville National Bank, which at that point had grown to serve approximately 30,000 people in five Hall County locations. By 1985, First Atlanta was acquired by Wachovia Corporation, a leading interstate financial services company with dual headquarters in Atlanta, Georgia and Winston-Salem, North Carolina, serving the southeastern, national and international markets.

Wachovia had total assets of $65.8 billion and deposits of $39.7 billion as of September 30, 1999. Wachovia, with more than 20,900 employees, has a heritage of more than 100 years of providing dependable and quality personal, corporate and institutional financial services, backed by in-depth expertise and resources.

The name "Wachovia" is the English form of the German word "Wachau" given by Moravian colonists in 1753 to the tract of land they acquired in what is now the Piedmont region of North Carolina, where the original bank of Salem was founded.

In Hall County, Wachovia counts total deposits of $356.8 million a 21.5 percent share of the Hall County market as of June 1999.

Wachovia, with seventy-five employees in Hall County, has four branches and full financial service capabilities spanning consumer, commercial, and capital markets, overseen by an area executive and a nine-member local board of advisors. The company encourages community involvement among its workers, who give generously of time and contributions to the Gainesville Symphony, Brenau University, Challenged Child, the Arts Council, the American Heart Association, the YMCA, the United Way, and North Georgia Community Foundation, among others.

With growth in deposits that has outpaced the market, Wachovia attracts customers with the stability of the institution, the reliability of its services and the quality of its people.

WACHOVIA BANK

Below: The management staff of Gainesville National Bank, 1961. From left: Thomas Sheffield, James Lewis, Edward Wayne, Jimmie Bryson, President Oscar Lilly, and Sue Pierce.

Bottom: The management staff of Wachovia, Northeast Georgia, 2000. Standing (from left): CEO Michael Whitmire, Leslie Jones, John Cook, Gail Schneider, Chip Frierson, Sandy Salyers, Jeff Norris. Seated (from left): Craig deCastrique, Steve Taylor, Shade Story, and Russ McEver.

GAINESVILLE COLLEGE

Dr. Martha T. Nesbitt (center) is the third president of Gainesville College. Since taking over leadership of the institution in 1997, she has been enhancing the College as a regional education, economic, and cultural center for the citizens of Northeast Georgia. Dr. Hugh M. Mills (right), the founding president, came on board in 1965 and played a major role in the development of the College in all areas from that date until his retirement eighteen years later. In 1983, Dr. J. Foster Watkins (left) became the second president of the institution. The College and the community benefited from his dedication and determination until his retirement in 1997.

For more than thirty years, Gainesville College has led the way in preparing Northeast Georgia students for life.

The persistence and leadership of a group of Gainesville's community leaders brought Gainesville College to Hall County in the mid-1960s, when then-Governor Carl Sanders established the Commission to Improve Education. Gainesville poultry businessman James Dunlap, then chairman of the state Board of Regents, was appointed to head up the new commission, and successfully campaigned with a group of local leaders for the establishment of Gainesville Junior College in Oakwood, at a 175-acre site of former cotton fields near Interstate 985.

Led by founding president Hugh Mills, Gainesville Junior College—which became Gainesville College in 1987—opened in the fall of 1966 with an enrollment of 419, nearly double the number anticipated. The following year, students moved from makeshift classes in and around the Gainesville area to facilities on the new campus.

By 1999, enrollment reached an all-time high of 3,000 students, and the college has enjoyed a reputation for exceptional student satisfaction, modern facilities and above average academic performance among Georgia's two-year colleges. With an extensive curriculum that offers two-year degrees in over thirty fields of study and a faculty of ninety dedicated professionals, Gainesville College is ready to prepare its students for career opportunities in the new millennium.

Dr. Mills was succeeded in retirement by Dr. J. Foster Watkins in 1983. During his thirteen-year tenure, Watkins guided the institution through enormous growth and development. Dr. Martha Nesbitt, who continues the traditions of academic excellence and service to the students, succeeded Watkins.

Gainesville College takes pride in its small class sizes—an average of under twenty-five students—its relatively low tuition rates and the individual support students receive from instructors. Those factors contribute to Gainesville College's superior retention rates among the thirty-four institutions in the University System of Georgia. Serving traditional and non-traditional students alike, the college grants more than 400 scholarships each year, in addition to the one-third of students who turn to the Georgia HOPE scholarship for financial assistance.

The 1990s has been a decade of remarkable physical growth on the Gainesville College campus. The Continuing Education/Performing Arts Center was completed in 1991, the first addition since 1974. In 1995, the $3.2 million Academic III building was opened, and the 60,000-square-foot Natural Sciences and Technology building, the largest facility on campus, was completed in the summer of 2000.

Gainesville College has contributed to the success of the Northeast Georgia community, and the community has responded in kind. With an endowment of over $6.5 million, Gainesville College boasts the largest foundation of any public two-year college in the state. The college recently established an Eminent Scholar position in history, made possible by $500,000 in private donations and a matching contribution from the State of Georgia.

From the cotton fields to the fields of learning, Gainesville College has cemented its status in the history of Hall County.

Founded in 1948 in the basement of Mary Battle's Hall County home, Gainesville Whiteprint has served the imaging needs of planners and architects for more than a half-century of building in the region.

In the 1940s, Buford Battle was executive vice-president of First Federal Savings, where he had frequent dealings with house builders of the day. Builders mentioned to Battle that there was a local need for a service to provide blueline prints in Gainesville, and he and his wife Mary seized the opportunity, buying a used Ozalid ammonia development blueprint machine.

The machine was set up in the Battle family's basement, where Mary learned to operate it. Mary would continue to operate the business out of her house for the next three decades, working with the U.S. Army Corps of Engineers on the plans for Lake Lanier and helping provide blueprints for the wave of growth brought on by the poultry industry in the 1950s and 1960s.

As one of the oldest providers of blueprint documentation in the Southeast, Gainesville Whiteprint has been central to the growth in Hall County, developing lasting relationships with architects, surveyors, and builders who have helped make Northeast Georgia the thriving commercial and residential region it is today.

In 1983, with Mary's son Tréce joining the business, the company was finally moved out of the Battle home and into an office on Spring Street located near Brenau University. Gainesville Whiteprint expanded to provide drafting and blueline printing equipment and supplies.

Shortly afterward, manual drafting gave way to computer-assisted drafting, or CAD.

After Mary's death in 1995, her son Al joined the business. Together, Tréce and Al pooled their assets and purchased the company's present Bradford Street building, a former office supply store. There they have offered myriad, diverse services and products, from topographical maps and trade show displays to small format and xerographic printing.

Since 1995 the company has changed gears dramatically, repositioning itself as a central paper plan depository for the Association of General Contractors of America's Georgia Branch. Gainesville Whiteprint now stores thousands of architectural plans for reference by contractors, and has assumed management of the Association of General Contractor's plan room in Atlanta.

In addition, the Battle brothers have embarked on a new concept made possible by the Internet revolution-computer plan rooms. Now available via the Internet, this innovative concept allows contractors to view plans maintained by Gainesville Whiteprint online. Now more than 100 pre-bid projects in Georgia can be viewed in the Internet plan room at anytime—well over ninety percent of all pre-bid plans in Georgia.

With a business that has grown from one employee eighteen years ago to twenty-six today, Gainesville Whiteprint looks to expand its services as technology continues to change the face of the imaging industry. Gainesville Whiteprint, a local institution since 1948, continues to play an integral role in the growth of Northeast Georgia.

GAINESVILLE WHITEPRINT

Above: Mary Battle founded Gainesville Whiteprint Company in 1948.

Below: Gainesville Whiteprint's offices on Bradford Street.

WARD'S FUNERAL HOME

The qualities that have made Ward's Funeral Home a Gainesville fixture for sixty-six years still define the business—a community-spirited attitude that combines compassionate care with reliable and affordable service.

Founded as Newton and Ward Company by H. Bryce Ward in 1934, Ward's moved into its present location at 758 Main Street in 1953. It continued in family hands through 1988 when the Sentinel Group bought the business. SCI acquired Ward's in 1991, and three years later Ward's became part of Houston-based Carriage Funeral Services. In May 2001 Ward's Funeral Home came back under local ownership and management of Gainesville native Jimmy Brewer.

Ward's staff has deep roots in the Gainesville and Hall County community. Raymond "Spider" Buffington has been an employee since 1954; Doyle McQueen and Haskell McQueen together represent many years of service. Jimmy Brewer and all of the caring staff of Ward's Funeral Home are ready to answer any quetions about at-need services or pre-need services.

Once again, Ward's offers the highest quality of service at the most affordable prices.

With street trees and wildflowers gracing the county's highways, the preservation of historic downtown buildings, and countywide scenic routes, The Jaeger Company played a major role in Hall County's late twentieth century movement to create more green space and preserve the past.

Founded in 1984 by landscape architect Dale Jaeger, The Jaeger Company's multidisciplinary structure allows the firm to work on cultural and ecological projects throughout the Southeast. The Jaeger Company guided several efforts in preparation for the 1996 Olympics, including creation of a countywide pedestrian trail system.

A result of the firm's 1997 Master Plan for the Rock Creek Corridor was a boardwalk over a native flower-filled wetland. The Jaeger Company's landscape design for the Civic Center incorporated a "living pergola" with Sycamore tree branches intertwined in a metal frame. Other projects include the Chicopee Woods Master Plan, Elachee Nature Center's native garden design, and Hall County's 1999 Recreation Master Plan.

THE JAEGER COMPANY

The Jaeger Company's Master Plan for the Rock Creek Corridor included this boardwalk crossing a recreated wetland in Wilshire Park.

The Longstreet Society was founded in 1994 to honor the life of Lieutenant General James Longstreet and his legacy of peace, brotherhood, understanding, and American patriotism.

One of the South's great military minds and an 1842 graduate of U.S. Military Academy, Longstreet commanded the famous Confederate First Corps of Robert E. Lee's Army and served as Lee's second-in-command and most trusted confidante. Lee called him "my old war horse." After the war, his was a voice for reconciliation. In 1875 he settled in Gainesville and purchased the forty-room Piedmont Hotel where his guests included General Joseph Johnston, Union General and New York Governor Daniel Sickles, author and editor Joel Chandler Harris, and future President Woodrow Wilson, whose daughter Jesse was born in the Piedmont.

By 2001 Society membership reached over six hundred scattered around the world. Its priority project remains the restoration of the Piedmont Hotel to include the Society headquarters and a museum/interpretive center to house Longstreet memorabilia and papers and to honor President Wilson's efforts to establish the League of Nations. An informative newsletter is published six times per year and the Society website, www.longstreet.org, was described by *Civil War News* as a model for other organizations. An annual seminar, popular among students of Civil War history, is held at one the National Military Parks. The Society maintains the lighting and assures the upkeep of the General's grave at Alta Vista Cemetery, now a popular tourist attraction.

THE LONGSTREET SOCIETY

MATTHEWS PRINTING COMPANY

From hot type to the computer era, Matthews Printing Company has been a commercial printer offering quality printing in almost all areas. Four color brochures, catalogs, presentation folders, letterheads, envelopes, business cards, office forms, foil stamping, and embossing are all produced on-site in its modern print shop.

Founded in 1948 by linotype operator W. E. Matthews, the company was the first in the Gainesville area to install offset printing equipment and has continued to offer the latest in printing technology.

Originally located on North Main Street behind the Princeton Hotel, the company moved in 1958 to its present location at 336 Northside Drive. Additions to the building were made in 1966 and 2000, making room for additional pre-press, bindery, and press equipment.

The heart of the company is its staff of twenty-five skilled craftsmen and women with many years of experience in their profession. As it was in the early years, the motto of the company remains, "Service that Satisfies."

ALLIED FOAM

In its more than twenty years in Hall County, Allied Foam has provided a quality product for construction throughout the Southeastern United States.

Founded by current President and CEO Jim Clark and partners W. T. Langston and Wiley Black in 1978, Allied Foam built its reputation on the manufacture of expanded polystyrene for insulation in poultry houses and other commercial uses. Over time the product and the projects in which it is used have grown more sophisticated.

Structural insulated panels, a cornerstone of Allied Foam's business, have become widely used in the construction of homes and commercial buildings, offering increased energy efficiency, inherent strength, durability and versatility. Clark, a member of the Association of Foam

Manufacturer's board of directors with thirty-two years of experience in the plastics industry, sees the use of structural insulated panels increasing threefold in the first decade of the twenty-first century. Allied Foam's goal is to keep up with that demand with an efficient, dependable product.

As Gainesville's poultry industry has expanded, so has the service and commitment of James Electric Company.

Founded by Ernest Bryant and Milton James in 1955, what began as Bryant & James Electric Company supplied industrial motors and service for an initial base of fifty customers from its Bradford Street location in Gainesville. Horace C. Land, owner and president of James Electric, began with the company in 1956. He and his wife, Virginia S. Land, who serves as secretary and treasurer, purchased the business in 1971.

Today the company, in its Industrial Boulevard location since 1971, serves nearly 1,000 customers and supplies motors, pumps, and service for a wide range of area industries. In addition to the poultry industry, James Electric serves the textile, food processing, construction, automotive manufacturing, food service, gas, and horticultural and dairy industries, among others. The company also works with governments to provide supplies and maintenance for sewage treatment facilities, schools, hospitals, and recreation facilities.

With a long-time relationship with Hall County's poultry processing plants and hatcheries, James Electric takes pride in Gainesville's prominent role in the broiler industry.

James Electric looks forward to the continued growth of area business as it maintains its focus on customer satisfaction.

JAMES ELECTRIC COMPANY

Horace and Virginia Land, owners of James Electric Company.

Founded in 1975 by Myron Gress, his son Ronald and nephew Peter Gress, Gress Foods has grown from a modest poultry portions operation employing 30 people to a multi-million dollar international company with more than 700 employees in Hall County alone.

As a contributor to the economy of Hall County's number one industry, Gress Foods processes chicken breast fillets, wing cuts and other portions for institutional, international and retail sales. In Hall County, its seventy-five-thousand-square-foot facility on Industrial Boulevard has a yearly payroll of $16 million and annual sales of $125 million.

With its integrated growing and feed mill operations, Gress Foods has retained a niche in the poultry portioning enterprise, In 1999, Gress Foods merged with Koch Meat Company of Chicago, creating a company with close to $600 million in sales and 3,000 employees in Georgia, Ohio, Illinois, and Tennessee.

With an eye toward continued stability and growth, Gress Foods hopes to reach $1 billion in sales in the first years of the new century.

GRESS FOODS

DUNCAN EXTERMINATING

The Duncan family of Duncan Exterminating (from left): Service Supervisor Matthew Duncan, co-founders Sherry and Floyd Duncan, and General Manager Brett Duncan.

Duncan Exterminating, Gainesville's largest locally owned pest control business, has built its reputation in treating customers with utmost respect and honesty while providing excellent service.

Floyd Duncan, who worked his way up through the ranks of Orkin Exterminating and become Getz's Gainesville office branch manager. In 1980, after ten years with the company, Duncan decided to put his 1974 C-10 Chevy truck on the road, and with wife Sherry, founded Duncan Exterminating.

Duncan Exterminating, with twenty employees, provides residential, industrial and commercial pest control and termite services for the Northeast Georgia region within a ninety-mile radius of Gainesville.

"We believe that honesty and integrity have always been the cornerstones of our business, and at Duncan, this philosophy will never change," Floyd Duncan said. "With the coming changes in the industry, including new products, procedures and changing regulations, our customers must have complete confidence in our ability to choose the best materials and methods available for controlling their pest problem."

NORTH GEORGIA ELECTRIC COMPANY, INC.

·North Georgia Electric Company Owner and President Tommy Wood, at the company's Maple Street location.

Established in the 1940s during the birth of the Hall County poultry industry, North Georgia Electric has worked in tandem with the county's broiler producers in a lasting and fruitful relationship.

Carl Romberg, owner of City Ice, established North Georgia Electric as a modest pump repair operation on Gainesville's Main Street. In 1957, Grover Harbin bought the business. In 1960, Harbin sold it to Julian H. "Babe" Wood, who moved the business from its Main Street location to its present site on Maple Street. When Wood died in the mid-1970s, his wife Oretha took over the business with the help of her son Tommy. The determination of Oretha Wood kept the business from folding, and her son Tommy

became owner upon his mother's death in 1990.

Today, North Georgia Electric services poultry industry giants like Mar Jac, Wayne Farms, FieldDale, Harrison Poultry and ConAgra, as well as a wide array of manufacturing industries in Hall County and Northeast Georgia, is providing the next door-neighbor service for which it has come to be known.

As the first large-scale dry ice manufacturing operation in Hall County, Atlantic Dry Ice LLC provides more than 16 million pounds of dry ice annually for area poultry, medical and pharmaceutical industries. The company is a wholesaler of dry ice for use in short-term refrigeration, blast cleaning and other applications.

Former City Ice Manager Jim Doles and City Ice President Carl Romberg founded an offshoot of City Ice Company of Gainesville, Atlantic Dry Ice in 1995. With Doles as president and CEO of Atlantic Dry Ice, City Ice remains a major partner in the company.

The increased use of dry ice as a holdover refrigerant for poultry products has seen demand for the product in the Southeast increase markedly during the mid to late 1990s. Since moving into its Grove Street location, the company has seen extensive growth in sales volume, and is looking to enlarge its operations and double its work force in the next few years.

Atlantic Dry Ice considers its top-notch service and freshness of product as an advantage in the face of large-scale competitors. The company may not be the biggest, but it just wants to be the best.

ATLANTIC DRY ICE, LLC

SPONSORS

INDEX